Generative Grammar
without Transformations

Peter J. Binkert

Generative Grammar
without Transformations

Mouton Publishers
Berlin · New York · Amsterdam

CIP-Kurztitelaufnahme der Deutschen Bibliothek

Binkert, Peter J.:
Generative grammar without transformations / Peter J. Binkert. —
Berlin ; New York ; Amsterdam : Mouton, 1984.
   ISBN 3-11-009720-6

Library of Congress Cataloging in Publication Data

Binkert, Peter J., 1942—
   Generative grammar without transformations.
   Bibliography: p.
   1. English language—Grammar, Generative. I. Title.
PE1112.B49   1984   425   83-27034
ISBN 3-11-009720-6

ACKNOWLEDGEMENT

The ideas which form the basis of this book began to take shape during a course in advanced syntax that I taught at Oakland University in the winter of 1981. Originally, I intended to write an article on what I proposed would be improvements of Jackendoff's (1977) work on X′ syntax. That article (Binkert, 1981) was never published; however, I remain indebted to the students in that syntax course (Joanna Berger, Ann Clancy, Cynthia Cutrona, Patrick Dennen, Linda Hall and Kate Hallett), who encouraged me to continue my work, and to two anonymous reviewers of *Linguistic Inquiry*. During the summer of 1981 I wrote a second article which was subsequently combined with the first to form Chapters One through Five of the present book. Chapter Six was added during the winter of 1982; Chapter Seven, the following summer.

I am indebted to Donna Jo Napoli and Cindy Hart-Gonzáles, who read earlier versions of portions of the manuscript, and, especially, to Greg Carlson, who read the entire manuscript and provided many useful comments. All remaining errors are, naturally, my own.

I would also like to thank Bill Schwab, Chairman of Oakland's Linguistics Department and Lew Pino, the Director of Research Services. A special debt is owed Brian Copenhaver, who, as the new dean of the College of Arts and Sciences back in 1981, supported me unstintingly though we had only just met, and who continues to be a source of encouragement. I am also indebted to Oakland University for a Faculty Research Grant which permitted me to take off the spring of 1982 and continue my research.

Finally, I would like to thank H. P., A. A., and J. B. Without them, I don't know where I'd be.

Troy, Michigan.   P. J. B.
Summer, 1983

TABLE OF CONTENTS

CHAPTER ONE

1.0 BACKGROUND

Modern linguistics is concerned with two broad empirical problems which Bresnan (1978) has referred to as the grammatical characterization problem and the grammatical realization problem. Essentially, the former entails accounting for the linguistic competence of native speakers, while the latter entails accounting for their linguistic performance.

The theory of language that has most successfully described linguistic competence is the theory of transformational generative grammar (hereafter, *TG*), which was first articulated by Noam Chomsky in a manuscript, *The Logical Structure of Linguistic Theory*, in 1955. Since then, countless articles and monographs have appeared on TG, and the theory has undergone considerable revision. However, basic to all versions of TG is the argument that grammars of natural languages contain two major types of syntactic rules: phrase structure rules and transformations. Basically, phrase structure rules generate the "deep structure" of sentences from which "surface structures" can be derived via transformations (Chomsky, 1965; Culicover, 1976; Baker, 1978).

Deep structures are highly abstract structures. Constituents often occupy different positions in deep and surface structures. Further, deep structures often contain elements which do not appear in surface structure at all, i.e., elements which are deleted by some transformational rule. For example, consider the sentences in (1).

(1) a. John wants Bill to visit Mary.
     b. John wants to visit Mary.

Native speakers know intuitively that the subject of *visit* in (1b) is the same as the subject of *wants*, namely, *John*. One current version of TG (Chomsky, 1977, 1981) accounts for this knowledge by deriving the embedded infinitive *to visit* from a full clause containing a subject represented by the abstract element PRO. The deep structure of (1b) is (2).

(2) John wants [PRO to visit Mary]

Similarly, sentences like (3) and (4) are derived from (5) and (6), respectively.

(3)   Whom does John want to visit Mary?

(4)   Whom does John want to visit? (ambiguous)

(5)   John wants [whom to visit Mary]

(6)   a. John wants [whom to visit]
      b. John wants [PRO to visit whom]

A transformational rule, WH-movement, moves the WH-words from their embedded positions in (5)/(6) to the positions in (7)/(8), leaving behind a "trace" which is coindexed with the moved WH-word.

(7)   whom$_i$ does John want [t$_i$ to visit Mary]

(8)   a. whom$_i$ does John want [t$_i$ to visit]
      b. whom$_i$ does John want [PRO to visit t$_i$]

In this manner, TG accounts for the native speaker's knowledge that *whom* in (3) can be understood as only the subject of the infinitive, whereas *whom* in (4) can be understood as either the subject or the object of the infinitive. Thus TG seems to provide a very revealing account of the grammatical characterization problem.

In terms of the grammatical realization problem, however, the relevance of the above analysis is questionable. Thus, Brown (1973) observes that children use sentences like (1b) *before* they use ones like (1a). Since the above analysis derives (1b) from (2), analogous to (1a), an apparent paradox arises. Specifically, children use the derived forms before they use the "basic" forms. Some linguists, e.g., Bresnan (1978), have argued that this raises doubts about incorporating TG into a model of linguistic performance.

Even in terms of the grammatical characterization problem, the above analysis is not without difficulties. Consider (9) and (10), which are parallel to (3) and (4).

(9)   *Whom does John wanna visit Mary?

(10) Whom does John wanna visit? (unambiguous)

As these data indicate, *want* and *to* can contract to *wanna* over an intervening empty node PRO, but not over an intervening empty node "trace" (cf. (7) and (8)). Thus the above analysis entails distinguishing between empty nodes that are invisible to phonological rules and those that are not. This rather unnatural dichotomy raises serious doubts about the adequacy of TG also as a model of linguistic competence.

Given these rather fundamental problems with TG, both as a model of linguistic competence and linguistic performance, it seems natural to explore the possibility of constructing a generative grammar without transformations. The theory of "residential generative grammar" (heareafter, RG) described in this monograph is such an attempt.

RG solves the difficulties mentioned above by directly generating all of the examples via the base phrase structure component of the grammar. In particular, sentences like (1b) are base generated without an abstract underlying PRO as the subject of the infinitive. An independent command relation, which will be described below, accounts for the fact that the subject of the infinitive is the same as the subject of the main verb. Further, RG base generates "moved" constituents like *whom* in (3) and (4) in their surface positions and accounts for the native speaker's understanding of their function (subject or object) by establishing a "binding relation" between the WH-word and a base generated empty node. In RG, the examples in (3) and (4) have the structures (11) and (12), where [____] is the empty noun phrase bound to the WH-word.

(11) whom does John want [____] to visit Mary

(12) a. whom does John want [____] to visit
      b. whom does John want to visit [____]

In this analysis, the fact that *want* and *to* can contract only in (12b) is accounted for, since it is only in (12b) that *want* and *to* are adjacent. This explains the ungrammaticality of (9) and the nonambiguity of (10). Furthermore, Brown's observation regarding the order of children's acquisition of such sentences no longer poses any problems: (1b) is a base generated structure that does not contain PRO.

RG began as an attempt to deal with generalizations that operate across major syntactic categories like NP and S, in examples like (13).

(13) a. [the barbarians' destruction of Rome]
          NP

      b. [the barbarians destroyed Rome]
          S

Just as *barbarians* is the subject of *destroyed*, and *Rome* the object in (13b); so *barbarians* is the subject of *destruction*, and *Rome* the object in (13a). Further, (14) also occurs.

(14) a. [Rome's destruction (by the barbarians)]
          NP

      b. [Rome was destroyed (by the barbarians)]
          S

The active/passive relation in (13b)/(14b) seems also to be operative in (13a)/(14a).

In Chomsky (1970), a suggestion is made that cross-categorial generalizations like the above can be captured if grammatical relations are expressed without reference to specific categories like NP and S. Ultimately, this suggestion became known as the X′ convention, where X is any syntactic category; it is elaborated most throughly in Jackendoff (1977). Basically, each category is represented in a uniform three-level hypothesis: for example, the S node by V‴ and the NP node by N‴. One can then say that the active/passive relation in examples like those above operates within X‴, i.e., either V‴ or N‴. Accordingly, the cross-categorial nature of the relation is expressed generally, not in terms of specific syntactic categories.

Jackendoff's (1977) elaboration of the X′ convention runs into a number of difficulties which are addressed at various points in the following chapters. The solution to these difficulties has directly produced the theory of RG. As noted, RG contains no syntactic transformations which move constituents, delete constituents under identity, or replace some constituents with others. In effect, RG eliminates the transformational subcomponent of the standard theory (Chomsky, 1965) and the extended standard theory (Jackendoff, 1977; Chomsky and Lasnik, 1977). RG does contain some rules that are transformational in nature; however, all of these rules, as we shall see, affect specific morphological material: e.g., the rules for the affixation of *-ing* and *-en*; the rule for the insertion of *of* in noun phrases; or the rule for the deletion of *x-many* in comparatives. Further, since these rules are not dependent on any particular "stage of derivation" but, rather, apply to very "shallow underlying representations," they can all be incorporated into the phonological component. Indeed, the extent to which such "morphological" transformations are needed is itself unclear at present. Many may be able to be eliminated altogether.

Clearly, although RG contains no transformational subcomponent, it must still account for all those relations which, until now, have been captured by transformations. RG does this by directly incorporating such relations into the phrasal architecture of surface structure, eliminating completely the concept of syntactic derivation via (ordered) (cyclic) transformational rules. Accordingly, it has advantages over TG both as a model of competence and as a potential part of the model of linguistic performance. Specifically, we shall see that RG solves a number of problems which psychologists and linguists alike have noted are inherent in the TG model when it is proffered as a component of the model of linguistic performance (Fodor, et al., 1974).

1.1 ON WRITING A NONTRANSFORMATIONAL GENERATIVE GRAMMAR

There are three major problems which arise when one attempts to write a nontransformational generative grammar of English. The first, which I shall refer to as the Categorial Problem, is to devise a set of generalized phrase structure rules which can account not only for all of the traditional base structures, such as those in Jackendoff (1977), but also for all of those sequences of categories that generally have been assumed to be the result of some transformational operation such as movement. For example, we need rules that will generate (15a), or the equivalent, to account for (15b), and also rules that will generate (16a), or the equivalent, to account for (16b).

(15) a. NP — AUX — V — NP
      b. You must read that book.

(16) a. NP — NP — AUX — V
      b. That book, you must read.

Even a cursory consideration of the Categorial Problem reveals that the number of possible combinations of categories that exist in English surface sentences is enormous, such that appeal to the usual abbreviatory devices like curly brackets and parentheses produces a very unrevealing description of English phrase structure. Thus, along with examples like (15)/(16), we must account for (17)/(18).

(17) a. Brilliant, John definitely is not.
      b. Than John, there is hardly anyone more qualified.
      c. Hurriedly, John finished the report.
      d. Into his bedroom and under his bed, the frightened child ran.
      e. After the ball is over, let's get a pizza.

(18) a. John definitely is not brilliant.
      b. There is hardly anyone more qualified than John.
      c. John finished the report hurriedly.
      d. The frightened child ran into his bedroom and under his bed.
      e. Let's get a pizza after the ball is over.

Furthermore, various elements can "float" to a number of positions, thereby complicating phrase structure:

(19) a. All the students may have gone fishing.
      b. The students all may have gone fishing.
      c. The students may all have gone fishing.
      d. The students may have all gone fishing.

(20) a. Ultimately peace will prevail.
      b. Peace ultimately will prevail.
      c. Peace will ultimately prevail.
      d. Peace will prevail ultimately.

The second problem, which I shall refer to as the Level Recursion Problem, is to account for the sometimes infinite sequences of categories that are possible at each level of phrase structure, i.e., X''', X'', X', and X, both to the left and to the right of the head X, in such a way that makes possible all of the varieties of structural groupings which are necessary for correct semantic interpretation. For example, consider (21).

(21)   John met the energetic young men from Boston and Bill met
       a. the lazy ones. (ones = young men from Boston)
       b. the lazy ones from New York. (ones = young men)
       c. the lazy old ones. (ones = men from Boston)
       d. the lazy old ones from New York. (ones = men)

Notice that the correct interpretation of *ones* requires different structural groupings within the noun phrase *the energetic young men from Boston*. Similarly, consider (22) and (23).

(22)   You can not do that.
       a. You have the option of not doing that.
       b. You do not have the option of doing that.

(23)   You can not # not do that. (# indicates a heavy pause)

Example (22) is ambiguous as indicated, and, as (23) shows, both negatives are possible within the same sentence. Hence it must be possible to group a negative either with a preceding modal or a following main verb, or both.

Related to these examples are those which indicate that a wide variety of categories on different X levels can occur in construction either to the left or to the right of the head of their phrase:

(24)   a. available books/books available
       b. history teacher/teacher of history
       c. enough pudding/pudding enough (cf. Jackendoff, 1977)
       d. the easiest students to teach/the students easiest to teach
       e. as many too many marbles/as many marbles too many (cf. Bresnan, 1973)
       f. quite far down the street/down the street quite far
       g. enthusiastically accepted the award/accepted the award enthusiastically
       h. If he tries, he will succeed./He will succeed if he tries.
       i. That man over there, he is my friend./He is my friend, that man over there.
       j. The bagels that her mother bakes, I love almost as much as she does./I love, almost as much as she does, the bagels that her mother bakes.

To my knowledge, the variety of alternations like those in (24) has never received a general left-of-head/right-of-head description in transformational syntax.

The third problem, which I shall refer to as the Command Problem, is to provide a definition of such syntactic notions as *subject-of* and *direct-object-of* and a mechanism whereby the subjects and objects of verbs, as well as nouns, adjectives, participles, etc., the scope of quantifiers and the antecedents of various pronouns can be determined. Thus the Command Problem entails accounting for the data previously mentioned in (1) through (14), for the antecedent of *all* in (19), the scope of the negatives in (22), as well as a variety of other problems, including accounting for the triple ambiguity of (25) and the varying interpretations of the participles in (26).

(25)   John saw the man walking toward the railroad station.

(26)   John saw the girl standing over there undressing on the beach using his binoculars.

Clearly, the above problems are closely interrelated, and it is somewhat artificial to separate them as I have. Nonetheless, I think it may be helpful in understanding the difficulties in constructing a generative grammar without transformations, if the reader attempts to keep the problems distinct. Basically, the Categorial Problem arises from the number of possible linear combinations of categories, the Level Recursion Problem arises from the hierarchical arrangements of categories to heads, and the Command Problem arises from consideration of such matters as syntactic function, scope, reference, and the like.

1.2 A SHORT PREVIEW OF RG

To account basically for the Categorial Problem, RG recognizes two *super-categories* that are not found in TG: adjunct (A) and characterizer (C). Their relation to the major syntactic categories of X′ syntax, verb (V), noun (N), adjective (ADJ), and preposition (P), discussed in Jackendoff (1977, 31–33), is as follows:

(27)

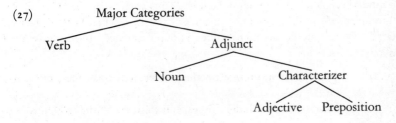

The most obvious justification for (27) in English is morphological: verbs alone carry tense, and nouns alone carry independent number. But there is syntactic justification as well. For example, adjuncts can occupy a wide variety of positions in phrasal hierarchies, whereas the position of verbs is highly constrained. Thus, while NP, ADJP, and PP may occur in initial position in simple sentences, VP cannot:

(28) a. That book, you must read.
     b. Brilliant, John definitely is not.
     c. Into the room, the frightened child ran.

(29) a. *Wash the clothes, you must.
     b. *Go home, John will.

Adjuncts can also serve as complements of *be*; bare verbs cannot:

(30) a. Those men are rebels.
     b. Those men are rebellious.
     c. Those men are up in arms.

(31) a. *Those men are go to war.
     b. *Those men are fight.

Characterizers are distinguished from nouns in that only the former can directly postmodify a nominal head:

(32) a. the student present
     b. the student in the room
     c. *the student presence (where *student* is the head)

Further, while most adjectives precede nominal heads, prepositions follow:

(33) a. *the student intelligent (cf. the student that intelligent, the intelligent student, *the that intelligent student)
     b. *the with the best grades student

Further justification of (27) will be provided as we proceed. Moreover, I shall ultimately expand the range of categories considered and provide an entirely syntactic feature matrix to distinguish the traditional parts of speech from each other. Although that matrix accounts for a wide variety of constructions, it is by no means complete and without difficulties. Thus, while sentences like (29) are ungrammatical, notice that there is an isolated case where VPs can occur initially: namely, in the second part of compound sentences following verbs of saying:

(34) a. John said you must wash the clothes, and wash the clothes you must.
     b. ?*John must wash the clothes, and wash the clothes you must too.

In short, categorial breakdowns like (27) will require modification as the inventory of examples is expanded.

To deal with the Level Recursion Problem, RG provides two mechanisms. The first involves the introduction of a new abbreviatory device into phrase structure schemata, the slash notation, which indicates items that are optional and that can occur on either side of a head X. Thus a rule like (35) is an abbreviation for the rules in (36).

(35) $X'' \rightarrow /A'''/X'$

(36) $X'' \rightarrow A''' - X' - A'''$
      $X'' \rightarrow A''' - X'$
      $X'' \rightarrow \qquad X' - A'''$
      $X'' \rightarrow \qquad X'$

This new notation is not to be understood as a disguised variation of a transformational operation such as movement. It is simply an abbreviatory device. Notice that both positions of A''' can occur simultaneously:

(37) a. The [best] students [available] are John and Bill.
          $\qquad A''' \qquad\qquad A'''$

      b. Mary [enthusiastically] sang [loudly].
          $\qquad A''' \qquad\qquad\qquad A'''$

The second mechanism is to introduce recursion of each X level into phrase structure directly, providing rules like (38).

(38) $X^n \rightarrow X^m$, where $m \leq n$

This mechanism will provide an account for examples like (39).

(39) a. the pretty little yellow house
      b. the operas that the library had that I recorded that Joe wants to rerecord
      c. the bird's migration from Canada to South America over the Rockies

The recursive property of a rule like (38) is, of course, impermissable in TG, even though a majority of texts on TG contain structures requiring such a rule, e.g., Culicover (1976) and Baker (1978). Since its inception, TG has placed a restriction on phrase structure rules so that they do not lead to ambiguity in constructing "trees of derivation" (Bach, 1964). A rule like (38), which allows a symbol to be rewritten as a string beginning or ending with itself, is therefore not allowed in TG. But this restriction has no meaning in RG, as we shall see; hence rules like (38) are premissable.

Combining these two mechanisms, RG provides one basic phrase structure schema for all phrases and sentences, as follows:

(40) $X^n \rightarrow /A''' - A'''/X^m$, where $m \le n$

Assuming that $n = m = 1$, rule (40) generates the following:

(41) $X' \rightarrow A''' - A''' - X' - A''' - A'''$
       $X' \rightarrow A''' - A''' - X'$
       $X' \rightarrow \qquad\qquad X' - A''' - A'''$
       $X' \rightarrow A''' - A''' - X' - A'''$
       $X' \rightarrow \qquad A''' - X' - A''' - A'''$
       $X' \rightarrow \qquad A''' - X' - A'''$
       $X' \rightarrow \qquad A''' - X'$
       $X' \rightarrow \qquad\qquad X' - A'''$
       $X' \rightarrow \qquad\qquad X'$

CHAPTER TWO

2.0 THE INTERNAL STRUCTURE OF NOUN PHRASES

2.1 ADJUNCTS ABOVE THE X′ LEVEL

As noted in Chapter One, I shall argue that the category adjunct subsumes all of the traditional syntactic categories except verb. There are two types of adjuncts: noun [+A, +Nominal] and characterizers [+A, −Nominal]. For convenience, I shall abbreviate the former as N and the latter as C. The category characterizer is discussed in the next chapter. Let us assume for the moment that it includes all categories except nouns and verbs.

Given the rule schema (40) of Chapter One and adopting the three level hypothesis of X′ syntax (Jackendoff, 1977, 36), the basic structure of a noun phrase with expansions of N‴ and N″ is (1).[1]

(1)

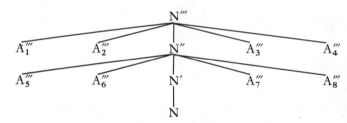

In a diagram like (1), I shall refer to positions appearing to the left of the head as "prehead" positions, and those appearing to the right of the head as "posthead" positions. Positions to the immediate left or right of the head will be referred to as *first* positions, and those adjacent to first positions, as *second* positions.

Adopting this terminology, we may say, for example, that A_2''' of (1) is an X‴ resident in first prehead position, and that A_8''' is an X″ resident in second posthead position. These positions will serve to distinguish the syntactic categories of English from each other. In fact, although I shall use traditional parts-of-speech terminology throughout this monograph for convenience, such terminology is actually unnecessary in the theory being developed here. For example, the definite articles simply comprise a group of words occurring as X''' residents in first prehead position in noun phrases, i.e., A_2''' of (1). Similarly, restrictive relative clauses are clauses generated in second posthead position on the X'' level of noun phrase, i.e., A_8'''. I shall return to a discussion of the advantages of this method of defining the syntactic categories of English at several points below.

Continuing to restrict our attention to the X''' and X'' levels of N''', let us explore the RG description of noun phrases like (2), which have the structure (3), and compare this description with those found in TG, particularly Jackendoff (1977).

(2)   a. all those many interesting books of John's which Mary has read
       b. a bunch of the twenty-five amazing men of courage approaching the platform

(3)

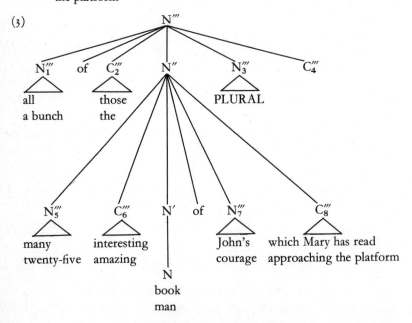

Position N_1''' (actually, $[+A, +\text{Nominal}]''')$ is the position of quantifiers like *all*, *each*, and *both*, and of measure nouns introducing the pseudopartitive construction like *bunch*, *lot*, *cup*, *foot*, *inch*, *pound*, etc.; position C_2''' (actually, $(+A, -\text{Nominal}]''')$ is the position of articles including *a*, *the*, *this* (*these*), *that* (*those*), and the phonologically null article $\emptyset$,[2] and of the possessive suffix *'s* (POSS). Position N_1''' is also the base position for possessivized nouns, so that instead of *all those* in (2a), we may have *Bill* POSS, i.e., *Bill's*.[3]

Position N_5''' contains cardinal and ordinal numerals and words such as *many*, *several, dozen*, etc., some of which can also occur in N_1'''. We thereby generate such examples as the following:[4]

(4) a. [the] [second] boy [on the left]
 　　　C_2　N_5　　　　C_8

　　b. [the] [one] man of [honor] [amongst us]
 　　　C_2　N_5　　　　N_7　　C_8

　　c. [John] [POSS] [three dozen] shirts
 　　　N_1　　C_2　　N_5

　　d. [a group] of [those] [three hundred] crazies
 　　　N_1　　　　　C_2　　N_5

　　e. [a large number] of people (*have* left)
 　　　N_1

　　f. [three inches] of molding (*is* needed)
 　　　N_1

　　g. [four feet] of [that] rope (*is* left)
 　　　N_1　　　　C_2

Position C_6''' is the position of descriptive adjectives. I assume that this position can dominate a sequence of conjoined descriptive adjectives to yield such NP as (5).[5]

(5) a. [John] [POSS] [several] [brief, but stunning and intricate]
 　　　N_1　　C_2　　N_5　　C_6

　　　arguments

　　b. [a] [big and furry and strong and utterly grotesque] monster
 　　　C_2 C_6

To generate C_6''' in (5), I shall adopt, without discussion, the compounding rule schema of Jackendoff (1977, 51), repeated here in (6).[6]

(6) $X^i \rightarrow X^i (CONJ - X^i)^*$

Comparing this description of prehead constituents in noun phrases with the one in Jackendoff (1977), we note a number of discrepencies. Jackendoff assumes a structure for N''' like (7).

(7)

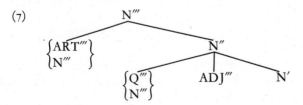

The major difference between (3) and (7) derives from the fact that Jackendoff follows a widely accepted tradition in TG of viewing entire possessive noun phrases like *John's* in *John's books* as alternatives to articles (cf. *the books*, **the John's books*, **John's the books*, and examples discussed in Stockwell et al., 1973). In the analysis presented here, only the possessive suffix POSS, which is actually a manifestation of CASE, is viewed as an alternative to the articles. That the ending should be entirely separated from the noun to which it is suffixed (by phonological rules) is indicated by its attachment to the entire preceding noun phrase:

(8)   a. the man standing over there with the stick's mother
       b. the soprano that was singing so shrilly's voice

(9)   a. *the man's standing over there with the stick mother
       b. *the soprano's that was singing so shrilly voice

Viewing entire possessive noun phrases as alternatives to articles also forces Jackendoff to make some rather strange category assignments. On page 104, he classifies *each, all, some*, etc., as articles, and on page 150 ff., he classifies *enough* as either a degree word or an article. The structures he is attempting to account for include the following:

(10)   a. the men, each man, all men
       b. *the each man, *those all men
       c. each of the men, all of those men, enough of the men
       d. enough men, men enough

His analysis on page 118 includes several *ad hoc* structures containing the element PRO, which are necessary, in particular, to generate (10c).

In the grammar being developed here it is not necessary to resort to such artificiality. Words like *each, all*, and *enough* are nouns, perhaps [+N, +Q], which freely occur in N_1''' of (3). If C_2''' is present in the form of an overt article, a rule of *of*-Insertion, which I assume is a spelling rule within the phonological component and which I shall discuss presently, applies, and (10c) is accounted for. If no overt article is present, then sequences like *each man, all men*, etc., are accounted for. The sequences in (10b) are ruled out because N_1''' does not have a C''' to its left. To rule out sequences like **each's book*, we can simply say that POSS cannot follow nouns that are +Q. Finally, sequences like *enough of the men* and *enough men* will exactly parallel *all of the men* and *all men*. Therefore, following Bresnan (1973), we may say that *enough* is a Q, or, more precisely, [+N, +Q]. I shall return to sequences like *men enough* presently.

With regard to words like *several, many*, etc., which Jackendoff (1977, 104) analyzes as Q, they are here treated as nouns which are either +Q or −Q, along with the numerals *two, three*, etc. When these words are +Q, they occur in N_1''';

when $-Q$, in N_5'''. We, therefore, are able to account directly for sequences like the following:

(11)   a. many of those men, those many men
        b. three of the men, the three men

Of course, this analysis means that phrases like *these many apples* are ambiguous, depending on whether *many* is in N_1''' or N_5'''. I believe that this is as it should be. Phrases like *these many apples* can have either a quantifier reading (*these many* an N′′′ within N_1''') or an adjective reading (*many* in N_5''', *these* in C_2'''). The former reading often occurs in responses to children's questions like *How many apples are there?* The reply may be either *There are these many* or *There are this many*. Often such sentences are spoken with an accompanying gesture, such as holding up the appropriate number of fingers. The latter reading, which seems to me primarily adjectival, occurs in sentences like *These many rotten apples will have to be thrown out*. Both readings occur in (12), which might be uttered while, say, holding up five fingers:

(12)   Take these/this many of these many rotten apples and dispose of them.

An immediate advantage of this analysis is that words like *each*, *many*, *two*, etc., being classified as nouns, can serve as the heads of noun phrases in partitive constructions, as we shall see shortly. It is precisely because they are not nouns in Jackendoff's theory that he must resort to the *ad hoc* element PRO, so that *each of the trees*, for example, becomes in his formulation (13).

(13)   [[each] PRO of [the trees]   ]
       N′′′ ART′′′   N′′′

The simplicity of the RG analysis is, I believe, a direct consequence of a very generalized investigation of the Categorial Problem. In every rule and diagram in Jackdendoff containing a Q, an N is offered via curly brackets as an alternative. This clearly suggests that N and Q are members of some larger syntactic category. Further, although Jackendoff himself notes the parallels between ART and DEG, he fails to point out the obvious difference between these two categories and ADJ: namely, that ART and DEG are prehead residents *on the X′′′ level*, ART in N′′′ and DEG elsewhere, whereas ADJ is regularly a prehead resident *on the X′′ level*. Facts such as these must be expressed if a grammar is to attain descriptive adequacy; further, expressing them, as always in the case of a real generalization, engenders simplicity and eliminates artificiality. Thus in RG, ART, DEG, and ADJ are all analyzed as members of C, each distinguished from the other in terms of their residency possibilities.

We now see that POSS can occur in C_2''' provided a $-Q$ noun is in N_1'''. Thus it occurs in the following environment:

(14) $[+N, -Q]$ ____ N′′

Phonological rules will, of course, provide the correct phonetic form of POSS. This accounts for the following examples:

(15)   a. John's book, the boy's many marbles, his shoes
        b. *John's the book, *that his car

Turning now to the insertion of *of* between N_1''' and C_2'', we see that *of* is inserted in just those cases where POSS cannot occur, a fact which has gone unnoticed in TG, to my knowledge. Specifically, *of* is inserted in the following environment:

(16) $[+N, +Q]$ ____ $C''' - N''$

Note that C''', in (16), can be the phonologically null article $\emptyset$, yielding pseudopartitives like *A bunch of flowers are on the floor*.

Summarizing these remarks, we can say that insertion of nouns into N_1''' produces examples like those in (17) and (18).

(17)   Where the noun is $-Q$
        a. John's mother
        b. the boy's three shirts
        c. her husband

(18)   Where the noun is $+Q$
        a. all of the men
        b. many of the flowers
        c. a bunch of flowers (*are* on the floor)

Assuming that (16) entails an optional phonological rule and observing the contents of Note 2, our grammar must contain the filters (19a, b) to account for (19c, d).[7]

(19)   a. $*[+N, +Q, +COUNT] - C''' - N''$
        b. $*[+N, +Q, -COUNT] - of - \emptyset - N''$
        c. a bunch of $\emptyset$ flowers/a bunch of the flowers
           *a bunch $\emptyset$ flowers /*a bunch the flowers
        d. *all of $\emptyset$ men/all of the men
           all $\emptyset$ men/all the men

Continuing our summary, we can say that the insertion of nouns into N_5''' position produces examples like those in (20).

(20)   a. these three men/a bunch of those three hundred men (are . . .)
        b. those many rotten apples/all (of) those many rotten apples

Turning to posthead position, consider first the X''' level residents. Position C_4'' in the theory being developed here is the position of appositive relatives, which will be discussed in Section 2.5, of comparative clauses, which will be discussed in Section 2.6, and of partitives such as the following:

(21) a. [these] [three] inches [of the twelve inches of molding we have]
           C_2 N_5 C_4

      b. [how many] cups [of the cups of sugar we filled]
          N_5 C_4

The *of* occurring in these partitives is, I believe, the head of a construction. That the *of* is a "full" preposition and not one introduced by some spelling rule is indicated by the fact that the entire phrase is separable from the head noun it modifies, as the following examples illustrate:

(22) a. Of the twelve inches of molding we have, only these three inches are straight.
      b. Of the cups of sugar we filled, how many cups will we need?

In contrast, position N_7''' contains noun phrases of various kinds that are introduced by an *of* which *is* the result of a spelling rule. Among these phrases are genitives of quality such as the following:

(23) a. [The] bunch of [flowers] is on the table.
          C_2 N_7

      b. [All] [these] [three] inches of [molding] are needed.
          N_1 C_2 N_5 N_7

      c. [All] of [these] [ten] cups of [sugar] are infested with ants.
          N_7 C_2 N_5 N_7

As the number on the verbs in (23) indicates, the heads of the subject noun phrases are, respectively, *bunch*, *inches*, and *cups*. The number on the pronoun of tag questions confirms this:

(24) a. The bunch of flowers is on the table, isn't it?
      b. All these three inches of molding are needed, aren't they?
      c. All of these ten cups of sugar are infested with ants, aren't they?

Now notice that these genitives of quality are not separable from the head noun:

(25) a. *Of flowers, the bunch is on the table.
      b. *All these three inches are needed of molding.
      c. *Of sugar, all of these ten cups are infested with ants.

These genitives of quality are essentially adjectival constructions, hence their residence on the X'' level.[8] Although I shall not discuss the matter here, I believe that ultimately they must be related to descriptive adjectives in prehead position to account for the following parallels:

(26)   a. a bouquet of exquisitely beautiful flowers
        b. an exquisitely beautiful floral bouquet

(27)   a. a man of exceptional courage
        b. an exceptionally courageous man

Now notice that, given the above description, we may produce NPs such as the following:

(28)   a. [these] [ten] inches of [molding]
             C_2 N_5 N_7
        b. ten of [these] inches of [molding]
                  C_2 N_7
        c. [all ten] of [these] [ten] inches of [molding]
             N_1 C_2 N_5 N_7

Of the five *of*-NP sequences in (28), only the first one in (28b) is a partitive; thus, the remaining four cannot be separated from the head:[9]

(29)   a. *of molding, these ten inches
        b. *of molding, ten of these inches
        c. *of molding, all ten of these ten inches
        d. *of these ten inches of molding, all ten

Specifically, (28c) cannot be a partitive, since one must have a part different from the whole to have a partitive construction. Hence, (29d) is semantically anomalous.[10]

On the other hand, the above description allows for structures such as as the following, which *are* partitives:

(30)   a. ten [of these inches of molding] (cf. (28b) and Note 9)
             C_4
        b. ten [of these fifteen inches of molding]
             C_4

These can be separated from the head:

(31)   a. Of these inches of molding, ten are straight.
        b. Of these fifteen inches of molding, ten are straight.

Summarizing, we have three occurrences of the word *of* in NP: (i) a pseudo-partitive-*of* occurring in prehead position on the X''' level; (ii) a genitive-of-quality-*of* occurring in posthead position on the X'' level; and, (iii) a partitive-*of* occurring in posthead position on the X''' level. Only the partitive construction is separable from the head. Further, the head of a phrase containing a pseudo-partitive follows *of*, whereas the head of a phrase containing a genitive of quality precedes the *of*. Further examples are as follows:

(32) a. [Ten cups] of([the]) sugar *is* needed.
         N_1 C_2
     b. [Both] of [these] [two] cups of [sugar] *are* needed.
         N_1 C_2 N_5 N_7
     c. [two] cups [of the ten cups of sugar] *are* needed.
         N_1 C_4
     d. *Ten cups *is* needed of (the) sugar.
     e. *Both of these two cups *are* needed of sugar.
         *Of these two cups of sugar, both *are* needed.
     f. Two cups *are* needed of the ten cups of sugar.

I believe that one of the major problems with analyses of partitives that I have seen, e.g., Selkirk (1977), is that little, if any, attention is paid to the following fact: a partitive construction must consist of a part which is less than the whole. It is for this reason that the following examples are infelicitous:

(33) a. *Of those two dozen cakes, all twenty-four were baked by Sue.
     b. *Both men will receive an award of the two men that were nominated.

However, the following *pseudopartitives* are not infelicitous:

(34) a. All twenty-four of those two dozen cakes were baked by Sue.
     b. Both of the two men that were nominated will receive an award.

Clearly, the above description will provide a wide variety of structures associated with an *of*-phrase in N‴, and all of them are necessary. In particular, phrases such as *many (five, several) apples*, where *apples* is the head, will have two structures, depending on whether the prehead adjunct is in N_1 or N_5. As noted, this seems necessary because words like *many (five, several)* have both $+Q$ and $-Q$ uses.

Continuing to investigate the variety of structures available, observe that we have such examples as the following:

(35) a. [all five] of [these] [five] pounds of [sugar] (*are* needed)
         N_1 C_2 N_5 N_7
     b. [these] [five] pounds of [sugar] (*are* infested with ants)
         C_2 N_5 N_7

Neither of these examples in (35) is a partitive:

(36) a. *All five of these five pounds are needed of sugar.
     b. *These five pounds are infested with ants of sugar.

    c. *Of these five pounds of sugar, all five are needed.

    d. *Of sugar, these five pounds are infested with ants.

Moreover, we have examples like the following, in which the head is not *pounds*:[11]

(37) a. [five pounds] of [ϕ] fruit (is needed)
          N_1 C_2

      b. [five pounds] of [ϕ] apples (are needed)
          N_1 C_2

These examples may be followed by partitives:

(38) a. Five pounds of fruit is needed of the ten pounds of fruit we have.

      b. Only five pounds of apples of all those pounds of apples you bought are left.

Lastly, we have these:

(39) a. [These] [five] pounds of [apples] [of all those pounds of apples
          C_2 N_5 N_7 C_4

        you bought] *were* the best.

      b. [These] [five] pounds of [fruit] *are* the best [of all those pounds
          C_2 N_5 N_7 C_4

        of fruit that you bought].

Within the framework of this description, a number of restrictions are necessary. For example, the "Partitive Constraint" mentioned in Selkirk (1977) must still be enforced. This constraint stipulates that only certain prehead adjuncts may occur within the partitive *of-* phrase, and that some may never occur there. It is necessary to rule out sequences like **five pounds of all apples*. Although I return to a discussion of partitives below, I shall not pursue the nature of these restrictions in this monograph.

Returning to our discussion of the diagram in (3), notice that position N_3''' dominates the abstract category NUMBER, i.e., [$\pm$ PLURAL]. I believe that such a category must be generated in most NPs, since most nouns can be inserted into base structures with a free choice of number. It seems intuitively correct to assign NUMBER to the category N, i.e., [+Nominal], rather than to the category C, i.e., [−Nominal], since, as we have seen, all words referring to number are [+N], e.g., *two, fifth*, etc. Another reason concerns the behavior of "floating" quantifiers, which occur in familiar paradigms like the following:

(40) a. All of the students could have been on time.

      b. The students all could have been on time.

      c. The student could all have been on time.

    d. The students could have all been on time.

    e. *The students could have been all on time.

The ungrammaticality of (40e) will be explained below.

For the present purposes, the crucial sentence to be discussed is (40b), and the question is, Where is the *all* generated?

Floating quantifiers can occur either in N_1''' of (3) or outside of the noun phrase; they cannot regularly occur in posthead position within a noun phrase, i.e., N_3'''. This explains why (41a) is grammatical, but (41b) is not.

(41)   a. I saw all of the men.

      b. *I saw the men all. (< [the men all])

                   N'''

Notice, however, that we do have the following:

(42)   a. I saw all of them.

      b. I saw them all.

What is the explanation for the grammaticality of (42b)? I believe it is as follows. Position N_3''' of most noun phrases is occupied by the category NUMBER, a free choice between singular and plural with count nouns. Therefore, quantifiers cannot float to this position, or, in our terminology, cannot be base generated in this position. It is filled. However, in a noun phrase whose head is a personal pronoun, this position is unfilled. Pronouns, unlike nouns, have inherent number which they bring with them from the lexicon during lexical insertion. Thus when a personal pronoun is the head of a noun phrase, position N_3''' is obligatorily empty of any number distinction and, accordingly, is free to contain a "floating" quantifier, explaining (42b). Notice that we also have sentences like (43) in some dialects, the interrogative having no number.

(43)   Who all did you see?

The present theory, thus, accounts for one rather mysterious fact about English syntax, namely, the differing status of (41b) and (42b). Furthermore, sentences like (44) can be explained: the *all* is based generated outside of the preceding noun phrase.[12] Compare (45).

(44)   We saw the children all playing happily together.

(45)   a. We saw the children, just as John said we would, all playing happily together.

      b. ?*We saw the children all, just as John said we would, playing happily together.

Now consider again the word *enough* in such expressions as (46), which are from Bresnan (1973, 285):

(46) a. We made pudding enough to last for days.

       b. We made puddings enough to last for days.

Bresnan observes that this postnominal use of *enough* is "contingent on the absence of an intervening determiner" (1973, 285). In our terminology, it is contingent on the presence of the $\emptyset$ article. If there is no noun in N_1''' of (3) and if there is no overt article in C_2'', i.e., if $\emptyset$ occurs, then choice of number in the noun phrase is predictable: the head must either be a mass noun like *pudding*, which is inherently singular, or a count noun like *puddings*, which must be plural. Observe that these are the only two types of noun phrases in which *enough* can occur if $\emptyset$ is present (cf. **enough book*). In essence, since the number of such noun phrases is *not* free, but predictably singular or plural from other considerations, position N_3''' is free to contain a base generated *enough* accounting for (46).

Consider now X'' residents in posthead positions. Position C_8''' is the position of postnominal modifiers, including not only adjectives and prepositional phrases, but also participles, infinitives, and restrictive relative clauses, whose internal structure I shall discuss in Chapter three.

Position N_7''', the home of the genitive of quality, is also the home of the double possessive construction, so named because of the presence of both *of* and POSS. Consider (47) and (48).

(47) a. Bills' friend

       b. a friend of Bill's

(48) a. the doctor's patient

       b. a patient of the doctor's

The most problematical feature of this construction is the fact that it is severely restricted. In particular, the head noun may not have any of the usual postnominal adjuncts. Compare (49) with (50).

(49) a. the man that Sue is going to marry's mother

         [the man that Sue is going to marry] [POSS] mother

         N_1 C_2

       b. the man with the beard's mother

         [the man with the beard] [POSS] mother

         N_1 C_2

       c. the man standing over there's mother

         [the man standing over there] [POSS] mother

         N_1 C_2

       d. the man present at noon's mother

         [the man present at noon] [POSS] mother

         N_1 C_2

(50) a. *(I know) the mother of the man that Sue is going to marry's[13]
     b. *(I know) the mother of the man with the beard's
     c. *(I know) the mother of the man standing over there's
     d. *(I know) the mother of the man persent at noon's

Moreover, I do not think that nouns in such constructions can even be pluralized. Consider (51) and (52).

(51) a. the children's mother
     [the children] [POSS] mother
     N_1 C_2

     b. the women's mother
     [the women] [POSS] mother
     N_1 C_2

     c. the boys' mother
     [the boys] [POSS] mother
     N_1 C_2

(52) a. *(I know) the mother of the children's
     b. *(I know) the mother of the women's
     c. ?*(I know) the mother of the boys' (cf. the mother of the boy's; the mother of the boys)

Now this double possessive construction cannot be derived from some source like that depicted in (53).

(53) a. a friend of John's friend(s)
     b. a friend of John's $\emptyset$

If this were the case, there would be no accounting for the ungrammaticality of (50) and (52). Notice that we do have phrases like *a friend of the man that Sue is going to marry's friend*, etc. (cf. Note 13).

The infelicity of (50) and (52) suggests the presence of some element which totally blocks posthead modification. I propose that that element is the case marker POSS, occupying second posthead position on the X''' level of such noun phrases, i.e., C_8''' of (3). The normal position for POSS is first prehead position on the X''' level, i.e., C_2''', the position of the definite articles. Since none of the definite articles occurs in posthead position, the position being suggested now for POSS is unusual. In any case, if we assume this to be correct, the structures associated with the noun phrases in (54) would be those diagrammed in (55).

(54) a. a friend of Bill's
     b. that meddlesome teacher of Mary's child's

(55)   a.

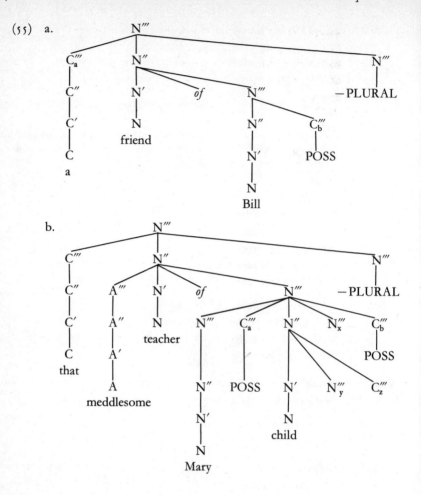

b.

If POSS occurs in C_a''', as it does in (55b), it simply follows the entire preceding N''' (in this case, *Mary*), in much the same way that *the* follows *all* in *all the boys*. If, on the other hand, POSS occurs in C_b''', as it does in both structures of (55), it is a characterizer which modifies the head of the noun phrase in which it occurs, i.e., *Bill* in (55a) and *child* in (55b). There is thus an important configurational difference between C_a''' and C_b''' in (55). Presumbaly, when POSS is in C_b''', positions N_x''', N_y''', and C_z''' cannot be filled in the structure. This will allow the possessive suffix to be attached directly to the head noun, as seems to be required in such cases.[14] This rules out (50) and (52), while allowing (49) and (51), as required.

In support of this analysis, notice that the double possessive construction also cannot contain nouns which normally fill N_1''' of (3):

(56) a. *the mother of all of the children's
      b. *the mother of a bunch of the men's

The explanation for these ungrammatical phrases is that nouns such as *all* and *bunch* require plural number in X‴ level posthead position, i.e., N_x''' of (55b). But N_x''' cannot occur in double possessive noun phrases, as we have just observed (cf. (52); hence, (56) will not occur. On the other hand, there is no reason to rule out the occurrence of a descriptive adjective in prehead position on the X″ level, as the following examples illustrate:

(57) a. the mother of the young child's
      b. a friend of a little boy's

What this amounts to in the terminology of RG is that the double possessive construction of English requires the presence of POSS, as a permanent resident, in second posthead position on the X‴ level. This prehead/posthead alternation of a syntactic category is, of course, one of the major features of RG. As we have seen, there are many cases where items can occur in either prehead or posthead position, such as *the available books* versus *the books available* or *enough pudding* versus *pudding enough*; POSS simply happens to be a special case of such alternations.

Summarizing, we have the following positions in noun phrases, some of which are yet to be discussed:

(58) a. X‴ LEVEL
      first prehead: definite articles and POSS
      second prehead: floating quantifiers and other +Q nouns as-
                        sociated with the pseudopartitive construction
      first posthead: NUMBER
      second posthead: appositive relatives, comparatives, partitives,
                        and, in the double possessive construction,
                        POSS

      b. X″ LEVEL
      first prehead: descriptive adjectives
      second prehead: cardinals, ordinals, *many*, *several*, *dozen*, etc.
      first posthead: genitives of quality and double possessives
      second posthead: postpositive adjectives, prepositional phrases,
                        participles, infinitives, and restrictive relatives.

Notice that nominal adjuncts (N) must precede characterizal adjuncts (C) in both prehead and posthead positions, on each level, when they both occur as in (3). We thus have a formal, totally syntactic way of distinguishing [+A, +N] from [+A, −N]. Misleading terminology such as *noun*, *article*, and *adjective* can therefore be supplanted with syntactic criteria such as first prehead position X″

level, second prehead position X''' level, etc. However, as noted above, I shall continue to use traditional terminology for convenience.

Notice also that the left-to-right order is strictly observed in both prehead and posthead positions. There are no noun phrases like the following:

(59)   a. *the all men
       b. *all of the pretty many girls
       c. *the most interesting men present of eloquence
       d. *the book that is yellow of John's[15]

2.2 A NOTE ON FORMALISM

As a step toward formalizing some of the above facts, I propose that the grammar contain "Phrase Structure Filters" (PSFs). These PSFs apply simultaneously, their function being to check the phrase structure for violations.

Making use of traditional terminology, we may say that items which occur in first prehead position on the X''' level belong to the class of characterizers, the degree words, where *degree word* is actually an abbreviation for a constellation of syntactic features like [−Nominal, +Prehead, +X''' level, ...] in the way that the symbol [i] stands for a sound that is [+Vocalic, −Consonantal, +High, −Back, +Tense, ...]. There are two major types of degree words: those like *a*, *the*, *this* (*these*), *that* (*those*), and $\emptyset$, which occur freely in noun phrases and which we shall informally refer to as articles (actually, [+____N]; and those like *too*, *as*, *so*, *that*, *this*, *how*, and *-er*, which occur mainly in comparatives and which we will formally distinguish as [−____N]. The lexical entries would then need to specify that the word *that* is [±____N], the word *the* is [+____N], and the word *too* is [−____N].

One PSF would then be the following:

(60)   If there are two adjuncts in prehead position on the same X''' level of a noun phrase, then the adjunct in first prehead position must be an article.[16]

At this point, there is no need to make statements like (60) any more formal than they are, and I will continue to use such language in the examples of PSFs in the next three chapters.

2.3 INFINITE SEQUENCES OF ADJUNCTS

Let us now turn to those adjuncts that apparently occur in infinite sequences in noun phrases, considering first those in prehead position on the X'' level. We have such examples as *these pretty little yellow houses* and *the tall slender graceful model*. Presumably, such strings of descriptive adjectives can be iterated indefinitely; however, their order is not completely free, as virtually every grammar of English notes, e.g., Quirk et al. (1972) and Frank (1972). I will not comment on the ordering restrictions here, as I assume that such restrictions can readily be incorporated into the PSFs of English. My purpose in mentioning such examples is to examine further the internal structure of NP.

Quite often, e.g., Jackendoff (1977, 74), rules such as (61) are proposed to generate these sequences, where the asterisk denotes that the item in parentheses can be iterated indefinitely.

(61) NP → (DET) (ADJ)* N

This rule clearly will not provide the needed structure for such strings of adjectives, as Culicover (1976, 185 ff.), among others, points out. He cites examples such as the following:

(62) John owns a sleek green metallic speedy Maserati,
    a. and Susan owns a sleek green metallic speedy one, too.
    b. and Susan owns a sleek green metallic one, too.
    c. and Susan owns a sleek green one, too.
    d. and Susan owns a sleek one, too.
    e. and Susan owns (*a) one, too.

To account for the behavior of *one* in (62), Culicover proposes the following structure:

(63)

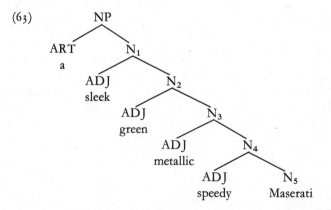

Clearly, the virtue of this structure is that it allows Culicover to say that *one* can refer to any N in a noun phrase. However, it must be noted that the structure violates the conventions of X′ syntax mentioned above (cf. Note 6).
Consider now the following examples:

(64)   a. John met the young man from Cleveland, and Bill met the one
from New York.

b. John met the young man from Cleveland, and Bill met the old one.

In (64a), *one* refers to *young man*; in (64b), it refers to *man from Cleveland*. Such examples cannot be accounted for with Culicover's analysis; however, the Det-Nom analysis of Baker (1978, Chapter 14) will do the job. The necessary structures for (64) are given in (65) in Baker's framework.

(65)   a.

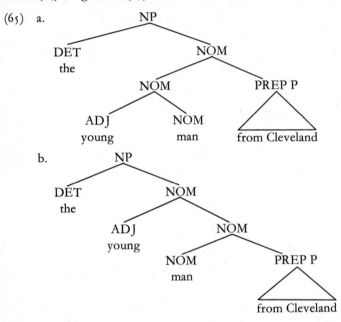

Baker does not provide any rules to generate structures like those in (65), and, since he is operating within the framework of the standard theory, it is not clear, in fact, how the rules could be provided without some very cumbersome notations. What is clear is that Baker's analysis, like that of Culicover's, violates the uniform three level hypothesis. Within our framework, (63) becomes (66), and (65) becomes (67).[17]

(66)

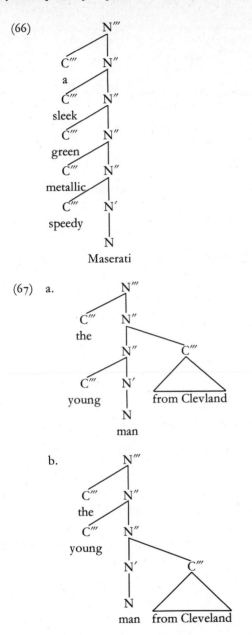

(67)   a.

b.

To generate (66) and (67), we need the rules in (68), a rather simple statement of the possible structures, provided we can further justify the category A, of which C is a member.

(68)   a. $X''' \rightarrow /A''' - A'''/ - X''$

b. $X'' \rightarrow /A''' - A'''/ - \begin{Bmatrix} X'' \\ X' \end{Bmatrix}$

Of course, (68b) violates the three level hypothesis in allowing a category on
one level, X'', to be rewritten as itself, just as the analyses of Culicover and
Baker do. As we shall see throughout the remainder of this monograph, the
three level hypothesis must be modified to allow rules like (68b).

As further examples of (68), consider the sentences in (69).

(69)   John met the energetic young men from Cleveland, and Bill met
    a. the lazy ones.
    b. the lazy ones from New York.
    c. the lazy old ones.
    d. the lazy old ones from New York.

The relevant N''' of (69) would receive the following diagrams respectively (the
circled N'' is the referent of *one*):

(70)   a.

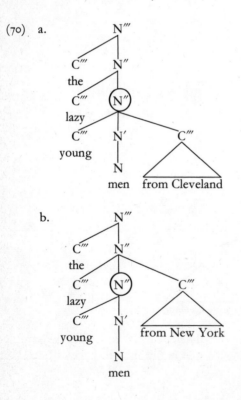

b.

c.

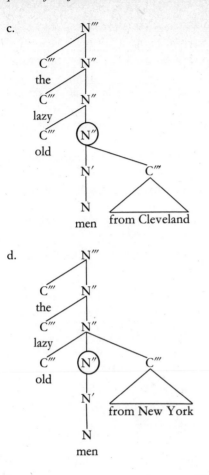

d.

In general, the word *one(s)* can refer to any N″ in a noun phrase provided an X″ level characterizer precedes or follows that N″. Observe the following, recalling that *many*, *dozen*, etc., can be X″ level residents (cf. (58)).

(71) a. *John met the man from Cleveland, and Bill met one from New York. (one = the man)

b. John met the man from Cleveland, and Bill met the one from New York.

c. *John met some of the many talented men from Cleveland, and Bill met all of the ones.

d. John met some of the talented men, and Bill met some of the inept ones.

e. John met some of the men from Cleveland, and Bill met some of the ones from New York.

f. *John met all the talented men from Cleveland, and Bill met three dozen ones from New York.

g. John bought only the books on sale, and Bill bought all the ones available.

h. John bought the books on syntax, and Bill bought the ones on phonology.

i. John bought the book that was on sale, and Bill bought the one that was not.

j. John bought the book stolen from the library, and Bill bought the one stolen from the bookstore.

k. John bought that book of Bill's, and Bill bought this one of John's.

l. John arranged that beautiful bunch of roses, and Bill arranged this ugly one of tulips.

m. *John bought the book(s), and Bill bought the one(s) too.

Observe also that we have examples like (72):

(72) a. *Sue met a man (from New York), and Joan met a one too.
      b. Sue met a man (from New York), and Joan met one too.

We can account for (72) rather simply by allowing the grammar to generate (72a) freely, and then have a local phonological rule for deleting *a* directly before *one*. Note (73), where *a* does not directly precede *one*:

(73) Sue met an energetic man, and Joan met a lazy one.

Finally, observe that *one(s)* cannot refer to any N level other than N″:

(74) a. *John bought the books, and Bill bought ones too. (referring to N‴)
      b. *John met the students of linguistics, and Bill met the ones of biology. (referring to N′)
      c. *John hired a good cleaning lady, and Bill hired a good cleaning one too. (referring to N)

Turning now to sequences of adjuncts in posthead position on the X″ level, we find that these can also be iterated indefinitely. Consider the following:

(75) a. those many books of Bill's that John read that I hated
      b. those books of John's about syntax that Sue read
      c. those books of John's about syntax in that library
      d. the best book of John's about syntax presently available
      e. the books about syntax of Chomsky's that the students had to read
      f. the house over there up the street on the hill with the HBO antenna that I would love to live in, that, unfortunately, my wife thinks is haunted ...

Such examples present no problems that I am aware of to the theory being proposed, and the behavior of *one(s)* in further examples like the following is explained:

(76) a. Sue read the three interesting books of John's that Bill hated and the four boring ones (that he liked) as well.

b. I will buy either that house over there up the street next to Fred's or the one (over here) (down the street) next to Harry's.

To conclude this section, we may note that the function of *one(s)* is to contrast descriptive and restrictive modifiers of the head, i.e., X″ level characterizal adjuncts. By accepting rule (68b), we can express this fact in a straightforward way.

2.4 ADJUNCTS ON THE X′ LEVEL

It seems that the phrase structure rule rewriting X′ must contain the same recursive property of the rule for rewriting X″. This is particularly evident in noun phrases, where in X′ level prehead position I propose to generate structures yielding complex nominals, and where in X′ level posthead position I propose to generate the complements of the head noun. I suggest, therefore, the rule (77), on the pattern of (68b).

$$(77) \quad X' \to |A''' - A'''| - \begin{Bmatrix} X' \\ X \end{Bmatrix}$$

Consider first the matter of complex nominals, which I claim are formed by adjuncts generated in X′ level prehead position. We have such examples as the following:

(78) a. history teacher
b. American history teacher
c. Spanish American history teacher

We should like to be able to relate these examples to their respective paraphrases in (79).

(79) a. teacher of history
b. 1. teacher of history who is American
2. teacher of American history
c. 1. teacher of history who is Spanish American
2. teacher of American history who is Spanish
3. teacher of Spanish American history

Within the framework being proposed here, the structures underlying (78a) and (79a) are as follows (recall that A = Adjunct):

(80)   history teacher:

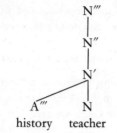

(81)   teacher of history:

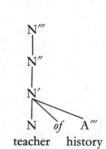

(81) requires a rule for the insertion of *of* in the context N___A [+Nominal].[18] The structure of (81), therefore, is straightforward; (80), however, requires some comment.

One might argue that complex nominals like *history teacher* should be dominated by their own separate node either in deep structure or after transformations (Levi, 1978). In other words, *a history teacher of children*, in such a theory, would be given a structure like (82), rather than (83), which I propose.

(82)

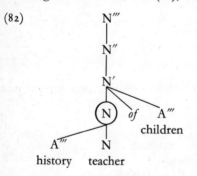

(83)

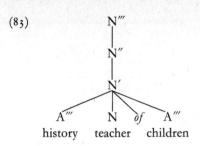

history   teacher   children

However, I can find no definitive syntactic argument for justifying the circled node of (82). As expected, it can never serve as the referent for one(s):

(84)   *John is the virology teacher of these medical students, and Bill is the one of those nurses.

We also do not have sentences like (85).

(85)   a. *John is a teacher of history, and Bill is one of archeology.
       b. *John is the teacher of history, and Bill is the one of archeology.

Such a node also cannot be gapped. Compare the grammatical (86) with the ungrammatical (87).

(86)   These friends of John's can be trusted more than those _____ of Bill's.

(87)   a. *These (history) teachers of the children are better trained than those _____ of the adults.
       b. *These teachers of history are more conscientious than those _____ of archeology.

Further, such nodes cannot be questioned or relativized. Compare (88) with (89).

(88)   a. You saw what of Bill's? (echo question)
       b. You met who(m) with a beard at the party? (echo question)
       c. the friend that I met of Bill's
       d. the man that I met with a beard

(89)   a. *You saw $\left\{ \begin{array}{l} \text{what} \\ \text{who(m)} \end{array} \right\}$ of the children?

       b. *You saw $\left\{ \begin{array}{l} \text{what} \\ \text{who(m)} \end{array} \right\}$ of history?

       c. *the history teachers that I met of the children
       d. *the teachers that I saw of history

In view of these facts, let us assume that (80) is the structure underlying the complex nominal *history teacher*. It follows that the remaining examples of (79) should receive the following structures:

(90) a. American history teacher (= teacher of history who is American)

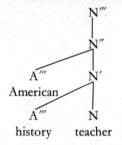

b. American history teacher (= teacher of American history)

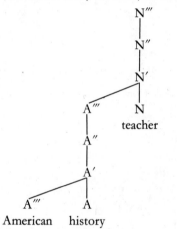

c. Spanish American history teacher (= teacher of history who is Spanish American)

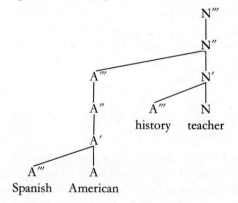

d. Spanish American history teacher (= teacher of American history who is Spanish)

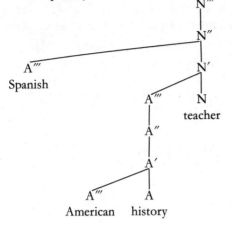

e. Spanish American history teacher (= teacher of Spanish American history)

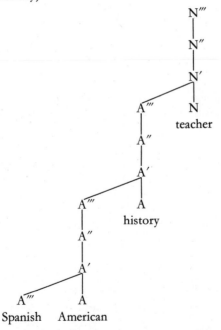

Notice that in some of the preceding diagrams I assume a reading where there are complex nominals inside of complex nominals. Thus, in (90e), *Spanish American* is a complex nominal inside of the larger complex nominal *Spanish*

American history, which, in turn, is embedded within *Spanish American history teacher*. This need not be the case; that is, sometimes *Spanish* or *American* can be understood as a descriptive adjunct on the X″ level, as *American* is in (90a). The possibilities multiply when one considers such nominals as the following:

(91) a. young Spanish American history teacher
      b. young Spanish American history teacher meeting
      c. long Spanish American history teacher meeting
      d. boring Spanish American history teacher meeting objectives
      e. boring Spanish American history teacher meeting objectives report
      f. and so on

In fact, Levi (1978) provides some truly astonishing complex nominals. Consider this mind-boggler from Chapter Three, page 67:

(92) lunar exploration project soil molecular analysis equipment failure

I attempt to diagram one reading for (92) in (93), using the framework I have suggested.

(93)

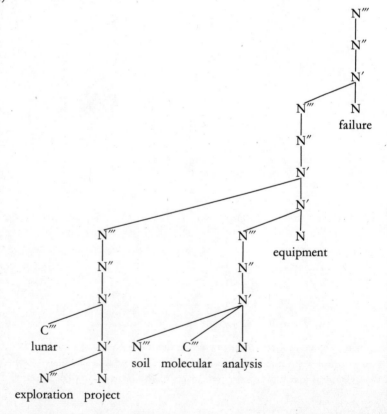

In the reading of (92) that I have chosen to diagram, the subject under discussion is *the failure of the lunar exploration project equipment for soil molecular analysis*. Notice that all the nodes of (93) are necessary, since we can fatten (92) to truly gargantuan proportions as follows:

(94)   all these many recent new lunar exploration project sandy soil fine molecular analysis mechanical equipment failures

In short, the descriptive power of the phrase structure rules proposed is not the result of an overestimation of possible structures. I hardly need to mention, however, that phrases like (94) have more shock value than content for most of us.

Turning now to posthead adjuncts on the X' level, which are the functional arguments of the head noun, we find such examples as the following:

(95)   a.   the nomination of Kennedy for the presidency so young
       b.   that bird's migration from Canada to Antarctica through wind and storm over mountains and valleys via the same route each year ...

In our framework, (95a) would receive the structure in (96).

(96)

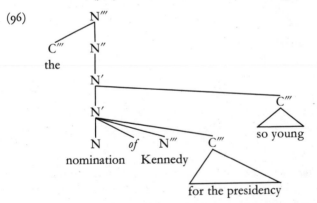

Although, for expository purposes, I must postpone discussion of the fact that *young* modifies *Kennedy* until Section 3.2, let me point out here that *young* does not modify *nomination* because adjective phrases modifying the head noun are generated on the X" level, i.e., off N", as we have seen. Thus, the ambiguity of *the issue of student grants* (from Quirk et al. (1972, 891)) is made clear in the following structures:

(97) a.

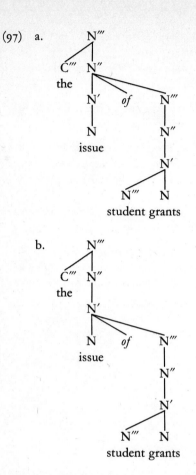

student grants

b.

In (97a), *student grants* (a complex nominal) is a genitive of quality, which occurs on the X″ level. In (97b), *student grants* is the complement of *issue*; hence, its occurrence on the X′ level.[19]

Similarly, the ambiguity of *an intellectual historian* is made clear in (98).

(98) a.

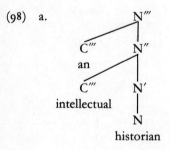

historian

b.

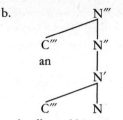

intellectual historian

In (98a), *intellectual* is a descriptive adjunct of the head; in (98b), it is part of the complex nominal *intellectual historian*.

Summarizing, the following phrase structure rules appear necessary to generate the full array of adjuncts:

(99) a. $X''' \rightarrow /A''' - A'''/ - X''$

  b. $X'' \rightarrow /A''' - A'''/ - \begin{Bmatrix} X'' \\ X' \end{Bmatrix}$

  c. $X' \rightarrow /A''' - A'''/ - \begin{Bmatrix} X' \\ X \end{Bmatrix}$

In each case, if two adjuncts occur on the same level, the first must be a noun and the second a characterizer.

Putting together the analyses above, we can assign such N''' as (100a) the structure (100b), under one of its several readings.

(100) a. all of those many expensive automatic electric food processors of Harry's that John bought that I wouldn't give you a dime for

b.

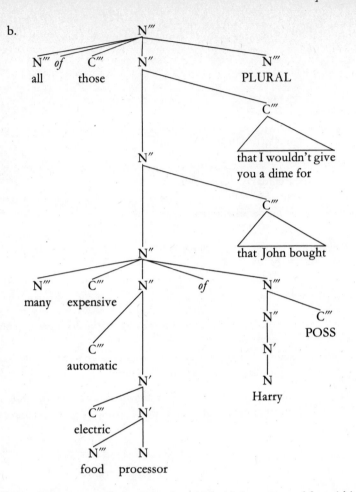

Further, perhaps more realistic, examples which can be accounted for within the theory being proposed are given in (101).

(101) a. that picture of Bill of theirs hanging on the wall
       b. those students of linguistics of Chomsky's present
       c. those books on syntax of Jespersen's available at a discount
       d. all those many interesting articles on phonology of Halle's
       e. his handing of the reports out to the stockholders one at a time
       f. the teaching of children about contraceptives so young
       g. those stories of war of great originality of Hemmingway's

As we noted above, the "semantic" order of adjuncts is not free: certain types of expressions must precede others. For example, it seems that genitives of quality must precede double possessives, for while we have (101g), we do not have (102).

(102)   *those stories of war of Hemmingway's of great originality.

Similarly, expressions of place normally precede those of time. We have *his arrival at the meeting late*, not *his arrival late at the meeting*. Some of these orders are predicted by the separation of levels within a phrase, others appear to have no real justification.

2.5 RELATIVE CLAUSES AND EXPRESSIONS OF QUANTITY

Among the rules in (99), the oddity is (99a), which lacks the recursive property of the other two rules. A more uniform set of rules would be (103), which, of course, we could abbreviate to (104).

(103)   a. $X''' \rightarrow /A''' - A'''/ - \begin{Bmatrix} X''' \\ X'' \end{Bmatrix}$

        b. $X'' \rightarrow /A''' - A'''/ - \begin{Bmatrix} X'' \\ X' \end{Bmatrix}$

        c. $X' \rightarrow /A''' - A'''/ - \begin{Bmatrix} X' \\ X \end{Bmatrix}$

(104) $X^n \rightarrow /A''' - A'''/ - \begin{Bmatrix} X^n \\ X^{n-1} \end{Bmatrix}$

The natural thing to do in this circumstance is to ascertain whether or not there is any evidence supporting (103a). I believe that there is. First of all, notice that the availability of multiple X''' levels will eradicate a serious problem in Jackendoff's analysis of appositive and restrictive relatives (Jackendoff, 1977, Chapter 7).

Jackendoff generates appositive relatives as daughters of N''' (X''' level posthead position, in our terminology), and restrictive relatives as daughters of N'' (X'' level posthead position). Without recursion, this analysis undermines a long-standing argument in generative grammar that pronouns replace (or refer to) entire nodes in trees, and cannot be part of the node they replace (or refer to) (Chomsky, 1965). In Jackendoff's framework each type of relative is often part of the node to which it refers.

To make clear what is at stake, consider first restrictive relatives such as the following:

(105)   a. the *many books* that I have read
        b. each of the *two operas of Verdi's* that the critics discussed

    c. all of the *children* that she had babysat for

    d. some of these *two dozen cakes* that I have iced

It seems to me that, in these examples, the relative pronoun refers to the italicized phrase, and only to that. In particular, X''' level prehead adjuncts are not included in the meaning of the relative pronoun, whereas X'' level prehead adjuncts are. Thus in (105 d), the *that* refers to *two dozen cakes*, not *some of these two dozen cakes*. Consider (106).

(106)   Some of these two dozen cakes of which I have iced all but one were baked by Fred.

The meaning here is clear: *I have iced all but one of two dozen cakes*, not *I have iced all but one of some of these two dozen cakes*. The facts are perhaps even clearer in examples that must be pseudopartitives, like (107).

(107)   All twenty-four of these two dozen cakes that Mary ordered of which I have iced all but one were baked by Fred.

The subject noun phrase of this sentence has the following diagram in our framework:

(108)

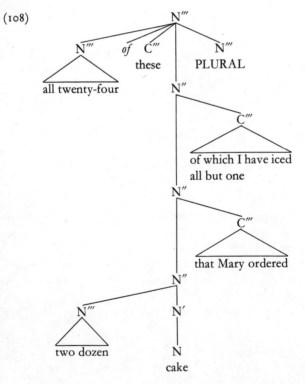

In this example, the sequence *all twenty-four of these two dozen cakes* is assigned the structure of a pseudopartitive, for reasons given in Section 2.1. The restrictive relative, *that Mary ordered*, is a daughter of N″, and the pronoun within the clause refers to the N″ that is a sister of the whole clause, *two dozen cakes*—an analysis made possible by the arguments presented in Section 2.3.

The restrictive relative *of which I have iced all but one*, which could also have an appositive reading, contains within it a partitive, i.e., the underlying structure in a TG before WH-movement is *I have iced all but one cake of which* (*which = two dozen cakes that Mary ordered*). Thus the referent for *which* is also the N″ that is the sister of the clause containing *which*. These relationships cannot be explained within Jackendoff's analysis of relatives. In particular, in our analysis, the referent for a restrictive relative pronoun is always the N″ that is the left-sister of the entire relative clause.[20]

A further problem for Jackendoff's analysis of restrictive relatives arises in connection with examples like (109).

(109)   all of these interesting books that John said he read

This phrase is ambiguous, in that the *that* can refer to either *interesting books* or *books* alone. The phrase is rendered unambiguous as follows:

(110)   a.

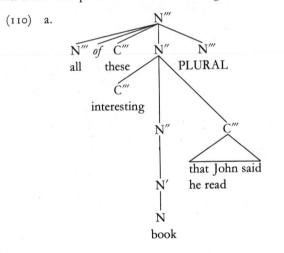

b.

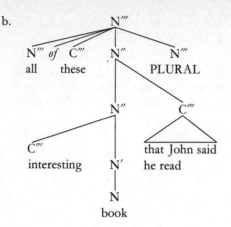

In (110a), John said he read *books* only; the person uttering the phrase has added the fact that they are *interesting*. The referent in this reading is only the N″, *book*. In (110b), John said he read *interesting books*; the referent for the relative is thus *interesting books*. Without some way to represent the reading in (110b), the following sentence is contradictory.

(111) All of those interesting books that John said he read are downright boring.

Compare now the sentences in (112); (112a) contains an appositive relative and (112b), a restrictive relative.

(112) a. All five of those five boys, who I happened to see set at the local Boys' Club, went on a hike.
b. All five of those five boys that belong to the local Boys' Club went on a hike.

It seems to me that the *who* in (112a) refers to *all five of those five boys*, whereas *that* in (112b) refers only to *five boys*. Rule (103b) will generate the correct structure for (112b): namely, (113b). What is needed is a rule like (103a) to generate (113a), which underlies the subject N‴ of (112a).

(113)   a.

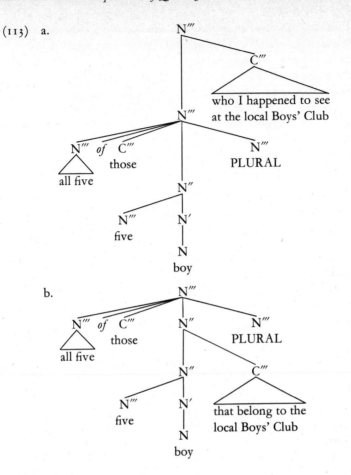

Thus if we accept (103a), we have what appears to be the appropriate structure for appositive relatives, and we may formulate the following principles:

(114)   a. Appositive relative pronouns refer to that N''' which is the left-
sister of the entire appositive relative clause.
b. Restrictive relative pronouns refer to that N'' which is the left-
sister of the entire restrictive clause.

So far in our theory, the N'' level may serve as the referent for either *one(s)* or a
restrictive relative pronoun.

It is worthwhile to point out explicitly that the theory being proposed has, in
the course of exposition, provided structures for stacked relatives. Such clauses
occur in (100), (108), and the following:

(115)   All those many books that John read that I hated were lost in the fire.

It is not necessary therefore to appeal to elaborate transformational machinery to describe the structure of stacked relatives, as has often been the case. (See Stockwell et al. (1973) for discussion.)

The straightforward analyses of relatives presented here seem to me to offer very positive gains in the theory of relativization, and therefore I believe they offer strong support for recursiveness on the N" and N''' levels.

Turning to prehead position on the X''' level, we find that expressions of quantification, of which I assume possession is one, can also be recursive. We have examples like (116).

(116)   a. all of John's friends are ...
        b. all of John's money is ...
        c. all twelve of John's twelve friends
        d. a small group of that bunch of John's many friends are ...
        e. John's wife's bunch of complaints are ...

These examples are interesting because they reveal that our theory has a way to render unambiguous the meanings of phrases containing multiple expressions of quantification. Consider first (117).

(117)   a. John's wife's bunch of complaints are identical to Bill's (wife's bunch of complaints).
        b. John's wife's bunch of complaints are identical to Mary's husband's (bunch of complaints).

Within our framework, *John's wife's bunch of complaints*, when interpreted as a pseudopartitive, has one of the following three possible representations:

(118)   a.

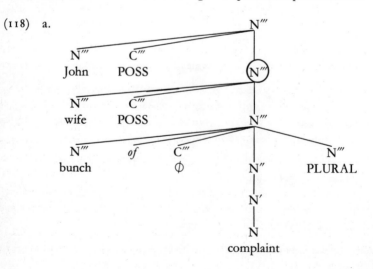

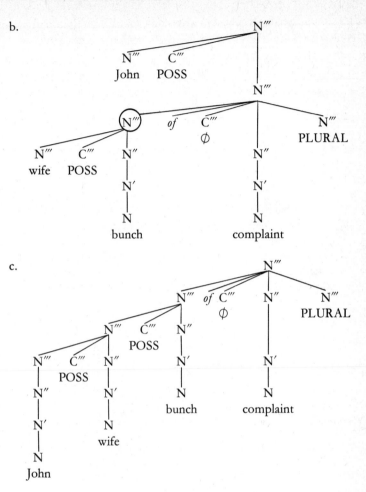

The usual structure assigned to multiple occurrences of prehead possessives is the left-branching structure of (118c) (cf. Chomsky (1965), Chapter 1)). However, this sort of structure will not account for the gapped sequences in (117), since the gapped items (those in parentheses) do not correspond to any one node in structures like (118c). On the other hand, the structure in (118a) does account for the gapping. The circled node is the one gapped in (117a); the N''' node below the circled node is the one gapped in (117b). It seems clear therefore that the grammar must contain structures like (118a).

It might be argued that structures like (118a) are counter-intuitive, since each noun in the chain of possessives is subject to co-occurrence restrictions which depend on each following noun. But this is not a good argument, for, as we have seen, it is generally the case that sequences of adjuncts are subject to co-occurrence restrictions of just this type, e.g., the order of prehead descriptive adjectives and the order of posthead prepositional phrases.

What then of the structures in (118b) and (118c)? I am unable to find any justification for such structures in the literature, and cannot think of any myself. For example, I know of no rule that will effect a node like the circled one in (118b). Since the only justification for having a node in a tree is that it must be mentioned in the structural index of some rule, I conclude that our grammar must contain the following PSF:

> (119)   *Any structure containing left-branching recursion of possessives in a prehead adjunct.

I suspect that the only reason structures like (118c) have occurred at all in the literature is that, until now, recursion through the head has not been available in generative grammar. Of course, this is one of the major features of RG. As we shall see shortly, (119) is part of a more general PSF regarding prehead nominal adjuncts.

Consider now examples like (120).

> (120)   all of the (many) men's (many) coats

Notice that the *all* in this phrase can refer to either *men* or *coats*. If it refers to *men*, then we can have an additional quantifier referring to coats:

> (121)   a. some of all of the men's coats (are ...)
>   b. a bunch of all of the men's coats (are ...)

Furthermore, whether *all* refers to *men* or *coats*, (120) can have either a pseudopartitive or partitive reading.[21] The four structures are as follows:

> (122)   a. Pseudopartitive; *all* modifies *coats*:

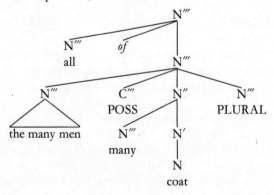

b. Pseudopartitive; *all* modifies *men*:

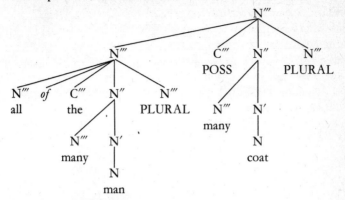

c. Partitive; *all* modifies *coats*:

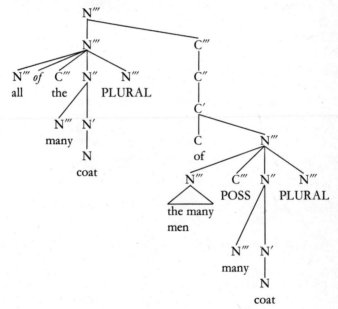

d. Partitive; *all* modifies *men*:

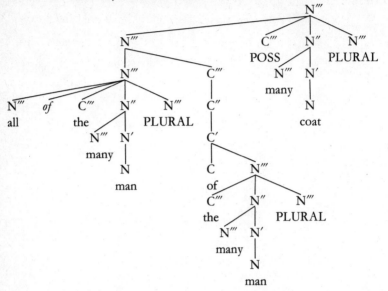

Using the above structures as a basis for discussion, notice first that rendering the pseudopartitives unambiguous is a straightforward matter. Thus (122a) is the structure which underlies examples like (123).

(123) a. *All of the man's many coats* are in that closet.
       b. *All of the man's money* is in that bank.

For (122b) we have examples like these:

(124) a. *Both of the men's money* is in that bank.
       b. All of *both of the men's money* is in that bank.

Turning to the partitives, examples with a structure like (122c) are the following:

(125) a. *All of the ones that I have seen of these many men's many coats* are hand-woven.
       b. *Of those many men's sixteen coats, all of these fourteen hand-woven ones* are exquisite.

The structure for which no grammatical sentences can be found is, interestingly enough, (122d)—at least when the genitive phrase (i.e., the whole) is present. Thus while we have examples like (126a), there are no sentences like (126b).

(126) a. Both of the men's money is in that bank. (= 124a)
       b. *These sixteen men of those twenty men's coats are hand-woven.

Preposing the partitive does not help:

(127)   *Of those twenty men, these sixteen men's coats are hand-woven.

In short, there can be no partitives in prehead nominal adjuncts. This, I believe, is related to filter (119). Accordingly, I modify (119) to (128).

(128)   *Any structure containing N‴ recursion in a *prehead nominal adjunct*, when either
a. the recursion involves the N‴ level of the adjunct (cf. (122d))
or
b. the recursion involves an additional prehead adjunct containing POSS (cf. (118b) and (118c)).

These filters will be formalized, simplified, and generalized as we proceed.

It follows from (128) that there should be no appositive relatives in the position occupied by the partitive in (122d), and that prediction of RG is exactly correct. While we have (129a), we do not have (129b).

(129)   a. the man that Sue voted for's mother
b. *the man, whom I happened to see at the store,'s mother

As we shall see in the next section, comparative clauses also cannot occur in the position under investigation.

Now observe that in all our diagrams with partitives and appositive relatives, these structures have been two levels above the X″ level. In other words, in the rewrite of N‴ to N″, there has never been a posthead characterizer as sister to N″. This fact was hidden in our initial discussion of the partitive in Section 2.1, because, at that point, we did not have recursion available. I believe that the grammar must therefore contain the following PSFs, which, after discussion of the category Characterizer in Chapter 3, we shall be able to simplify greatly.

(130)   a. Partitives, appositive relatives, and comparative clauses cannot occur on the last rewrite of N‴ as N″, as posthead characterizers.
b. The abstract category CASE must occur on the last rewrite of N‴, as a posthead characterizer.
c. The abstract category NUMBER must occur on the last rewrite of N‴, as a posthead noun.
d. The last rewrite of N‴, and only the last rewrite of N‴, may contain articles.

Filter (130a) follows from the above discussion.

Filter (130b) is a general feature of residential grammar. I shall have little to say about CASE here, except to mention that POSS, as we have seen, is generated in the position mentioned (see Binkert (in preparation)).

Filter (130c) ensures that noun phrases will have a number. The major exception we have seen is in connection with pronouns.

Filter (130d) prevents the iteration of articles, though it allows for the iteration of POSS on successive N‴ levels of the head only.

I believe that the above analyses offer compelling reasons for accepting recursiveness on every level of noun phrases. The rule (131) therefore seems justified.

$$(131) \quad X^n \rightarrow /A''' - A'''/ - \begin{Bmatrix} X^n \\ X^{n-1} \end{Bmatrix} \ (= 104)$$

Since there appears to be no need to make explicit intervening unbranching levels, we can simplify (131) to (132), which is the rule (40) of Chapter 1, and which produces such structure as (133).[22]

$$(132) \quad X^n \rightarrow /A''' - A'''/ - X^m, \ m \leq n$$

(133)   a.

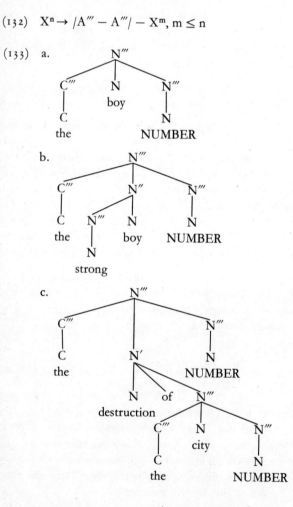

Of course, such a generalized P-S rule schema as (132) relies heavily on PSFs to ensure that phrases are well-formed. Should such filters prove empirically inadequate, the proposed theory will lose much of its generality. Obviously, I see no reason now that they should.

One further point requires discussion before I conclude this section. Notice that a rule like (132) allows a symbol to be written as itself, violating a long standing principle of generative grammar that a rule may not replace some element with a string beginning or ending with that element. (See Bach (1964) for discussion.) However, in the rewrite from the X″ and X′ level there is never any ambiguity in determining the head of the construction, even when the X″ and X′ levels are repeated. The reason is that all adjuncts will be X‴; thus, the number of primes will always serve to distinguish the head from the adjuncts.

It would appear that a problem arises, however, in the rewriting of X‴ as X‴ with some other X‴ adjuncts to its left or right. But any ambiguity here is solved by the PSFs; in fact, there will be no ambiguity, because the PSFs function to check the phrase for violations. For example, suppose we have the string N‴ − N‴ − N‴ realized with free lexical insertion as *man − the −* PLURAL. Such a string would automatically be marked as ill-formed since *the*, being an article, must precede a noun or an empty nominal category, and PLURAL must follow a noun or an empty nominal category. This arises from the fact that all articles must occur in first prehead position on the X‴ level, and number distinctions must occur in first posthead position on the X‴ level. Further, nouns preceding articles must be [+Q], giving us the pseudopartitive construction. *Man* is not such a noun.

In short, by itself rule (132) might lead to ambiguity if it were not for the fact that the grammar contains phrase structure filters. Since our grammar does contain PSFs, this problem is solved.

Lastly, it is worthwhile observing the following. The normal use of language involves the simultaneous integration of a wide variety of linguistic facts. Certainly, the speed of the communicative process would appear to preclude extensive derivation via ordered transformations, following ordered phrase structure rules. This is one reason many psycholinguists have abandoned transformational grammars as models of performance, however adequate they are as models of competence. (Cf. Fodor et al. (1974) for a review of the matter.) Thus transformational grammars are "unrealistic" as models of performance, in the sense of Bresnan (1978).

The grammar described here has no ordered rules at all. Much of the information regarding phrase structure—some general (perhaps, universal), some idiosyncratic—is incorporated into PSFs, all of which we may view as applying simultaneously. Thus, we need not say that a phrase is generated and then checked for violations; rather, in the course of the actual generation of a structure, the PSFs are in force, as conditions on well-formedness. This seems to me to comport well with what is known about linguistic performance, so that the grammar of competence here described might also serve as a realistic model of linguistic performance. I will return to these matters in more detail in Chapter 6.

2.6 COMPARATIVES

Continuing to assume that all other traditional categories than *verb* belong to the category A, consider now the behavior of comparatives, in particular, *more*. This word, like other comparative nouns, differs from the quantifiers discussed in the last section in a number of important respects. First, unlike *all*, *both*, etc., *more* can be directly associated with a partitive. Compare (134) with (135).[23]

(134)   a. All of these twelve men are over fifty.
        b. *Of these twelve men, all are over fifty.
        c. Both of these two men are over fifty.
        d. *Of these two men, both are over fifty.

(135)   a. More of these twelve men than you think are over fifty.
        b. Of these twelve men, more than you think are over fifty.

Second, comparative expressions like *more* are always associated with some unexpressed quantity which is the point of comparison. Following Bresnan (1973), I shall represent this number with the article "x". Thus, underlying (135a), I propose there is a string like (136).

(136)   more x-many men of these twelve men than you think x-many men of
        these twelve men are over fifty—are over fifty

Notice that there is no need to postulate a similarly abstract structure for sentences like (134a); say, (137).

(137)   all x-many of these twelve men are over fifty

The reason is clear: *all* in (134a) actually means or stands for *twelve*; that is, *all of these twelve men* signifies *twelve of these twelve men*. The same, however, is not true of *more* in (135a).

Third, the word *more* is itself a complex lexical item, serving as the comparative of both *much* and *many*. There are no forms *mucher* and *manier* or sequences *more much* and *more many*. Following Bresnan (1973, 277) and Selkirk (1970), I therefore incorporate the paradigms (138) and (139) into the theory proposed here.

(138) as   much bread   as   little bread
       too   much bread   too   little bread
       that much bread   that little bread
       so   much bread   so   little bread
       -er   much bread [> more]   -er   little bread [> less]

(139) as   many people   as   few people
       too   many people   too   few people
       that many people   that few people
       so   many people   so   few people
       -er   many people [> more]   -er   few people [> fewer]

As a result of all of the above, I propose a structure like (141) underlying
(140).

(140)   more of the men's coats than (of) the women's (coats)

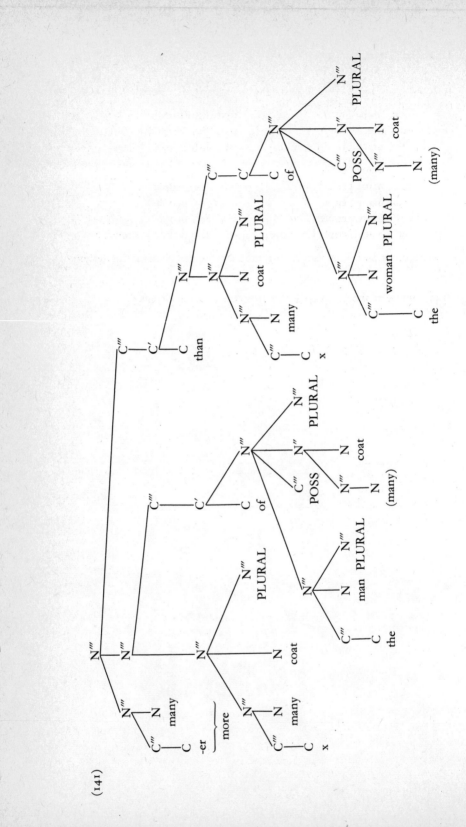

(141)

If we substitute various numbers for the parenthesized occurrences of *many* in (141), we can derive such sentences as the following:

(142) a. More of the men's sixteen coats (that were brought to the cleaners) than of the women's twenty-three coats were ruined.
       b. More of the men's two dozen coats than of the women's fifteen were ruined.
       c. More of the men's than of the women's thirty coats were ruined.

What the above analysis demands, of course, is that no numerical expression be inserted on the X'' level of any noun phrase containing an x-phrase; either x-*much* or x-*many*. Ruling out such expressions with x-*much* appears to be a straightforward, isolated matter. Since *much* cannot occur with count nouns, there can be no sequences like *much three men. But I believe that the reason is even more general than that: there simply are no pseudopartitives associated with comparatives. In every case where an *of*-phrase follows a comparative, that *of*-phrase can be interpreted as a partitive:

(143) a. Of the men, more than I expected showed up.
       b. Of the twelve men, more than I expected showed up.
       c. Of those men that I invited, more than I expected showed up.

Thus, while we have (144), we do not have (145).

(144) a. all twelve men
       b. all two dozen shirts

(145) a. *many twelve men
       b. *many two dozen shirts

Furthermore, just as we cannot have a numerical expression with x-*many*, we cannot have one with *how many*:

(146) a. *how many twelve men
       b. *how many two dozen shirts

The reason for (146) is that *how* takes the place of x in forming the interrogative. Thus, it is as contradictory to have a number in a noun phrase whose number is being questioned, i.e., *how many*, as it is to have a number in a noun phrase whose unknown number is represented by x-many. It follows that the phrases underlying (145) would be (147), which are contradictory.

(147) a. *many x-many twelve men
       b. *many x-many two dozen shirts

In short, all comparatives must contain some x-phrase, which is the point of comparison. Since this phrase is unknown as regards number, there can be no numerical expression on the X'' level below the x-phrase; hence there are no pseudopartitives associated with comparatives, and comparatives are essentially a partitive-type construction. I do not believe that the importance of these observations has been realized in the work on comparatives that I have seen.

Notice that in examples like the above the essentially partitive meaning of the comparative extends to cases where the area on the coats, rather than the amount of coats, is the subject of discussion. Consider (148).

(148)   More of the man's coat than could be repaired was ruined.

In (148), *more* derives from *-er much*, not *-er many*; an analysis made possible by the paradigms from Bresnan and Selkirk mentioned above. As predicted, we have (149), which is a partitive.

(149)   Of the man's coat, more than could be repaired was ruined.

The above analysis of *more* extends to other comparative noun phrases. The relevant examples using *as many* are these:

(150)   a.   As many of that man's assistants as you need *are* available. (< as
             many x-many assistants of that man's assistants as you need x-
             many assistants)
        b.   As much of that man's assistance as you need *is* available. (< as
             much x-much assistance of that man's assistance as you need x-
             much assistance)

(151)   a.   Of that man's assistants, as many as you need are available.
        b.   Of that man's assistance, as much as you need is available.

Other matters regarding *more* now fall into place. In particular, of the four structures associated with *all of the men's coats*, discussed in the last section, only one type can be associated with *more of the men's coats*, which I claim is unambiguous, and derives from *-er many x-many of the men's coats*.[24] Structures like (122a) and (122b) are ruled out because there is no pseudopartitive associated with comparatives. Structures like (122d) are ruled out, because the comparative, which is essentially a partivive-type construction, would require N''' recursion in a prehead nominal adjunct, thereby violating filter (128a). The only type of structures possible are those like (122c), e.g., (141).

For these reasons, we do not get examples like (152).

(152)   *more of the men than of the women's coats

The lack of a possessive suffix on *men* would only be possible if it were possible to compare elements other than the head; that is, if structures like (122d) were not blocked.

If we accept the above analysis, we can allow partitive recursion through the head, and thereby produce structures of much greater simplicity than have been proposed. For example, for the sentence (153), Bresnan (1973, 342) proposes (154).

(153)   Mary swam as many more laps than Joan (swam) as Linda (swam).

(154)

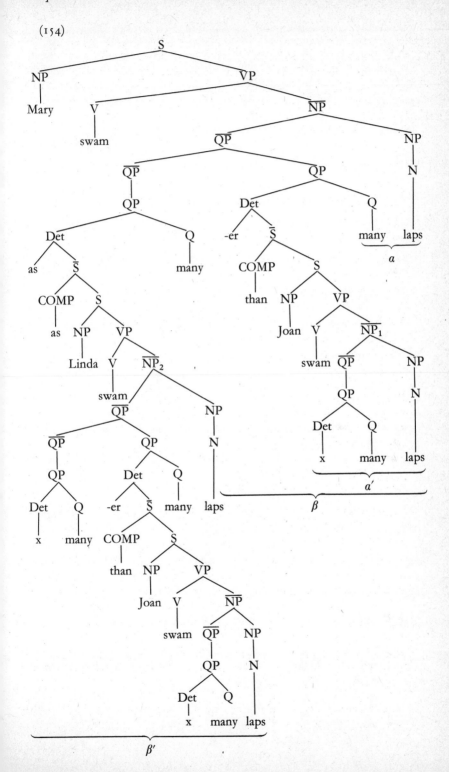

In our framework, the relevant noun phrase is as follows:[25]

(155)

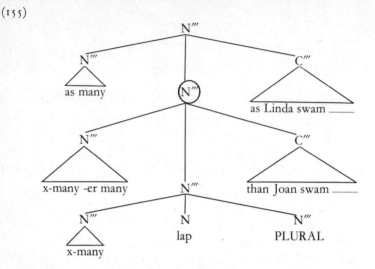

In each case of the above, the gap in the comparative is filled by the left-sister N''' of the entire comparative clause, in very much the same way that referrents for relative pronouns were specified in the last section.

In addition to the above arguments, notice that we now have a way to explain the contrasts in (156), which are similar to Bresman's examples (1973, 290) repeated here as (157).

(156)   a. Mary swam as many more laps than Joan swam as Linda.
        b. Mary swam as many laps more than Joan swam as Linda.

(157)   a. as many too many marbles
        b. as many marbles too many

In (155) there is no posthead nominal adjunct off the circled N'''. (There is only one number to each head, and that occurs on the last rewrite of N'''.) Therefore we may simply allow comparative noun phrases like *-er many* and *too many* to be base generated in this empty posthead nominal position.[26] Previous arguments explain why (156b) is the only possible variant; we can not have (158), because the order of adjuncts must be nouns before characterizers.

(158)   *Mary swam as many laps than Joan more as Linda swam.

Notice that the structure in (155) is a self-embedded one (Chomsky, 1965). As is usual with self-embedded structures, they lead to unacceptability the third time around. Compare the following:

(159) a. John has more marbles than Bill.
       b. ?John has too many more marbles than Bill to hold.
       c. ???John has as many too many more marbles than Bill to hold as Harry.

(160) a. I met the woman that the man married.
       b. ?I met the woman that the man that the dog bit married.
       c. ???I met the woman that the man that the dog that the cat chased bit married.

(161) a. That John left early annoyed Sue.
       b. ?That that John left early annoyed Sue worried Bob.
       c. ???That that that John left early annoyed Sue worried Bob pleased Helen.

(162) a. When John fell, Sue laughed.
       b. ?Because when John fell Sue laughed, Frank got angry.
       c. ???Even though because when John fell Sue laughed Frank got angry, Bill was unperturbed.

The level of difficulty in understanding a sentence like (159c) seems appropriate, given the self-embedded structure that we propose underlies it. On the other hand, left-branching structures for comparatives, such as those posited by Jackendoff (1977, 159), do not seem appropriate. For a phrase like (163), Jackendoff proposes the structure (164).

(163)   as many times more feet too tall

(164)

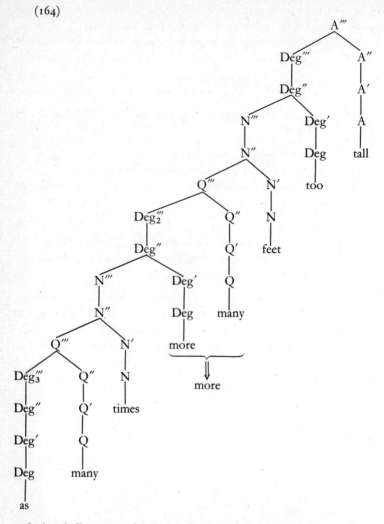

Jackendoff requests that his readers supply a context for (163). Suppose we opt for the following progression:

(165) a. Fafner is too tall to get into Valhalla.
  b. This dragon is more feet too tall to get into Valhalla than Fafner is (too tall to get into Valhalla).
  c. That giant is as many times more feet too tall to get into Valhalla than Fafner is (too tall to get into Valhalla) as this dragon is (more feet too tall to get into Valhalla than Fafner is too tall to get into Valhalla).

In Jackendoff's extraposition theory of comparatives, and also those theories of Bowers (1968) and Selkirk (1970), the most deeply embedded comparative clause is unfortunately the one furthest to the right after extraposition. Thus in the above example, the *as*-clause is the Deg_3''', the *than*- clause in Deg_2''', and the *to*-phrase in Deg_1'''. This entails a novel operation of the cycle, if I understand these theories correctly: since the extraposition proceeds in stages, the higher degree clauses and phrases must be extraposed first making room for those one cycle down to move up. In any case, this seems to be one of the reasons Jackendoff abandons the extraposition theory in favor of an interpretive theory that has the degree clauses and phrases generated in surface position.

On the other hand, Bresnan's theory runs into difficulty because it requires nonconstituent identity, as Jackendoff (1977, 216) points out. Notice what the constituents in (154) are, in particular, those referred to by the Greek letters.

Within our framework, none of these problems arise. The structure for (165c) is as follows:

(166)

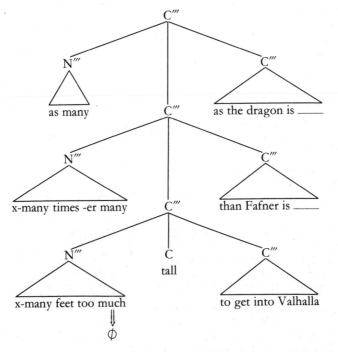

Accepting Bresnan's (1973, 278) rule of *much*-deletion, the structure in (166) seems to me to correctly represent the sense of the examples in (165). Thus, in (165b), the meaning is that Fafner is some number of feet too tall to get into Valhalla, and that the dragon is even more than that number of feet too tall.

Going up a level to get (165c), the meaning is that the dragon is some number of times more number of feet too tall, and that the giant equals that.

The most attractive feature of allowing comparative recursion through the head is of course the ease with which the gap in the comparative can be supplied. In all cases, it is the X ‴ that is the left-sister of the entire comparative clause or phrase. Beyond that, we need no extraposition transformations, and we have underlying representations that conform in complexity to the difficulty in comprehension. Notice that the left-branching sequence in (164), Jackendoff's representation, should be much more difficult to understand than it is. (See Chomsky (1965) for discussion.)

2.7 CONCLUDING REMARKS

In view of all the above arguments, it seems to me that rule (40) of Chapter 1, with which we began this inquiry, must be accepted. It provides underlying representations that are very close to surface structures; eliminates the need for a considerable number of transformational operations; and, most importantly I think, generates structures that conform in complexity to difficulties in comprehension.

NOTES TO CHAPTER 2

1. The diagrams included in this monograph often contain subscripts on categories, circled nodes, broken lines, arrows, etc., which are for expository purposes only.

2. In this monograph, it is assumed that ϕ occurs obligatorily before mass (including proper) nouns, e.g., *butter* and *John*, and before plural count nouns having no overt article, e.g., *men*. For a somewhat different approach to ϕ, see Quirk et al. 1972, 128. The bases and consequences of our assumption will be discussed at several points in the following chapters.

3. The availability of two positions for possessives in (3) will produce strings like *Bill's many interesting books of John's which Mary has read*, which seem to me ungrammatical, though interpretable. Binkert (in preparation) discusses a "redundancy condition" intended to account for cases of pleonasm like this, as well as the following:

(i)   *the available books available (cf. the books available/the available books)
(ii)   *The men all may all have all gone. (cf. The men all may have gone./The men may all have gone./The men may have all gone.)

Though difficult to formalize, the redundancy condition is a necessary part of every complete grammatical theory since phrases containing some types of pleonasm are clearly anomalous.

4. To avoid clutter, I shall eliminate the prime notation in examples containing labelled brackets like (4). Unless otherwise indicated, all categories labelling square brackets are to be understood as X‴.

5. I shall discuss sequences like *pretty little yellow Cape Cod house* below. The adjectives will be discussed in Section 2.3; the complex nominal, in Section 2.4.

6. This rule schema violates the three level hypothesis of Jackendoff (1977, 36) in allowing a category to be rewritten as the same category *at the same level*. Schema (40) in Chapter 1 does the same, casting doubt on the general omission of same level recursion in phrase structure. I return to this very important matter at several points below, particularly in the conclusion to Section 2.5.

7. I have no explanation for these filters at present. In Chapters 6 and 7 I shall discuss the status of such filters in RG.

8. As we have just seen (cf. (5)), descriptive adjectives occupy X'' level prehead position. Some descriptive adjectives can also occur in C_8''', e.g., *available, present, afloat,* etc. (see Quirk et al., 1972). Position C_8''' also can contain present and passive participles, e.g., *The baby sleeping is content* and *The man murdered was a thief*, and adjectives preceded by degree words, e.g., *A man that intelligent is a nuisance*. Note also examples like *A baby happy is a joy*. There are many restrictions on postmodification by adjectives, which will not be discussed in this monograph. The relevant point at present is that X'' level residents are generally adjectival or adverbial in nature (cf. the discussion of manner adverbs below).

9. There is actually a recursion involved in example (28b), as we shall see. The representation is
[[[*ten*]] [*of* [[*these*] *inches of* [*molding*]]]]. This is not the case in (28c), i.e., the representation
N''' N''' N C_4''' N''' C_2''' N_7'''

is not [[*all ten inches*] [*of these ten inches of molding*]]. Note the ungrammaticality of (29d). The
N''' N''' C'''

recursiveness of (28b) will be clarified in Section 2.5 below.

10. To avoid confusion, I should perhaps mention that the partitive is *not* within the *of*-phrase. The partitive is made up of elements preceding the *of*-phrase, which is the *genitive of the whole*. The classical grammarians are very clear on this matter (cf. Smyth, 1956, and Woodcock, 1959).

11. Unfortunately, I know of no way to prove that the head is not *pounds* in an example like (37b), since the number on *pounds* and *apples* is the same. Thus *apples* could be a genitive of quality, and *pounds* the head (cf. *One pound of (those) apples is/are enough*).

12. A position for the *all* within the participial phrase will be discussed in Chapters 3 and 4.

13. Observe that one can say *the mother of the man that Sue is going to marry's friend*; however, in this case, the POSS goes with *man* (cf. *the mother of the man's friend*). Similar remarks apply to the remaining examples in (50).

14. I believe that this is related to the contraction of negatives in the auxiliary, which I shall discuss in Chapter 4, Section 4.2 (cf. the difference between sentences like *John* [kænnat] / [kæn ≠ nat] *go*; only [kænnat] contracts to [kænt]). This similarity between POSS and a negative suggests that POSS must at some level be analyzed as a quantifier. Notice that if this can be justified, we have an explanation for the fact that the noun in (14) must be −Q. A +Q noun followed by POSS, also +Q, violates the Redundancy Condition mentioned in Note 3.

As regards the insertion of *of* in these constructions, see Section 2.4 and Note 18.

15. The ungrammaticality of this example indicates that the double possessive noun phrase is within the relative clause, not to the right of it (cf. *The book that I read of John's*). I shall discuss phrases like *the book about syntax of John's* in Section 2.3.

16. Note that (60) is, essentially, a context sensitive phrase structure rule. It might be written in the form (i).

(i) $C \rightarrow$ article / A''' _____ N''

I shall discuss PSFs in more detail in Chapters 6 and 7.

17. In the diagrams that follow in the remainder of this monograph, I shall omit categories irrelevant to the discussion, e.g., NUMBER in (67).

18. The insertion of *of* in the context given is a rule of wide generality applicable in all of the following cases:

(i)   a book of John's

(ii)   a man of eloquence

(iii)   the love of money

(iv)   the destruction of Rome

(v)   the giving of such long assignments to students

The rule should probably also be generalized to the following cases of [-Nominal] adjuncts, i.e., to all adjuncts, in order to account for examples like the following, but I shall not pursue the matter here.

(vi)   proud of her husband/aware of the facts

(vii)   because of John/out of his mind

In verbs, of course, there is no insertion of *of*; however, as we will see below, the proposals being made here for nouns extend to verbs. Thus *bartend* has the structure (viii) and *tend bar* the structure (ix).

(viii)

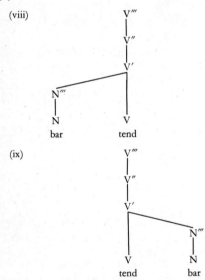

(ix)

19. Notice that our theory can also generate the complex nominal *student grants issue*, which has the structure in (i).

(i)

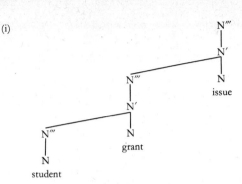

20. Such an analysis is impossible in Jackendoff's theory because he generates restrictive relatives on the same level as he generates pseudopartitives. See Jackendoff (1977, 119 ff.)

21. The partitive reading is actually connected, in each case, with the word *many* on the X″ level. For reasons mentioned above, *all*, strictly speaking, cannot occur in a partitive. There are no examples like *Of these men, all are named John*. I return to this matter in the next section, which involves comparatives.

22. Note that each adjunct must begin at the X‴ level, a feature that separates adjuncts from verbs, as we shall see. Although intervening unbranching nodes are not explicitly mentioned in structures, I believe their presence can be implied, that is, although there may be no N″ between N‴ and N′ explicitly, one is there implicitly.

23. The ungrammatical sentences in (134) should not be confused with sentences like *Of these twelve men, all that we can hire are six*, where the initial *of* goes with *six*.

24. I mean unambiguous as regards structure. There is an ambiguity, but it has to do with whether *more* derives from *-er much* or *-er many*, as just discussed. This ambiguity is not relevant here.

25. It may appear that these structures are related to filter (128b), since we have *x-many* as a prehead adjunct on the X‴ level of a phrase whose head is *many*. However, careful consideration of filter (128b) will reveal that there is a difference between this example and those discussed earlier. *X-many* is not an attempt at recursion; if it were, we would be able, presumably, to have a comparative clause associated with it. There are only two comparative clauses possible in (155): one associated with *-er many*; the other, with *as many*.

26. A restriction is necessary, however: the first comparative in a sequence of comparatives must occur in prehead position, if the head of the phrase is an adjunct. If the head is a verb, then both the comparative noun phrase and the comparative clause are generated in posthead position (cf. *John swims more than he used to* versus **John more swims than he used to*). An explanation for this dichotomy will be given in Chapter 4, Section 4.4.

CHAPTER THREE

3.0 THE CATEGORY CHARACTERIZER

In Chapter 2, Section 2.2, I summarized some of the advantages of considering degree words and articles as members of a higher class[1] which, in turn, is a member of the category characterizer. Treating articles and degree words in this manner, at the very least, accounts for the fact that there are two articles that are homophonous with degree words: *this* and *that*.

Including adjectives and adverbs in the same category as articles and degree words—namely, the category characterizer—seems to me a straightforward matter. The members of [+DEG] are X''' level residents, whereas adjectives and adverbs are X'' level residents. In prehead position, adjectives are distinguished from adverbs in that adverbs are restricted to verb phrases. One happy consequence of this analysis is that it now seems entirely natural that many languages inflect characterizers such as *that*, other demonstratives, articles, and adjectives in like manner, i.e., they all agree in number, gender, and case with the noun that forms the head of the phrase they reside in.[2]

Since these matters seem straightforward, let me turn now to a more controversial idea; namely, that prepositions, conjunctions, and complementizers, including *that*, also belong to the category characterizer. I shall however have little to say about subordinating conjunctions, since the idea that they belong to the same category as prepositions is not so new, even within the framework of X' syntax. (Cf. Jackendoff (1977) for discussion.)

Basic to the theoretical approach of RG are the arguments supporting the contention that all sentence embedding is accomplished by one rule, namely, (1).[3]

(1) $X' \rightarrow /V^n/ - X$

The X in (1) can be a member of any category governing adjuncts on the X' level. These are specified as [+COMP] in Table 1, which expresses the interface between the traditional categories and the terminology employed in RG.[4] The feature [+PREHEAD] means the category can occur in prehead position; [+POSTHEAD] means it can occur in posthead position. The feature

	VERB	NOUN	NUM	TNS	CASE	DEG	ART	ADV	ADJ	PREP	CPL	CONJ
						CHARACTERIZER						
NOMINAL	−	+	+	−	−	−	−	−	−	−	−	−
NEIGHBOR	+	+	−	−	−	−	−	−	−	−	−	−
PREHEAD	+	+	−	+	+	+	+	+	+	−	+	−
POSTHEAD	+	+	+	−	+	+	−	+	+	+	+	+
|___/N	+	+	+	−	+	−	+	−	+	+	+	+
X''' LEVEL	−	+	+	+	+	+	+	−	−	+	+	+
COMP	+	+	−	+	−	−	−	−	+	+	+	+

(ADJUNCT)

TABLE 1

[+/___/N] means that the category can modify a head noun. The feature [+X″′ LEVEL] signifies categories that can occur as daughters of X″′.

The feature values, plus and minus, in Table 1 pertain to English only; further, they refer to the expected cases typically representative of the category, not the exceptions. For example, notice that prepositions are assigned the feature [−PREHEAD]. This is exactly right, given the behavior of most prepositions and prepositional phrases in English. There are however a few isolated cases in which prepositions and prepositional phrases can occur in prehead position. We have such examples as He *downshifted to first gear*, where *down*, a preposition (or particle), forms with *shift* the compound verb *downshift*. Also there are expressions like *an out-of-the-way place*, *an off-color joke*, etc., in which the (idiomatic) prepositional phrases function like adjectives in X″ level prehead position (cf. *a remote place*, *a risque joke*, etc.). However, English does not regularly contain any expressions like *the in the room man*, *a with a scrawny beard man*, etc. This is a peculiarity of English, no doubt related to other factors regarding word order. It is not a universal feature of language, since there are languages which permit expressions of this type. For example, in Ancient Greek, there occur phrases like ἀπὸ τῶν ἐν τῇ Ἀσίᾳ πόλεων Ἑλληνίδων (literally: 'from the in Asia cities Greek,' i.e., 'from the Greek cities in Asia'). (See Smyth, 1956, 294, for discussion.)

3.1 V″′ AND S

Jackendoff (1977) argues that the V″′ node should be equated with the S node of the standard theory (Chomsky, 1965). Such an equation allows him to generalize notions like "subject-of" to both noun phrases and sentences. This, as we noted in Chapter 1, was one of the original motivations of the X′ convention. However, in Jackendoff's theory, the equation of V″′ with S, together with other factors, causes many difficulties; principally, it begets massive structural overgeneration. Recall that Jackendoff's theory contains the initial rule (2), the deverbalizing rule schema (3), and the rule (4).

(2) $V''' \rightarrow (N''') - (M''') - V''$

(3) $X^i \rightarrow af - V^i$

(4) $X \rightarrow \triangle$

Schema (3) yields rules such as those in (5).

(5)   a. $V''' \rightarrow COMP - V'''$
      b. $V'' \rightarrow ing - V''$
      c. $V'' \rightarrow to - V''$

d. $N''' \rightarrow ing - V'''$
e. $N'' \rightarrow ing - V''$
f. $N' \rightarrow ing - V'$

Of course, these rules will produce infinitely recursive structures like (6).

(6) a.

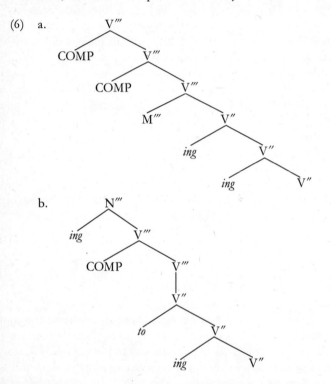

b.

In addition, the unnecessary number of complement *types* that this system will generate makes it unacceptable. For example, there is no reason for a grammar of English to contain both a rule which allows no subject node at all, (2), and one which allows a subject node to be empty, (4). In short, while there is much support for the equation of V''' with S, within Jackendoff's overall framework, this creates many problems.

Within RG, we can achieve the original goal of the X' convention and, at the same time, avoid Jackendoff's difficulties. Thus, extending previous discussions, I propose that the structures underlying (7a) and (7b) are, respectively, (8a) and (8b).

(7) a. the barbarians' destruction of Rome.
     b. The barbarians' destroyed Rome.

(8) a.

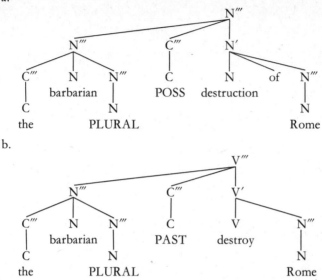

b.

Given structures like those in (8), it is clear that we can generalize relations like *subject-of* and *direct-object-of* to noun phrases and sentences. The internal structural configurations of the N''' in (8a) and the V''' (= S) in (8b) are identical. Further, notice that we are now in a position to equate POSS with TENSE; both are X''' prehead characterizers, the former, a distinguishing feature of noun phrases, the latter, a distinguishing feature of sentences. In characterizers, this position is empty. Finally, notice that, with the availability of X''' recursion, we can account for subordinate clauses and the "fronted" constituents mentioned in Chapter 1. These are merely adjuncts of higher V'''. I return to these matters in the next chapter.

Notice that rule (1) allows for the embedding of all V levels, from the bare verb up to complex sentences, as complements of prepositions, subordinating conjunctions, relative pronouns, and complementizers. We will, therefore, be attempting to justify such structures as the following in this chapter:

(9) a.

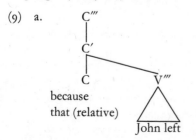

b.

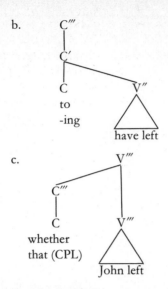

Accepting these premises, we can zero in on the heart of the matter by examining the complementizers *to* and *for*. In particular, if these words can be shown to function like prepositions, then we are but a step away from considering them characterizers.

3.2 COMPLEMENTIZERS AS PREPOSITIONS

Let me begin this section of the inquiry by giving some examples of prepositional phrases in our current framework. The basic structure generated by rule (40) of Chapter 1 is as follows:

(10)

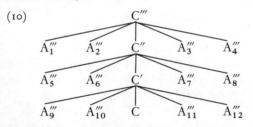

In accordance with principles discussed above, when two adjuncts occur on the same level, their order is [+Nominal], [−Nominal], i.e., N, C. In characterizer phrases like the above, as in noun phrases, position A_1''' contains quantifiers like *much*, *little*, *far*, etc. Position A_2''' is obligatorily empty, as just mentioned. There are no sequences like **as too tall*, **more so angry*, **more too behind the times*. Thus, a further distinction between nouns and characterizers is that nouns have articles in A_2''', whereas characterizers have nothing in A_2'''.

Turning to X''' level posthead position, we note that characterizer phrases, of course, lack NUMBER. Accordingly, positions A_3''' and A_4''' are free to contain quantifiers and comparative clauses (and phrases), respectively, just as position A_3''' of noun phrases can contain a quantifier, if there is no NUMBER at the same level, and position A_4''' of noun phrases contains comparative clauses (and phrases); see (156) and (157) in Chapter 2. We therefore have examples like the following, some of which contain recursion of C''':

(11)   a. [quite far] down the road
          A_1

        b. down the road [quite far]
                           A_3

        c. [so much] [x-much] behind the times
          A_1 A_1
          [as to be downright ancient]
          A_4

        d. [more] [x-much] out of his mind
          A_1 A_1
          [than he used to be]
          A_4

        e. [pretty much] out of the question
          A_1

        f. [a little bit more] [x-much] up the street [than I thought]
          A_1 A_1 A_4

        g. [x-much] up the street [a little bit more]
          A_1 A_3
          [than Harry was (x-much up the street)]
          A_4

The deletion of *much* before adjectives and adverbs is fairly regular; however, Bresnan (1973) notes its optional deletion before some adjectives, e.g., *different* and *alike*. Before prepositions, the behavior of *much* is somewhat erratic. In some cases it can be optionally deleted, as in (11c); in others it cannot, as in (11e). Perhaps the behavior of *much* in (11e) derives from the fact that *pretty* is not a normal degree word, since we do have the following:

(12)   a. This is so (much) out of the question that I refuse to discuss it.
        b. ?Just how (much) out of the question is this?

Turning to examples like (11d), notice than we can have further C''' recursion to produce (13a) from an underlying (13b).

(13)   a. He is so very much more out of his mind than he used to be that he
           is actually nonfunctional.
       b. He is so very much [[[x-much] [-er] [much]] [x-much] out of his
           mind ...

The underlying structure is diagrammed in (14).

(14)

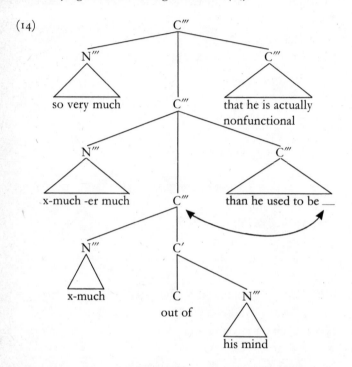

As with (155) and (166) in Chapter 2, each level of (14) except the uppermost
begins with an x-phrase, indicating the point of comparison.

   In short, the theory presented above can quite naturally be extended to
characterizer phrases, including those containing prepositions.[5]

   Let us turn now to the question of the complementizers *to* and *for*. In what
follows, I have endeavored to find evidence that is independent of the theory
being described, thereby hoping to strengthen our argument.

   To begin with, the idea that the complementizers *to* and *for* are actually
prepositions seems justified semantically. These complementizers have much in
common with the normal prepositions *to* and *for*. Compare, for example, the
following pairs of sentences:

(15)   a. He consented to a review of his book.
       b. He consented to have his book reviewed.

(16) a. He aspires to fame.
      b. He aspires to become famous.

(17) a. He pressed them to a reconciliation.
      b. He pressed them to reconcile.

(18) a. John is praying for the apocolypse.
      b. John is praying for his savior to come.

(19) a. John is waiting for Bill.
      b. John is waiting for Bill to come.

(20) a. John longs for Sue.
      b. John longs for Sue to come.

Second, observe that the rules of contraction involving the complementizer *to* must be extended to the preposition *to*. Consider the following:

(21) a. He is going to go. (going to = [gowəna])
      b. He is going to New York. (going to = [gowəna])

(22) a. He has gone to buy a present. (gone to = [ganna])
      b. He has gone to New York. (gone to = [ganna])

(23) a. He's proposed to go. (proposed to = [prəpowstə])
      b. He's proposed to Sue. (proposed to = [prəpowstə])

Third, there are a few other prepositions in English that also take the bare verb as a complement:

(24) a. He will do anything except sing.
      b. He will meet anyone except Sue.

(25) a. He did everything including sing.
      b. He met everyone including Sue.

(26) He wanted to sing instead of dance.

(27) What can he do besides sing?

Similarly, other prepositions than *for* are often used to introduce the "subject" of infinitives:

(28) a. They pleaded *with* John to do it.
      b. I will rely *on* you to do it.
      c. Let's put our trust *in* Bill to do it.

Fourth, as Jespersen (1961, V, 212) points out, English is peculiar in the severe restrictions it places on the prepositions that may occur before infinitives (i.e., the bare verb). In other languages we have expressions like *ohne zu warten*, *uden at vente*, *sans attendre*, *senza aspettare*, etc., quite freely. In such cases, English normally requires the gerund, e.g., *without waiting*. Thus, we may view English as a language which has standardized the use of one preposition, in most cases, before the verb.

Fifth, as Van Riemsdijk (1978) has observed, one of the most remarkable features about prepositions in English is that they can be stranded. But this is also true of the complementizer *for*:

(29)   What did John leave for?

Possible answers to (29), include both (30a) and (30b).

(30)   a. He left for beer.
       b. He left to get beer.

The complementizer *to* may be "stranded" through deletion, but not movement, since "Move *a*" (Chomsky, 1981) applies only to adjuncts:

(31)   a. Leave, if you want to.
       b. Bill wants to go more than Harry wants to.
       c. *What do you want to?

Turning now to one of the major theory internal arguments, notice that more structure is required of infinitive complements than is ordinarily given them. We have examples like the following:

(32)   a. *Just* to place in the finals would be gratifying.
       b. *Even once* to see her happy would be a joy.
       c. For them *still not* to have paid their taxes is outrageous.
       d. For them *deliberately* to refuse to go is shocking.
       e. I am praying *more* for John *simply* to place in the finals *than* for him to win.

Clearly, the italicized elements in (32) would have no home if the complementizers are merely inserted into TENSE or COMP, as is usually the case. The theory presented above provides a home for all of these elements, as we will see.

In view of the above, let us adopt the position that complementizers are a member of the category characterizer.

3.3 THE COMMAND PROBLEM

We are now in a position to discuss the RG solution to the Command Problem sketched in Chapter 1. Recall that this problem entails identifying subjects and direct objects, and accounting for the antecedents of various pronouns. The two command relations used in RG are as follows:

(33) L-command (for Left-of-head command)
A category X L-commands a category Y, if the first branching category Z^n above X dominates Y, and if
a. Y is an adjunct and Y is to the left of the head of Z^n
or
b. Y is not an adjunct and X is to the left of Y.

(34) R-command (for Right-of-head command)
A category X R-commands a category Y, if the first branching category Z^n above X dominates Y, and if
a. Y is an adjunct and Y is to the right of the head of Z^n
or
b. Y is not an adjunct and X is to the right of Y.

These command relations, which are based on the work of Klima (1964), Langacker (1969), and Reinhart (1976), are a distinguishing feature of RG and will be used to account for a wide variety of ostensibly different syntactic phenomena. In fact, it is a claim of RG that failure to distinguish the left-of-head/right-of-head characteristics explicit in these two command relations has made the phenomena seem more different than they really are.

To illustrate the operation of (33) and (34), I shall use the following pair of sentences:

(35) a. The students may both want to visit each other.
     b. The students may want both to visit each other.

In RG, these sentences have the following respective structures:

(36) a.

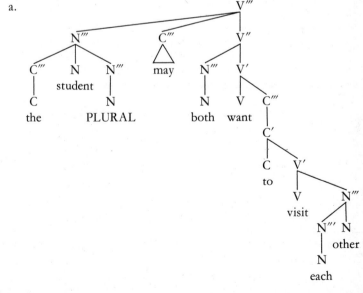

b.

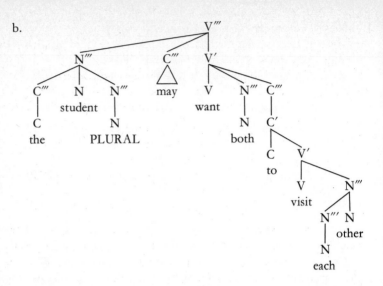

With regard to (35), a descriptively adequate grammar of English must account for the following facts:

(37)   a. In both sentences, *the students* is the subject of *want.*
      b. In (35a), *the students* is also the subject of *visit.*
      c. In (35b), *both* is the subject of *visit.*

(38)   a. In both sentences, *each other* is the object of *visit.*
      b. In (35a), *want* has no direct object.
      c. In (35b), *both* is the direct object of *want.*

(39)   a. In (35a), the antecedent of *both* is *the students.*
      b. In (35b), *both* has no sentence internal antecedent.

(40)   a. In (35a), the antecedent of *each other* is *the students.*
      b. In (35b), the antecedent of *each other* is *both.*

All of this information can be accounted for by the following definitions:[6]

(41)   The subject of a verb is the N‴ that most immediately L-commands it.

(42)   The direct object of a verb is the N‴ that most immediately R-commands it.

(43)   The antecedent of a "floating" quantifier is the N‴ which most immediately L-commands it.

(44)   The antecedent of a reciprocal is the N‴ which most immediately R-commands it.

To simplify matters first, consider both structures in (36), ignoring the presence of the word *both*. In this case the structures are virtually identical. To identify the subject of *want* in this case, we proceed as follows: the first branching category above *students* is V‴, the topmost node; the head of V‴ is the verb *want*; *students* is to the left of *want*; hence *students* is its subject. To identify the direct object of *visit*, again ignoring the presence of *both*, we proceed in this way: the first branching category above *other* is V′; the head of V′ is *visit*; *other* is to the right of *visit*; hence *other* is its direct object.

Now consider (36a) with *both* present. *Both* is now the N‴ that most immediately L-command *want* and *visit*; however, *both* is a "floating" quantifier. The antecedent of *both* is *the students*, the N‴ which most immediately L-commands *both*; hence *students* is ultimately the subject of both *want* and visit.[7]

Now consider (36b) also with *both* present. In this diagram, *both* simultaneously R-commands *want* and L-commands *visit*; hence it is the object of *want* and the subject of *visit*. Furthermore, *both* now R-commands *each other*, so it is the antecedent of *each other*. Lastly, *students* cannot be the antecedent of *both*, since it does not L-command *both* (*both* is not to the left of the head of V‴, i.e., *want*).

All relevant information is thus accounted for.

Further, as we shall see in the next chapter, since a noun like *destruction* is [[destroy] [tion]] in RG, (41) and (42) also account for the pair (8a)/(8b), N′V   N
thereby accomplishing directly one of the original goals of X′ syntax.

It is now possible to explain why *so young*, in phrases like *the nomination of Kennedy for the presidency so young*, goes with *Kennedy* and not with *nomination* or *presidency*. This example, (96) in Chapter 2, I repeat here for convenience:

(= 96 in Chapter 2):

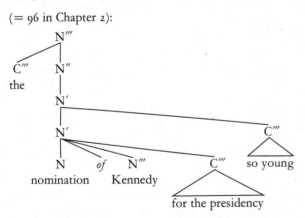

In every case that I have examined in English, the operation of the command relations (33) and (34) is never sensitive to rewrites of the same category at the same level—that is, "n" in "Z^n" of both (33) and (34) must be constant. Given this, observe the following: the first branching category above *Kennedy* is N'; N' also dominates *young*; *young* is an adjunct; and, *young* is to the right of *nomination*, the head of N'. Therefore *Kennedy* R-commands *young*. But, by exactly the same definition of R-command, *young* R-commands *Kennedy*. In short, these two adjuncts R-command each other in complement position of *nomination*.

Suppose now that we say that items which R-command each other on the X' level are given "coreferential interpretation", meaning that they have the same referent. Thus, in this case, for some x, x is the referent of both *Kennedy* and *so young*. This extension of R-command can be applied in all cases of objective complements, so that we can say the two adjuncts in each of the following have the same referent: *eat the food raw*; *consider the man smart*; *see the man walking*; *put those down*; *paint the house red*; *push the door open*; *elect the man senator*; *want the problems eliminated*; and, with the same head, *have the children in*, *have the cars washed*, *have the baby quiet*. Clearly, the precise interpretation of these examples depends on the semantic character of the head—in particular, whether its meaning is essive, inchoative, causative, or neutral.[8]

Given this, we may say that *so young* "goes with" *Kennedy*, leaving the exact specification of the nature of the relationship to further semantic interpretation which must consider the meaning of the head.[9] Such matters are pursued in Chapter 6.

Once familiar with the new terminology, the reader can see that RG provides a simple and direct method for solving the Command Problem. Further, no transformations are involved at all, and the grammar does not have to contain abstract elements like PRO and TRACE.

Now observe that the claim that *both* is simultaneously the object of *want* and the subject of *visit* in (36b) is exactly what a grammar of English must do. This approach, which has never been proposed in TG to my knowledge, directly explains two conflicting facts: while the subject of the infinitive is under co-occurrence restrictions bound to the verb within the infinitive, that subject is nonetheless in the accusative (or objective) case, in all languages having case or remnants thereof. This accounts for the oddity of (45) and the case of the pronoun in (46).

(45)   Mary wants the man to become pregnant.

(46)   Mary wants him to go. (cf. *Mary wants he to go.)

Before proceeding with further examples of the command relation, I must discuss another important difference between RG and TG. In all versions of TG, including those cast within the framework of X' syntax, no distinction is made structurally between predicate nominatives and direct objects. In RG, this is not the case. Predicate nominatives are posthead residents on the V" level, while direct objects, as we have seen, are posthead residents on the V′ level. This distinction will be used below to account for a number of different facts. For the present, the following examples will, I trust, indicate the need for making some structural distinction between predicate nominatives and direct objects:

(47) a. The boys made good cakes.
      b. The boy made good cakes.

(48) a. The boys made good cooks.
      b. *The boy made good cooks.

Clearly, without some way to distinguish the direct object *good cakes* from the predicate nominative *good cooks*, the ungrammaticality of (48b) is not accounted for. Notice that, essentially, (48b) is ungrammatical because of a failure of agreement: predicate nominatives must agree with the subject in number:

(49) a. *The boy is good cooks.
      b. *The boys are good cook.

If we specify that only posthead residents on the V″ level, not the V′ level, are subject to agreement rules, then we can account for the above data in a straightforward way.

Consider now the slightly more complicated pair of sentences in (50) and the respective structures our theory would assign them in (51).

(50) a. John appeared to Bill to (have) fix(ed) the sink.
      b. John appealed to Bill to fix the sink.

(51) a.

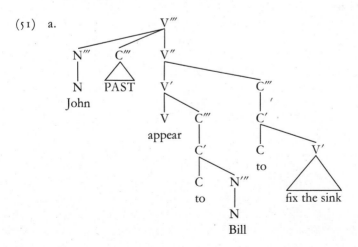

b.

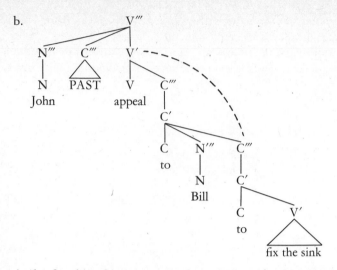

In (51a), the first branching category above *Bill* is C′, which dominates neither *appear* nor *fix*. Thus, though *Bill* is to the right of *appear*, it is not its direct object; also, though *Bill* is to the left of *fix*, it is not its subject. Applying the command relations, *John* turns out to be the subject of both verbs. Further, *appear* has no direct object.

Turning to (51b), *John* is clearly the subject of *appeal*; further *appeal* has no direct object. The problem is accounting for the fact that *Bill* is the subject of *fix*. I have indicated two possible points of attachment for *to fix the sink*. The one, indicated by the unbroken line is a structure like that found in such pre-positional phrases as *to Bill in New York, down the street toward Bill*, etc. (See Jackendoff, 1977, 78–9, for discussion.) The other, indicated by the broken line, is one that would require V′ recursion (not shown), since there cannot be two characterizers in posthead position on the same level. Of the two, the one that seems to me to be correct is the former, which I shall refer to as *the unbroken structure*.

In support of the unbroken structure, notice first that the non-infinitive *to*-phrase can be fronted when the main verb is *appear* to produce sentences like (52a); however we do not have (52b), which, if grammatical, would presumably require that *appeal* occur in a structure like the one indicated by the broken lines in (51b) so that it would parallel (51a).

(52)   a.   To all those who saw him, John appeared to be in the process of fixing the sink.

       b.   *To everyone who he thought could do the job, John appealed to fix the sink.

(52a) seems possible because the non-infinitive *to*-phrase is a single constituent in structures like (51a). Given the broken structure in (51b), we would likewise expect (52b) to be possible.

Second, and more important, the same *to*-phrase can be eliminated in sentences containing *appear*, but not those containing *appeal*:

(53)   a.   John appeared to have fixed the sink.
       b.   *John appealed to fix the sink.

These two facts follow from the unbroken structure in (51b). Furthermore, if we assume the unbroken structure to be correct, then *Bill* is clearly the subject of *fix*. The first branching category above *Bill* is C′, which, in turn, dominates *fix*. *Bill* is to the left of *fix*, so *Bill* is its subject. The broken structure in (51b), which would require some modification of the command relations, is therefore unjustified.

Consider now the following pair:

(54)   a.   John started to fix the sink.
       b.   John started fixing the sink.

To account for this pair, it seems natural to assume that *-ing* is also a characterizer, which, we may assume, is ultimately affixed to its following verb by a phonological rule. The structure indicated is (55).

(55)

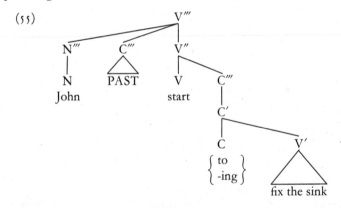

Assuming the above, we now have a way to elucidate the triple ambiguity of (56), which has the three structures in (57).

(56)   John saw the man walking toward the railroad station.

(57) a.

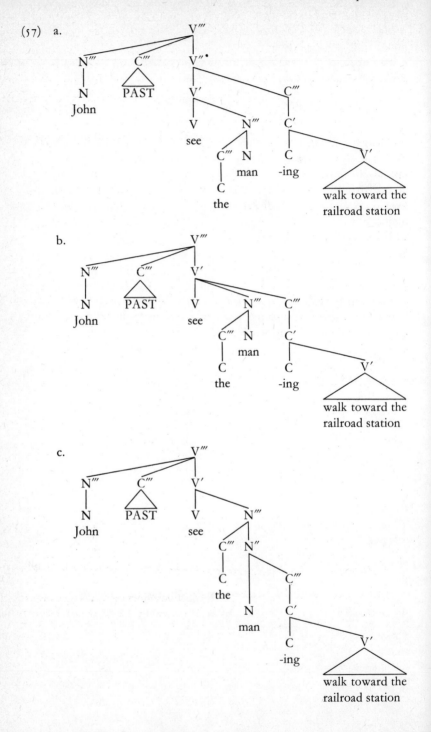

In (57a), the participial phrase modifies the subject since it is in predicate nominative position (off V″); further, *John* is the subject of *walk*, since it is the only noun that L-commands *walk*. The sentence means roughly, *John saw the man while he (John) was walking toward the railroad station.*

Sentences having a structure similar to (57a) include the following:

(58) a. A man appeared *to fix the sink.*
      b. A review appeared *of that book that John wrote.*
      c. A picture arrived *of the bride and groom.*
      d. A man arrived *that we should hire.*
      e. *A picture arrived *of John's.*

In every case of (58), the underscored elements refer back to the subject, since they are in predicate nominative position. (58a) is ambiguous depending on whether *appear* means "show up" or "seem." If it means the former, the infinitive phrase is purposive; if the latter, the infinitive phrase is not purposive. (58b) and (58c) are grammatical because the of-phrase is introduced by a true preposition, whereas (58e) is ungrammatical because the *of* of double possessives is the result of *of*-Insertion.

In (57b), *the man* is simultaneously the object of *see* and the subject of walk, and the sentence means roughly, *John saw the man while the man was walking toward the railroad station.* This structure parallels (36b) above.

In (57c), the participial phrase is essentially an adjective modifying *man*, which is the subject of *walk*. The sentence means roughly, *John saw the man who was walking toward the railroad station.*

Consider now the following sentences:

(59) a. John saw the man while walking toward the railroad station.
      b. Mary always yells at her daughter when cleaning the house.
      c. Jane met Sue after graduating from college.

As these sentences indicate, the subject of a temporal participial phrase must always be identical to the subject of the matrix sentence. This is not the case in full temporal clauses. Thus, in the following examples, the pronoun can refer to either of the two preceding nouns:

(60) a. John saw the man while he was walking toward the railroad station.
      b. Mary always yells at her daughter when she is cleaning the house.
      c. Jane met Sue after she graduated from college.

The grammar must therefore contain a PSF which blocks the generation of any sentence containing a temporal participial phrase in positions such as those occupied by the participial phrases in (57b) and (57c). In short, a sentence like (59a) can only be assigned an underlying structure like (57a), which, in turn, serves also as the underlying structure of one reading of (56). One way to account for that reading would be to assume that the grammar contains a local rule for deleting temporal conjunctions, when they occur between V′ and -*ing*. The rule might be as follows:

(61) Temporal Deletion:
      Delete a temporal conjunction in the environment V′ _____ ing.

But a filter blocking temporal participial phrases from structures like (57b) and (57c) is still needed, e.g. (62):

(62) Temporal PSF:
      *[V ... N^n — C — *ing* ...], where C is a temporal conjunction
      V′

Notice that the deletion rule (61) and the filter (62) are in complementary distribution. This is an unwelcome redundancy. Essentially the grammar is accounting for the same fact twice, namely, that participial phrases can only be introduced by a temporal conjunction when they modify the subject. I shall propose a solution to this problem at the end of this section.

Consider now the following sentences:

(63) a. John saw the man walk toward the station.
      b. *John saw the man to walk toward the station.
      c. The man was seen to walk toward the station.
      d. *The man was seen walk toward the station.

(64) a. John made the man walk toward the station.
      b. *John made the man to walk toward the station.
      c. The man was made to walk toward the station.
      d. *The man was made walk toward the station.

(65) a. John let the man walk toward the station.
      b. *John let the man to walk toward the station.
      c. *The man was let to walk toward the station.
      d. *The man was let walk toward the station.

(66) a. *John allowed the man walk toward the station.
      b. John allowed the man to walk toward the station.
      c. The man was allowed to walk toward the station.
      d. *The man was allowed walk toward the station.

(67) a. *John dared the man walk toward the station.
      b. John dared the man to walk toward the station.
      c. The man was dared to walk toward the station.
      d. *The man was dared walk toward the station.

I now propose that the (a) sentences in (63)–(67) have an underlying structure which is parallel to (36b), except that the verbal complement is directly embedded via rule (1) giving us the structure (68).

(68)

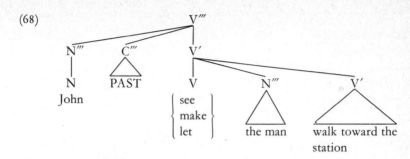

We may then say that preception verbs like *see*, and causatives like *make* and *let*, obligatorily take a "bare" verbal complement (when they are active). *Allow* and (transitive) *dare*, like *want*, on the other hand, take the expected (unmarked) construction in (36b), where *to* must be present in both the active and the passive, if the verb has a passive, which *want* does not have, presumably because it is stative. Perception verbs and causatives may therefore be considered a marked class which obligatorily take the "bare" verbal complement in the active. Both (65c) and (65d) are ungrammatical, because *let* does not have a passive, again presumably because it is stative.

The really important question here is, Why don't perception verbs and causatives take the bare verb when they are passive? I believe that there are two reasons. First, when an infinitive phrase is in predicate nominative position, as it must be in the passive according to our theory (it modifies the subject), the *to*, like *-ing*, can never be absent.[10] There are no sentences like (69).

(69)   a.   *A man arrived fix the sink.
       b.   *A man fix the sink arrived.

The reason the sentences in (69) are ruled out is that verb phrases can never serve as adjuncts in posthead position off X''' or X''. Verb phrases can only be embedded on the X' level, i.e., in the position of complements or functional arguments. This is made possible by rule (1).

The second reason why perception verbs and causatives do not govern bare verbs in the passive is that the past participle of the passive is essentially an adjective, and adjectives never take bare verbal complements.[11]

Summarizing the previous discussion, we see that the command relations in (33) and (34), together with the definitions in (41) through (44), attain a higher level of descriptive adequacy than TG in terms of the Command Problem. The principal reasons are that TG must resort to a variety of devices to account for the same data; must treat the data as though they were unconnected in many cases; and often simply has no explanation for the data. When transformations, as a formal object, are eliminated and phrase structures are enriched, as they are in RG, these deficiencies disappear; and yet the relevant facts are accounted for.

For example, recall what the interpretation of sentences like (35) entails within a TG framework: (i) a definition of the functional notions "subject" and

"object" in terms of structural hierarchy (Chomsky, 1965); (ii) postulation of an abstract underlying structure consisting of a full sentence containing the nodes COMP and PRO, i.e., [COMP [PRO to [visit each other]]], (Chomsky, 1973,
$$S$$
1977, 1981); transformational rules, or similar devices, to account for the positions of *both* and *each*; some rule or filter for the deletion of the COMP *for* (Chomsky and Lasnik, 1977; Chomsky, 1981); and some principle for explaining *to* (Chomsky, 1981). All this, and still facts are left unaccounted for, e.g., the fact that *both* in (35b) cannot refer back to the subject. Further, the TG system cannot be extended easily to account for, say, the triple ambiguity in (56) or the data regarding perception verbs and causatives presented in (63)–(67). Lastly, we shall see in Chapter 5 that additional data the TG system attempts to handle can be described in a very natural way within RG.

Before pursuing the Command Problem any further, we must pause to consider another difference between RG and TG. In RG, a distinction is made between two important types of residents in phrase structure; permanent residents and free residents. They have the following characteristics:

(70) Permanent Residents:
   a. R-command their anaphors
   b. must obligatorily occur
   c. establish a domain which extends from the resident through all items it R-commands and L-commands and over which a binding relation cannot be formed.

(71) Free Residents:
   a. L-command their anaphors
   b. may optionally occur
   c. establish a domain which extends from the resident through all items it L-commands and over which a binding relation cannot be formed.

As examples of residency, English contains the following:

(72) a. John wondered whether Bill saw WHOM? (an echo question)
      b. *Whom did John wonder whether Bill saw ____?

(73) a. John claimed (that) Bill saw WHOM? (an echo question)
      b. Whom did John claim (that) Bill saw ____?
      c. *Who did John claim that ____ saw Bill?

Example (72) contains an indirect question, governed by the word *wonder*. An important feature of all indirect questions is that they contain some complementaiizer as a permanent resident. There are no sentences like (74).

(74) *John wonders did Bill see Jane?

Since *whether* is a permanent resident, a binding relation cannot be established between *whom* and the gap in (72b). Accordingly, the sentence is ungrammatical.

Example (73), on the other hand, contains an indirect statement. The complementizer introducing such statements is normally a free resident. Hence, a binding relation can be established between *whom* and the gap in (73b), since the gap is not L-commanded by *that*. However, in (73c), the gap is L-commanded by *that*; thus a binding relation cannot be established, and (73c) is ungrammatical. If *that* does not occur, sentences like (75) are possible, since the free resident is absent.

(75)   Who did John claim _____ saw Bill?

The examples (72b) and (73b), with the free resident *that* present, are diagrammed in (76a); example (75), in (76b). In both of these diagrams, the reversal of the order of C''' and N''' on the V''' level is viewed in RG as a principled exception to the normal order used in English to signal questions. I return to this below.

(76)   a.

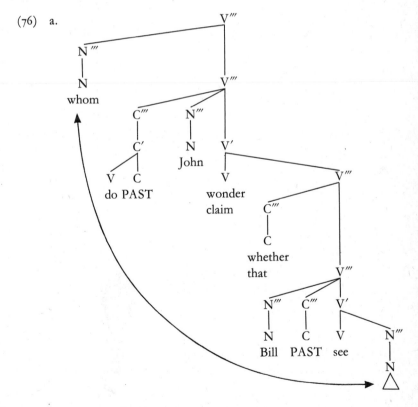

b.

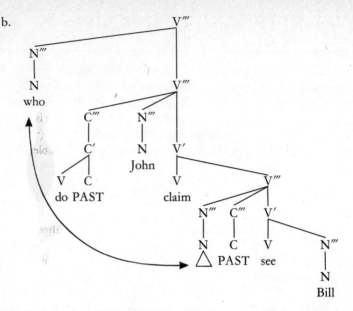

Applying all of the above RG principles to the data originally considered in Chapter 1 yields the following structures:

(77)   a.   Whom does John want to visit Mary?

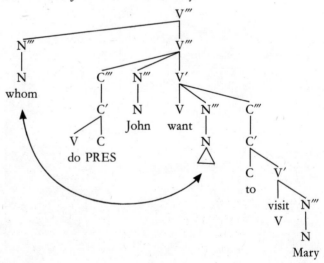

b. Whom does John want to visit?

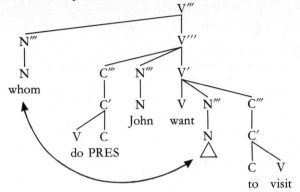

c. Whom does John wanna visit?

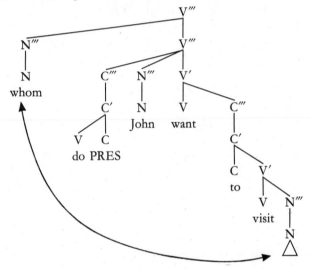

In (77a), *John* L-commands *want*, so it is its subject. Further, the empty node R-commands *want* and L-commands *visit*, so it is the object of *want* and the subject of visit. This same analysis applies to (77b).

In (77c), *John* L-commands both *want* and visit; therefore, it is the subject of both verbs. Further, *want* and *to* are adjacent only in (77c); thus only in that structure can they be contracted, and *Whom does John wanna visit* is unambiguous, as we have discussed.

These examples indicate that (41)–(44) should be refined to allow for the possibility of a *chain of binding*—that is, sequences of anaphors and antecedents that are linked. Therefore let us replace (41)–(44) with (78)–(81), respectively.

(78)   The subject of a verb is the N''' which most immediately L-commands the verb or which itself is the antecedent of an anaphor that most immediately L-commands the verb.

(79)   The direct object of a verb is the N''' which most immediately R-commands the verb or which itself is the antecedent of an anaphor that most immediately R-commands the verb.

(80)   The antecedent of a "floating" quantifier is the N'''' which most immediately L-commands either the quantifier or an anaphor that is bound to the quantifer in a chain.

(81)   The antecedent of a reciprocal is the N''' which most immediately R-commands either the reciprocal or an anaphor that is bound to the reciprocal in a chain.

Note that in all of the above, "anaphor" includes empty nodes.[12] Further, note that these more refined definitions give a more explicit specification of the subject of (35a) and of the function of *whom* in (77).

Returning to the main discussion, consider now all of the sentences in this section in light of the rule WH-movement, which I shall ultimately completely reject. We have the following examples:

(82)   a.   What does John want to fix?
             (cf. (36a))
       b.   What does John want Bill to fix?
             (cf. (36b))
       c.   What did John appear to Bill to have fixed?
             (cf. (51a))
       d.   What did John appeal to Bill to fix?
             (cf. (51b))
       e.   What did John start to fix?
             (cf. (55))
       f.   What did John start fixing?
             (cf. (55))
       g.   What did John see the man walking toward?
             (cf. (56))
       h.   *What did John see the man while walking toward?
             (cf. (59a))
       i.   *What did John see the man while he was walking toward?
             (cf. (60a))
       j.   What did John see the man walk toward?
             (cf. (63a))
       k.   What was the man seen to walk toward?
             (cf. (63c))

    l.   What did John make the man walk toward?
        (cf. (64a))
    m. What was the man made to walk toward?
        (cf. (64c))
    n. What was the man seen walking toward?

As these examples illustrate WH-movement of the object of *to*-infinitives and bare infinitives is free in all the structural positions diagrammed. Notice also that WH-movement is also free to apply in most cases to the object of *ing*-participles. In particular, in (82g), the sentence can still have either of the readings associated with (57a) or (57b). The more common, of course, is the one associated with (57b). But I believe that the one associated with (57a) is also possible. It will not do simply to rule out that reading, for extraction of objects of "extraposed" participles that refer back to the subject occurs in each of the following:

(83)   a. What did John die saying?
        b. What did John go away carrying?
        c. Who did the man start fighting against?

Notice also that we have (82n), above.

I believe that our theory has an explanation for the difficulty of applying a (57a) reading to (82g). It is, namely, that *man* does not L-command *walk*, even though it precedes it. Thus, despite the expectations set up by the left to right order of the elements, speakers must understand that *man* and *walk* are on different levels, that *man* does not L-command *walk*. This problem does not arise in connection with (83), there being no intervening direct object. When the object does intervene, as in the reading under discussion, expectations are not met. In the reading associated with (57b), *man* does L-command *walk*. Expectations are met, and the reading can be grasped without difficulty.

Observe now that the reading associated with (57c) cannot be applied to (82g). The reason follows directly from the residency requirements of RG. Recall that the article or POSS is a permanent resident of all noun phrases on the X''' level. Even when it appears not to be present, it is present in the form of $\emptyset$, the phonologically null article, mentioned earlier. Thus no items falling within the domain of the article or POSS can be bound to an item outside of the domain. Accordingly, we have none of the following:[13]

(84)   a. *Who do they support the education of?
        b. *Whose did they meet children of?
        c. *What did they trip over the man to fix?
        d. *What did they trip over the man from?
        e. *What did the dog jump on the man reading?

Note that (84e) unambiguously contains the construction in question; hence the reading (57c) for (82g) is blocked.

Returning to the remaining examples of (82), we can block (82h) and (82i) by noting that *while*, like all subordinating conjunctions, is a permanent resident. This is obvious: without clairvoyance, it is impossible to determine the meaning of a subordinate clause or phrase if the conjunction is absent. Accordingly, no item within the domain of a subordinating conjunction can be bound to another item outside the domain. Further, we can now avoid the redundancy in (61) and (62), keeping only (62), by proposing that (57a) is a base generated structure, i.e., it is not derived from some underlying temporal participial phrase. To these latter phrases, we now assign the structure in (85) (cf. (9a)).

(85)

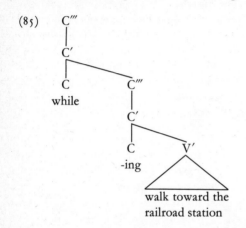

To conclude this discussion, we observe that the RG analysis of the examples in (82) involving bound empty nodes, which are anaphors (see note 12), surpasses a WH-movement analysis in terms of descriptive adequacy. All relevant facts are accounted for principally on the basis of the command relations (33) and (34), and the residency requirements (70) and (71). This includes the possible readings for (82g) and the ungrammaticality of (82h) and (82i).

Now observe that the additional structure given to participial phrases by RG is necessary:

(86)   The president addressed the nation more ignoring current problems that actually confronting the issues.

The structure of the participial phrase in (86) parallels (14), which in turn parallels examples (155) and (166) in Chapter 2.

Second, observe that it is possible to have a participial phrase in all three positions of (57) at once:

(87)   John saw the man walking toward the railroad station rowing a boat in the lake yesterday using the new binoculars he got for Christmas.

Third, observe that we can have a participial phrase in all three positions of (57) and still a temporal participial phrase after them:

(88)   I unexpectedly saw the girl standing over there undressing on the beach last night looking through my binoculars while scanning the area for my lost son.

Lastly, notice that we now have a way of rendering unambiguous such sentences as *John wants the girl to impress his mother*, which can have any of the three readings associated with the structures in (57). In addition, the question *Who does John want the girl to impress?* strongly favors the reading associated with (57b); cannot at all have a reading like the one associated with (57c); and can only with difficulty have a reading such as the one associated with (57a). So far as I am aware, no other theory is able to explicate examples like these, either with or without transformations. Accordingly, I conclude that there is much to be gained by considering *to* and *-ing* a subclass of the category *preposition*, which in turn is a subclass of the category *characterizer*.

NOTES TO CHAPTER 3

1. For convenience, I shall refer to this class as [+DEG] with the understanding that [+DEG] is merely an abbreviation for a feature matrix which includes [+A, −Nominal, +X‴ Level,...]. Recall that the articles, in addition, are [+___N].

2. For further discussion of the categorial breakdown of the parts of speech in English and other languages, see Binkert (in preparation). Observe that the similarity, overall, in the behavior of comparatives in both noun phrases and characterizer phrases argues for collapsing these two categories into one category, Adjunct (cf. (155) and (166) in Chapter 2). As I noted in Chapter 2, Section 2.6, the behavior of comparatives in verb phrases is different.

3. As we shall see shortly, (1) allows for the embedding of infinitives and participles, among other things. The direct embedding of verb phrases as posthead adjuncts on the X′ level is necessary for perception verbs like *see, hear, watch*, etc.; causatives like *let* and *make*; and a few other verbs like *dare* (cf. *He didn't dare go*.). Direct embedding of V^n in X′ level prehead position is necessary to account for nominals like [[[*push*] [*cart*]]] and [*a* [[*who-do-you-think-you-are*] [*tone*]] *in his N‴ N′ V N N‴ N′ V‴ N voice*]. I return to these matters below.

4. The abbreviation "CPL" refers to complementizers. The feature [±NEIGHBOR] will be discussed in the next chapter, and a more detailed feature system will be presented in Chapter 7.

5. Notice also that compound prepositions can be derived, though in a much more limited way due to the closed nature of the category, in exactly the same manner as compound nouns and compound adjectives like *carefree* (cf. *free of*/*from care*), *life supporting* (cf. *supporting life*), etc., and

compound verbs like *downplay* (cf. *He downplayed his role/He played down his role/He played his role down*). Thus we are able to account for compound prepositions like *aside from*, *together with*, *in relation to*, and so on. That these are compounds and not sequences of individual prepositions as has been suggested (Jackendoff, 1973, 1977) is clear from the following data:

(i)   simply because of
      *because simply of

(ii) directly outside of the house
      *outside directly of the house

(iii) totally aside from that
      *aside totally from that

6. Notice that in the following definitions the subject of a verb and the antecedent of a floating quantifier are defined in terms of the L-command relation, and that the object of a verb and the antecedent of a reciprocal are defined in terms of the R-command relation. This is surely not an accident, given the fact that floating quantifiers are restricted, for the most part, to subjects, and that reciprocals must be associated with the direct object. This very important conflation of facts has, I believe, been made possible because of the RG framework itself; in particular, because of the central position it gives to the concept *head of a phrase*. Thus (33) and (34), together with these definitions, offer very strong support for the RG model of competence. Notice, in addition, that it is impossible to state (33) and (34) in any other current version of X′ syntax; therefore it is not surprising that the facts in (33) and (34) have been completely missed by transformational grammarians. I return to these matters in Chapter 6.

7. I shall sharpen statements like "is ultimately the subject" below in connection with a concept called *chain of binding*.

8. Note how ambiguous an example like *put those down* is:

(i)   A man should never put down his son verbally.

(ii) John put the book down on the table.

(iii) Let me put it down to inexperience.

(iv) He put down the drink in one gulp.

Further note that we can employ coreferential interpretation to eliminate the rule of particle movement from the grammar, while still accounting for the relationship the rule is intended to express. In *put N‴ down* and *put down N‴*, *down* and N‴ R-command each other in X′ level complement position and are therefore subject to coreferential interpretation. The left to right order of the particle and the noun phrase is rendered irrelevant. Thus the interpretation of particles and their associated noun phrases collapses with the interpretation of objective complements. In this case RG attains a higher level of descriptive adequacy than TG: it eliminates a rule and expresses the relationship the rule was designed to capture in terms of a more general relationship. I return to these matters in Chapter 6.

9. As we shall see below in Chapter 4, the suffiix *-ion* is considered the head in RG. The root *nominate* is analyzed as a verb embedded in X′ level prehead position by rule (1) of the present chapter in very much the same way as complex nominals were formed in Chapter 2. Thus RG makes no real distinction between complex nominals and nominalizations, any more than, say, generative phonology distinguishes archiphonemes from phonemes.

10. The idea that the infinitive phrase in the passive is a daughter of V″ follows naturally from the fact that it refers to the subject and must therefore be in predicate nominative position. If this is correct, it means that the passive transformation, if it exists, must move complements of the direct object from the X′ level to the X″ level when it moves the direct object to subject position. This

seems an extraordinary thing for a transformation to do; hence I consider this another argument against the passive relationship being expressed transformationally. Perhaps this is one reason that TG has never attempted to distinguish direct objects from predicate nominatives structurally.

11. Notice that these remarks obviate the need for a rule of *to*-deletion, which other theories would have to have in order to relate pairs like (63a) and (63c), assuming that those theories derived sentences from underlying respresentations containing COMP. I shall substantiate the claims made regarding the adjectival nature of the passive participle in the next chapter.

12. In the trace theory of movement rules, traces have frequently been interpreted as "anaphors" (see Chomsky, 1980b, 174 ff., for discussion). In our theory, there is no trace, because there are no movement rules. It seems natural therefore to argue that empty nodes, which replace trace, are anaphors in RG. Structures containing empty nodes which cannot either be bound to some antecedent or given an arbitrary interpretation are ungrammatical. Thus empty nodes are treated in the same manner as elements, like reciprocals and floating quantifiers: all are anaphors. In this regard, one can view the RG analysis as a notational variation of the trace theory of movement rules. I return to these matters in Chapter 6.

13. Great care must be exercised in selecting examples like those in (84) to ensure that all items are within the same N'''. Thus, for (84e), one cannot substitute *What did John see the man reading*, because *reading* here need not be analyzed as part of the same N''' as *the man*.

CHAPTER FOUR

4.0 PASSIVE AND THE AUXILIARY

If the analysis of the present participle presented in the last chapter is correct, it follows that the past participle, which I shall signify with the general ending "-en," should have a structure like (1).

(1)

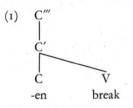

Then the ambiguity of the sentence *The jar could be broken* can be resolved by associating the adjective interpretation with (2) and the passive interpretation with (3).[1]

(2) broken = adjective

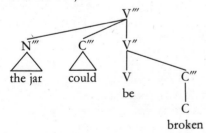

(3)   broken = passive

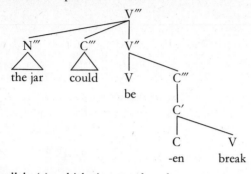

(3) parallels (4), which, in turn, has the same structure as *The jar could start breaking* (cf. (55) in Chapter 3).

(4)

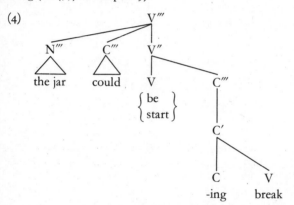

The question is, of course, Is there any independent evidence for such structures? I believe there is. Recall that quantifiers like *all* and *both* can be base generated in a variety of positions, provided they are L-commanded by their antecedent. We have examples like those in (5).

(5)   a.   The two men both could have been linguists.
      b.   The two men could both have been linguists.
      c.   The two men could have both been linguists.
      d.   *The two men could have been both linguists. (= a)[2]

In (5), the head of the sentences is *been*; accordingly, *both* must occur to its left in order to be L-commanded by *the two men*. Now consider these:

(6)   a.   The two men both could have been fishing.
      b.   The two men could both have been fishing.
      c.   The two men could have both been fishing.
      d.   *The two men could have been both fishing.

(7) a. The two men both could have been injured.
     b. The two men could both have been injured.
     c. The two men could have both been injured.
     d. *The two men could have been both injured.

Similarly, we have (8).

(8) a. The two men both could have started falling.
     b. The two men could both have started falling.
     c. The two men could have both started falling.
     d. *The two men could have started both falling. (= a)

It is clear from these examples that the head of the sentences in (6) and (7) is *been*, just as the head in (5) is *been*, and the head in (8) is *started*. This supports structures like (3) and (4).

As additional support for this analysis of passive and progressive *be*, consider the following examples involving *there*:

(9) a. There could have been many people aware of the problem.
     b. There could have been many people fishing in the lake.
     c. There could have been many people injured in the storm.

These, of course, are related to (10).

(10) a. Many people could have been aware of the problem.
      b. Many people could have been fishing in the lake.
      c. Many people could have been injured in the storm.

Now it is clear that there can be no predicate nominatives or adjectives in a sentence without something for them to refer back to in subject position, at least in English. While we have (11a), we do not have (11b).

(11) a. Many people are aware of the problem.
      b. *Are aware of the problem many people.

Accordingly, *there* is a permanent resident in (9) and, as such, must R-command the noun phrase it substitutes for. It is for this reason, I believe, that *many people* must occur to the right of *been* in all of the examples of (9). This is exactly what the structural change of the *there*-insertion transformation effects (Baker, 1978, and many other references). However, in TG, it is a complete accident that the subject noun phrase ends up to the right of the first occurrence of *be*. In RG, using the concept *permanent resident*, this is of course exactly what is expected. Hence, in RG, we have a clearer picture of the relationship that *there*-insertion was invented to express. Moreover, in RG, the relevant structures are well motivated. Those associated with (9) are diagrammed in (12).

(12)

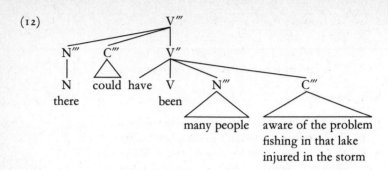

In TG, the output of *there*-insertion has produced highly unmotivated structures which are non-structure preserving in the sense of Emonds (1976). For this reason, I believe, many texts on TG (e.g., Baker (1978), Culicover (1976)) either do not mention data like (9) or discuss *there*-insertion without providing diagrams of its output. But there is no embarrassment at all in RG: once it is realized that the verb *be* is the head of these sentences and that *there* is a permanent resident, the only place that the "moved" noun phrase can occur grammatically is to the right of *be*. Further, this analysis generalizes easily to cases like *There arose a clamor in the hall*, where *arose* is clearly the head. I return to the importance of these observations in Chapter 6.

Notice that structures like (12) allow for the ambiguity of the participles in examples like (13a), which can have an adjectival reading like (13b) or a passive reading like (13c).

(13) a. There could have been many people injured.
      b. There could have been many people injured for hours without medical attention.
      c. There could have been many people injured by his lack of consideration.

It follows from this discussion that the structures for the examples in (14) are those in (15).

(14) a. The jars could be being broken.
      b. There could be jars being broken.

(15)   a.

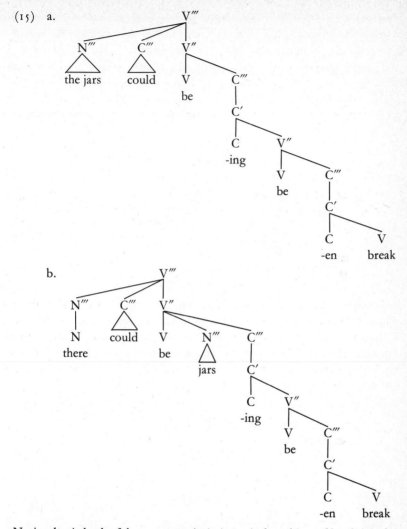

Notice that in both of the structures in (15), *jars* is the subject of *break*: it is the noun phrase that most immediately L-commands *break*. Thus, a distinct advantage of RG is that *be* can be the head of both sentences in (14), and yet, at the same time, there is no difficulty in determining that *jars* is the subject of *break*. Further, we have distinguished *lexical* passives like (2) from *transformational* passives like (3). Lastly, we are able to account for both (16a) and (16b), but for the moment only in transformational terms.

(16)   a.   The jars were all being broken.
       b.   *The jars could be all being broken.

(16a) derives from *the jars PAST do all be ing be en break*; after *do*-replacement, the *all* ends up to the right of *were*.[3] In (16b), *be* must be the head since the sentence contains *could*; therefore, *all* cannot occur after *be*.

Ignoring perfective *have* for the moment, let us turn now to the elements TENSE, *do*, and Modal. Continuing to assume that these elements occupy X''' level prehead position in V''' the way articles and POSS occupy X''' level prehead position in N''', we may posit structures like (17) for *John did/could go* and *John went*.

(17)

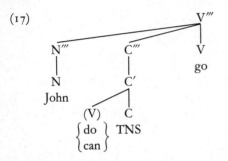

This structure has a number of advantages. First, treating TENSE as a characterizer like *-ing* and *-en* will clearly aid in generalizing the structures involved in what TG describes with the rule, affix hopping (Baker, 1978). Second, structures like (17) will aid in capturing the effect of TG's *do*-replacement since one verb, *do*, is being replaced by another verb *be*. Thus the structure for *The jars are big* might be (18).

(18)

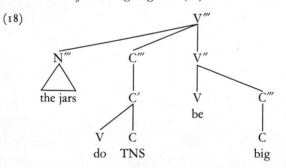

Third, (17) and (18) directly incorporate all the advantages of a *do*-replacement analysis, such as the fact that TENSE, *do*, and modals do not occur in infinitives and participles, i.e., in V'' structures:

(19) a. *to can go
   b. *to was going
   c. *doing go to the party
   d. *wasing at the party

In fact it may be possible to eliminate *do*-replacement altogether, but retain its effects. For instance, we might base generate *be* where *do* is in (18) and leave the main verb slot empty. A binding relation can then be established between *be* and the empty main verb node. I shall pursue this alternative directly.

Consider now the perfective *have*. First, notice that this verb in its auxiliary use never functions as the head of a sentence. We have (20) but not (21).

(20) a. They have all gone.
      b. The three men could have all gone.

(21) a. *There could have many men gone.
      b. *There could have many men been going.

Notice that *all* in (20) should not be to the right of *have*, if *have* is the head; further, *many men* should be acceptable to the right of *have* in (21), if *have* is the head. This follows from a careful consideration of the data in (5)–(9), and how such data would be represented in any generative grammar—transformational or otherwise.

Second, perfective *have* cannot only be generated with TENSE, *do*, and modals within an AUX constituent, because unlike these elements *have* does occur in infinitives and participles:

(22) a. for him to have gone
      b. having gone

Third, notice that perfective *have* does not parallel progressive and passive *be* in regard to gapping, particularly when it is contracted to [əv]. We have both (23a) and (23b), but not (23c).

(23) a. John could have been fishing, and so could Bill (have (been (fishing))).

      b. John could have been fishing, and so could $\begin{Bmatrix} \text{have} \\ [\text{əv}] \end{Bmatrix}$ Bill (been (fishing)).

      c. *John could have been fishing, and so could $\begin{Bmatrix} \text{have} \\ [\text{əv}] \end{Bmatrix}$ been Bill (fishing).

Similarly, while we have (24), we do not have (25).

(24) a. John could have seen this play, and so could $\begin{Bmatrix} \text{have} \\ [\text{əv}] \end{Bmatrix}$ Bill (seen this play).

      b. This play could have ended early, and so could $\begin{Bmatrix} \text{have} \\ [\text{əv}] \end{Bmatrix}$ that one (ended early).

(25) a. *John could be seeing this play, and so could be Bill (seeing this play).
   b. *This play could be ending early, and so could be that one (ending early).
   c. *This play could be finished, and so could be that one (finished).

Fourth, in some dialects, including those that are spoken here in The Water Winter Wonderland, one often hears questions like (26a), but even Michiganians reject (26b).

(26) a. Could $\begin{Bmatrix} \text{have} \\ [\text{əv}] \end{Bmatrix}$ Bill gone?
   b. *Could be Bill going?

All of these facts suggest that perfective *have* should *not* be given a structural analysis that parallels progressive and passive *be*, as is widely the case in TG (Chomsky, 1955, 418 ff., 1957, and many another analyses since then). Furthermore, what is needed is a theory which would allow *have* to be ambiguously analyzed by speakers, so that it can be as easily grouped with preceding verbal elements as it can with those that follow. Also, however *have* is analyzed, the past participle affix associated with it must always remain with the verb phrase (V″) proper. In other words, although *have* may occur in initial position as it does in questions, the past participle affix always remains in the main verb phrase. I believe that our theory provides a solution to these problems along the lines of structures such as the following:

(27)

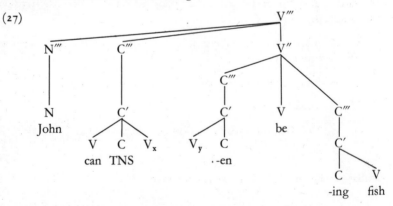

In a structure like (27), *have* can occur in either of the two positions, V_x or V_y. If it occurs in V_x, we account for those cases in which *have* seems to function as part of the AUX. Such a position requires no extension of our theory: we have seen that verbs can be directly embedded in X′ level posthead position. If *have* occurs in position V_y, we account for all those cases in which it seems to be part of the main verb phrase. This position also does not require an extension of our theory. Rule (1) of Chapter 3 allows specifically for verbs to be embedded in X′ level prehead position. This position is necessary to account for several aspects of derivational morphology, which, as we have seen in the case of complex nominals, are directly incorporated into the syntax in RG. For example, Rule (1) of Chapter 3 will allow for the direct generation of the following structures:

(28)   a.   phrases like *the new go–cart*

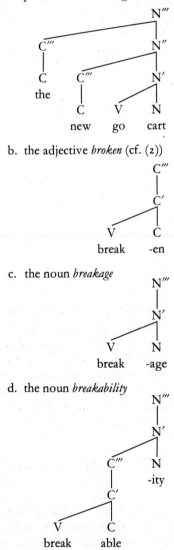

b.   the adjective *broken* (cf. (2))

c.   the noun *breakage*

d.   the noun *breakability*

Structures similar to those in (28) will be used in Chapter 6 to describe various nominalizations in English; in particular, phrases like (29a) and (29b).

(29)   a.

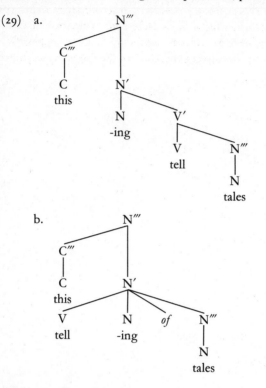

These structures follow directly from the arguments presented in Section 2.4. The difficulty with generating *have* in position V_y of (27), in an effort to account for those cases in which *have* functions as part of the main verb, is that the *-en* is always attached to the following verb, never directly to *have*. In other words, the prehead verb *have* and the affix do not merge in the way the prehead modal or *do* merge with TNS, or the way *break* merges with *-en* in (28b) to produce the adjective *broken* (cf. (2)). Thus the generation of V^n in X′ level prehead position is not the issue here. Such structures are needed elsewhere in the grammar. A further example occurs in (30).

(30)   She had [a [[why-don't-you-help-me] [look]]] on her face.
                N‴   N′V‴   N

The issue is that *-en* is always attached to the following verb, never to *have*.

It appears that we must treat the behavior of *-en* as an exception to expected cases, perhaps occasioned by the duplicity of structures like (27). Alternatively, we might look for evidence that *have* and *-en* are actually not part of the same phrase, even though they are adjacent. To this end, consider (31).

(31) a. Could these two men both have gone?
      b. Could these two men have both gone?

The arguments presented thus far indicate that the structure associated with (31a) must be (32a) and that associated with (31b) must be (32b).

(32) a.

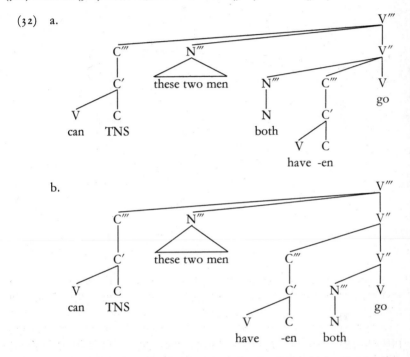

b.

Notice that in both of these structures the quantifier *both*, which refers back to the subject, is a daughter of V″. This seems to be perfectly natural in view of what has been discussed. Thus predicate nominatives, which are R-commanded by the subject, are daughters of V″ in posthead position. We now say that "floating" quantifiers like *all* and *both*, which are L-commanded by the subject, are daughters of V″ in prehead position.

Now notice that, in structure (32b), the quantifier *both* intervenes between *-en* and *go*, making it very difficult to merge the two to form *gone* by some local phonological rule. Furthermore, there are other items that can occur between the two as the following examples indicate:

(33) a. Could they have inadvertently offended the host?
      b. Could the two men have both inadvertently offended the host?

   c. Could the two men have, inadvertently, both offended the host?[4]

   d. Couldn't they have simply not accepted the invitation?

To account for these data, suppose we say that *have* and *-en* belong to separate phrases, and, in the manner suggested above to account for the *do-* replacement cases, generate, first, an empty node where the *-en* is in (32b) and, second, a separate node containing *-en* bound to the first. Exploring this possibility, consider the structure (34).

(34)

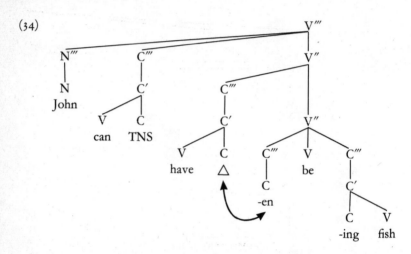

Assuming (34), we revise (32a) and (32b) to (35a) and (35b), respectively. The revision (35b) places *-en* directly before *go*, thereby avoiding the problem of the intervening *both* in (32b). Thus, in all cases, we now have the affixes either directly after a verb or directly before a verb. Further, the behavior of *-en* is now prefectly regular in all structures. The major advantage of structures like (35), therefore, is that affixes that are the heads of characterizer phrases or noun phrases are always associated with the preceding or following V node.

(35)   a.

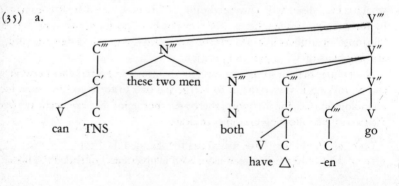

b.

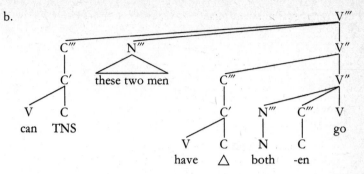

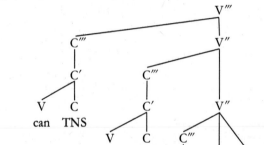

Summarizing, we may say that the structure for a sequence like *(could) have been being chased* is either (36), (37), or (38).

(36)   *have* in the verb phrase

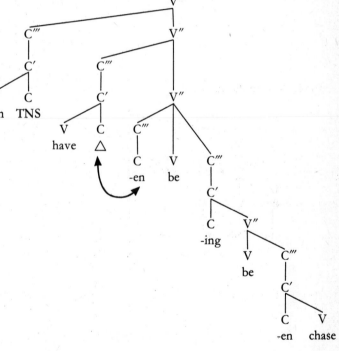

(37) *have* in the auxiliary

(38) *have* in the auxiliary

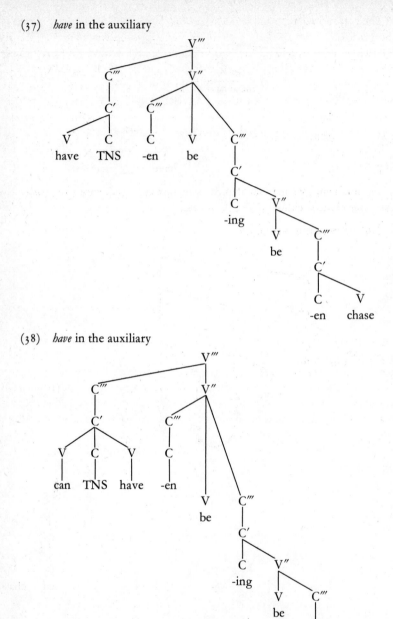

The typical structures are (36) and (37). In these, TNS is always attached to the preceding verb, and the affixes *-en* and *-ing* are always attached to the following verb. Structures like (36) underlie all sentences in which *have* functions as part of the main verb phrase, e.g., *Could they have all gone?* The typical cases in which *have* is part of the AUX is accounted for by (37), e.g., *Have they all gone?* A rather exceptional structure is (38), which occurs only in those cases in which *have* can be part of the AUX when the AUX already contains a modal, e.g., (23b), (24), and the dialectal (26a).

While the structures in (36)–(38) are admittedly more complex than those underlying an affix hopping analysis, it must be noted that these structures have been suggested in an attempt to account for a great deal more than the affix hopping analysis can. In particular, the affix hopping analysis, based on a sequence like (39), cannot account for the adjectival nature of the present and past participles, necessary in English to relate *the young child*, *the sleeping child*, and *the adored child*, and crucial in many other languages, e.g., the Romance languages, to account for the concord between participles and the subject in compound tenses (see Binkert, in preparation).

(39)   TNS — (Modal) — (have — en) — (be — ing) — (be — en)

Furthermore, recent modifications of Chomsky's 1955, 1957 analysis involving implicitly or explicitly a rule of *do*-replacement (Jackendoff, 1972; Emonds, 1970, 1976; Culicover, 1976; Akmajian et al., 1979) fare no better in this regard. Also, even these analyses must have an extra transformational rule for moving *have* into the AUX when the AUX already contains a modal as Jackendoff (1972) suggests. Finally, none of these analyses can account for data like (6) and (7), which are pivotal.

The above analysis extends to participles like *having gone*, which has the structure (40).

(40)

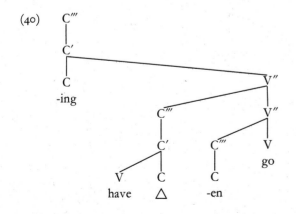

As an added advantage, we now have parallel structures for the examples in (41), which are (42), respectively.[5]

(41)   a.   to have both gone/having both gone
       b.   both to have gone/both having gone
       c.   to both have gone

(42)   a.

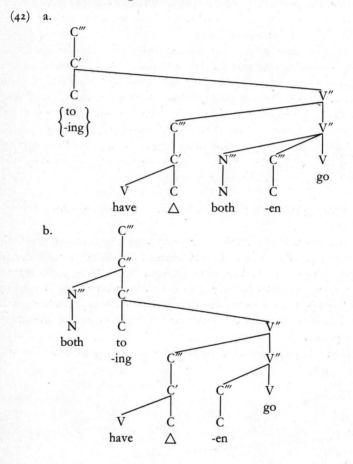

c.

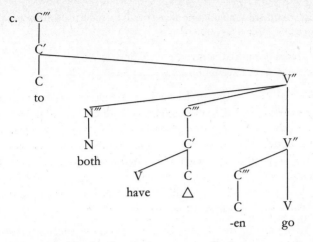

Given structures like the above, we can now eliminate our own need for *do*-replacement, as suggested above in connection with (19), by adding the following PSFs to the grammar:

(43)   a. If *be* occurs in X′ level prehead position before TNS, it must be bound to an empty main verb node.

        b. If *do* occurs to the left of TNS, there can be no *have* or *be* in the same V‴, except that *do* can occur with the main verb *have*.

The principal advantage of (43a) over a *do*-replacement analysis is that it treats all occurrences of *be* equally accounting not only for (44), but also for (45).

(44)   a. Was John going?

        b. Was John seen?

(45)   Was John happy?

In particular, the RG analysis avoids generating counter-intuitive surface structures containing a VP node without a V node, as in the case in the TG derivation of (45).

Further, (43a), by *not* mentioning any binding relation for *have* when it occurs as part of the AUX, accounts for the different behavior of perfective *have* and main verb *have* in American English, which allows (46a), but not (46b). Perfective *have* is never associated with the main verb node; main verb *have* is always so associated.

(46)   a. Has John gone?

        b. *Has John a house?

Quite simply, no main verb can occur in AUX, other than *be*.

(43b) is necessary to rule out (47), but allow (48).

(47)   a. *Does John have gone?
       b. *Does John be nice?

(48)   a. Does John have a house?
       b. John does have a house.

Since there is no TG version of the auxiliary that has yet attempted to account for all of the above data, I shall postpone to future discussion further comparisons between RG and TG in regard to those facts which *do*-replacement is designed to account for; however, we shall return to a discussion of the auxiliary in Chapter 7 to formalize the required filters. As we shall see below, quite apart from the *do*-replacement issue, there are further advantages of the RG analysis. In particular, we can eliminate the rule VP-fronting suggested in Akmajian et al. (1979) to account for (49).

(49)   a. They all said that John was being obnoxious, and *being obnoxious* he
           definitely was ____.
       b. They all said that John was being obnoxious, and *obnoxious* he
           definitely was being ____.

Since the structures are at hand, let me just point out here that these "fronted" constituents are bound, in our terminology, to an empty postverbal adjunct. This accounts for the following:

(50)   a. They all said that John was being chased, and *chased* he definitely
           was being ____.
       b. They all said that John was being chased, and *being chased* he
           definitely was ____.
       c. They all said that John would be a good doctor, and *a good doctor* he
           definitely $\begin{Bmatrix} \text{is} \\ \text{has become} \\ \text{appears to be} \end{Bmatrix}$ ____.

In both (50a) and (50b) the "fronted" constituents are C'''; in (50c) the "fronted" constituent is an N'''; thus, what occurs in initial position is an A'''.

A major advantage of the above analysis is that we can account for the ambiguity of a word like *searching* (adjective or participle) or *nominating* (derived nominal or gerundial nominal) in a way that exactly parallels cases like *broken* (adjective (cf. (28b)) or participle (cf. (3))). The structure for the adjective *searching*, the derived nominal *nominating*, and the adjective *broken* are, respectively,
$\underset{C'''}{[}\ \underset{C'}{[}\ \underset{V}{[\text{search}]}\ [\text{-ing}]]]$, $\underset{N'''}{[}\ \underset{N'}{[}\ \underset{V}{[\text{nominate}]}\ [\text{-ing}]]]$, and $\underset{C'''}{[}\ \underset{C'}{[}\ \underset{V}{[\text{break}]}$
[-en]]]. The structure for the participle *searching*, the gerundial nominal *nominat*-
C

ing, and the participle *broken* are, respectively, [[[-ing] [search]]], [[
                          C‴ C′ C   V   N‴ N′

[-ing] [nominate]]], and [[[-en] [break]]]. Notice that, in the former trio
N   V   C‴ C′ C   V

of words, the verbal root is embedded in X′ level prehead position, whereas, in
the latter trio, the verbal root is embedded in X′ level posthead position.
Accordingly, an ambiguous phrase like *the imposing Avon lady* is directly rendered unambiguous in phrase structure; furthermore, this is accomplished in a
way that treats both the adjective *imposing* and the participle *imposing* as modifiers, i.e., in *the imposing Avon lady*, *imposing* is an N″ level prehead characterizer. Conversely, in the transformational derivation of the participle *imposing*
via relative clause reduction and modifier shift (Baker, 1978), it is a complete
accident that *imposing*, which derives from a present progressive, i.e., *the Avon
lady who is imposing*, should occur in surface prenominal position, where adjectives normally occur. The problem for TG, essentially, is that it is not possible
to generate the participle *imposing* apart from the progressive, just as it is not
possible to generate the participle *broken* apart from the passive. In RG, such
forms can occur with *be* to form the progressive and passive, respectively; yet
they can also occur independent of *be*. Thus in (3), we can have *get* in place of *be*,
yielding *the jar could get broken*; similarly, in (4), we can have *start* in place of *be*,
yielding *the jar could start breaking*. In identical ways, we can generate *the jar
broken by the child, the jar broken beyond repair, students both interesting and interested,
the Avon lady both imposing in size and commanding in appearance*, etc., in which all of
the relevant forms are characterizers embedded on the N″ level and are interpreted accordingly as modifiers of the head. In short, the major disadvantage of
the affix hopping analysis is that it binds the present and past participles to the
progressive and passive, respectively, thereby making it impossible to formulate any generalized statements regarding both adjectives and participles.
Accordingly, to account for the parallels between *a sick man, a murdered man*, and
a sleeping man, transformational grammarians must allow modifier shift to apply
to both adjectives and verbs, and no reason can be given to explain why verbs
should undergo this strange shift in position (cf. Baker, 1978, Chapter 13). This
problem is completely solved in the RG analysis, which treats all participles as
characterizers. Further, the relationships which transformations were intended
to capture are directly captured by the phrasal architecture: items on the X″
level, whether full relative clauses, adjectives, participles, infinitive phrases,
etc., are all modifiers of the head (cf. *the books which are available, the available books*,
and *the books available*).

    Before turning to other matters directly related to the above, note that the
attachment of the affixes in the examples given seems to require a rule that
functions like a syntactic transformation. One might also say this about the

insertion of *of* and the deletion of *x-many* in Chapter 2. It therefore seems appropriate to reiterate the claims of RG. As noted in Chapter 1, RG does not stipulate that a generative grammar cannot contain a rule which has any of the properties attributed until now to transformations. Clearly, some morphological and phonological rules have transformational properties like deletion. What this monograph seeks to show is that syntactic transformations, forming a separate subcomponent within the syntactic component and turning abstract deep syntactic structures into surface syntactic structures, are unnecessary and, in fact, by their very nature, preclude the attainment of descriptive adequacy. The relations that the transformational subcomponent of TG was designed to capture can be directly incorporated into phrasal architecture through the assignment of specific functional relations to specific positions, e.g., all N″ level adjuncts are descriptive modifiers of the head N.

It is interesting that, from my own research, the only rules remaining that look at all like transformations are those that directly involve specific morphological material and which, I assume, are to be incorporated into the phonological component. Included here are rules like *of*-insertion, as well as rules for the deletion of morphemes like *x-many*. Further research may, in fact, eliminate these, perhaps along the lines with which *do*-replacement was eliminated.

Let us now turn again to a consideration of "floating" quantifiers.

The above analysis of auxiliary verbs, as we noted, accounts for the interpretation of quantifiers that refer to the subject from prehead position of verb phrases. Consider now examples like (51).

(51)   a.   These two men both could [have gone].
                                          V″

       b.   These two men could both [have gone].
                                          V″

The question I wish to raise now is, Where are the occurrences of *both* in (51) generated? The full structure of AUX (= X‴ level prehead characterizer of V‴), without recursion, is given in (52).

(52)

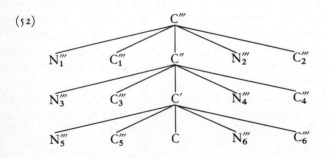

Following the above arguments, notice first that since AUX is a characterizer, position C_1''' must be empty. Second, positions N_3''' and N_4''' in all characterizer phrases are never filled with (numerical) noun phrases that directly modify the head. There are no examples like (53).

(53) a. *several pretty
      b. *out of their mind many

I propose therefore that positions N_3''' and N_4''' are free to contain quantifiers that refer back to the subject, producing examples like (51) as well as (54) to be discussed below.

(54) a. The two men may both [not want to go].
                             V''
      b. The two men both may [not want to go].
                             V''

Notice that in all of these examples the X'' level quantifiers refer back to the subject. We may, therefore, formulate the following PSF:

(55) Nouns like *all*, *both*, etc., can be base generated in either X''' level prehead position of N''' or X'' level prehead and posthead position of C''' and V''', i.e., $[-\text{Nominal}]'''$. In all cases, these nouns must be L-commanded by their antecedent.

This principle accounts for the base generation of "floating" quantifiers in all of the following examples:

(56) a. Both of the players may have been six-feet tall.
      b. The players both may have been six-feet tall.
      c. The players may both have been six-feet tall.
      d. The players may have both been six-feet tall.

Furthermore, we now have an explanation for the ungrammaticality of (57).

(57) *The players may have been both six-feet tall.

In (57), *players* does not L-command *both*, since *both* is to the right of *been*. Consider now the example (58).

(58) The players are both six-feet tall.

Although in this sentence it seems that *both* is to the right of the head *are*, this is actually not the case. The structure for (58) is (59).

(59)

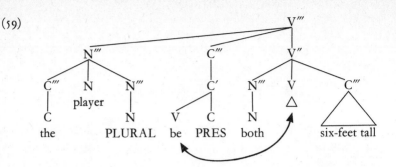

As we just discussed, the verb *be* in (58) is base generated to the left of TNS and is bound to the empty node under the head V, as (59) demonstrates. Thus *both* is, in fact, to the left of the head V. I believe that this example offers very strong support for the analysis we have suggested. It explains the difference between (57) and (58), which no version of the TG analysis of AUX would be able to (cf. *The two men are both gone/* The two men could have been both gone/The two men could have both been gone.*)

4.1 COMPLEX SENTENCES

If we combine the arguments presented in the preceding chapters, we can generate the structure for complex sentences which is diagrammed in Figure 1. This figure contains, in addition, expansions of the auxiliary and main verb.

As the dotted line in Figure 1 indicates, we can have infinite recursion of V''' nodes, at least theoretically. Limiting the number for expository purposes, I have included only two levels above the level usually represented as S, that is V_2''' in the diagram. This node, in our theory, dominates the subject N_5''', the auxiliary, C_5''', and the main verb phrase, V_0''. If only these three positions are filled, we have a simple sentence like *John went*. If we fill positions to the left and the right of V_2''' and those above V_2''', we produce such examples as the following:

(60) a. [If the weather is nice], he can go.
          C_3

      b. He can go, [if the weather is nice].
                      C_4

(61) a. [Since he so desperately wants to go], [if the weather is nice], he
          C_1 C_3

          can go.

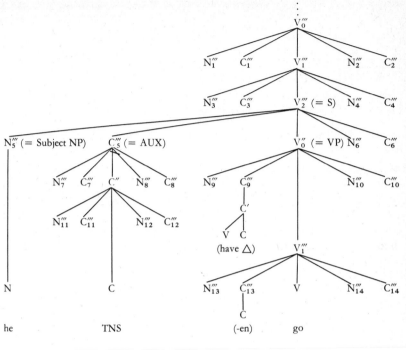

Figure 1

b. [Since he so desperately wants to go], he can go, [if the weather is
   C_3 C_4
   nice].

c. He can go, [if the weather is nice], [since he so desperately wants to
                C_4 C_2
   go].

As these examples indicate, the theory proposed provides exactly those positions necessary for adverbial subordinate clauses; they are prehead and posthead characterizers on the X''' level of V'''. Notice also that these structures give the correct interpretation for pronouns. The command relations discussed in the last chapter are not sensitive to rewrites of the same level: they refer to the first branching category Z^n with the restriction that n is constant. Thus in Figure 1, the first branching category above, say, N_{13}''' includes both V_1' and V_0'', but not V_2''' or anything higher. Accordingly, a noun in N_5''' can be the referent of a pronoun in a subordinate clause in C_4''', as the following example illustrates:

(62) John left after he saw Sue.

However, a pronoun in N_5''' cannot be the referent of a noun in C_4''' because, in such a case, the pronoun both precedes and commands its intended referent (Langacker, 1969; Ross, 1969).

Notice also that a movement analysis of dislocated constituents is unnecessary: these are base generated in prehead and posthead nominal position on the X''' level of V'''. Consider, for example, (63).

(63) a. [That child who has been creating such a fuss], [if the weather is
          N_3 C_3

          nice], he can go.

       b. [That child who has been creating such a fuss], he can go, [if the
          N_3 C_4

          weather is nice].

       c. [If the weather is nice], he can go, [that child who has been creating
          C_3 N_4

          such a fuss].

       d. He can go, [that child who has been creating such a fuss], [if the
                      N_4 C_4

          weather is nice].

Thus this analysis will enable us to combine those common aspects of dislocation and question movement which have been observed in the literature (see, especially, Chomsky, 1977). I return to such matters in the next chapter. In the remainder of this chapter, I shall consider a variety of specific details of English syntax in an attempt to show how the descriptive apparatus associated with RG can provide revealing solutions to some previously intractable problems.

4.2 NEGATIVES AND EMPHATICS

Most grammars of English, e.g., Quirk et al. (1972) and Frank (1972), note that a sentence such as (64) is ambiguous depending upon how the modal is interpreted.

(64) John can go.

If this sentence is negated, a further ambiguity ensues, which many grammarians fail to recognize:

(65) a. John cannot go. (= John doesn't have the option of going.)
       b. John can not go. (= John has the option of not going.)

A second negative can be introduced into (64) to yield (66).

(66)   John can't not go. (= John doesn't have the option of not going.)

Clearly, in (66) both the modal and the main verb are negated.

Transformational grammars do not generally contain rules for the generation of double negative constructions of any kind. The grammar presented in Akmajian, Steele, and Wasow (1979) is a notable exception. However, their rules will not generate (66) in a way that provides an unambiguous source for the *n't*.

One way to deal with this problem is to allow for the base generation of *not* in either C_8''' or C_9''' or both, in Figure 1, given that such a structure is available. In (65a) *not* is base generated in C_8''' as a constituent of C_5'' (= AUX); (65b) has *not* base generated in C_9''' as a constituent of V'' (= VP); and, (66) has *not* base generated in both of those positions.

Now notice that *not*, when it occurs in C_8''', is in complementary distribution to the emphatic use of *so* and *too*. If there is a negative in C_5''', the emphatics cannot be used:

(67)   a.   *You can't so go.
       b.   *He won't too do it.

Further, the position occupied by the emphatics in AUX is the same as that occupied by *not*, i.e., C_8''':

(68)   a.   You can't go.
       b.   You can so go.
       c.   You can too go.

(69)   a.   You can't not go. (*n't* in C_8'''; *not* in C_9''')
       b.   You can so not go. (*so* in C_8'''; *not* in C_9''')
       c.   You can too not go. (*too* in C_8'''; *not* in C_9''')

(70)   a.   *You can't not not go.
       b.   *You can't so not go.
       c.   *You can't too not go.

Several facts need to be accounted for in these data.

First, note that (68a) is unambiguous. It parallels only (65a). Hence contraction of a negative can occur only when the negative is base generated in C_8''' (or somewhere else in AUX). We may therefore formulate the following constraint:

(71)   Contraction of a negative is not possible unless the negative is in AUX (= C''').[6]

As confirmation of (71), consider the behavior of manner adverbs like *enthusiastically*. These adverbs are base generated as X'' level characterizers in verb phrases, i.e., C_9''' and/or C_{10}''' (cf. *John enthusiastically ran on to the playing field quickly*.) They can be modified by degree words such as *not* and by other adverbial phrases such as *not very*. Consider (72).

(72) a. He not very enthusiastically accepted the invitation.
      b. He accepted the invitation not very enthusiastically.
      c. He is not very enthusiastically filling out his tax return.

These adverbs cannot occur in AUX:[7]

(73) a. *He not very enthusiastically could have accepted the invitation.
      b. *He could very enthusiastically not have accepted the invitation.

Now consider (74).

(74) He couldn't very enthusiastically accepted the invitation.

(74) must mean (75a), not (75b).

(75) a. He couldn't accept the invitation very enthusiastically.
      b. He could accept the invitation not very enthusiastically.

The prediction of (71) is borne out. In order for (74) to mean (75b), the *not* would have to originate as a degree word inside the verb phrase. Contraction to *couldn't* would, therefore, violate (71). Thus the *not* originates in C_8''', and (74) means (75a).

The second fact to be noticed about the data in (68)–(70) is that we find the same words, *not*, *so*, and *too*, in other X''' categories. Consider the following:

(76) a. adjective: not unkind, so peculiar, too angry
      b. adverb: not quickly, so readily, too vigorously
      c. preposition: not without ambition, so behind the times, too off the wall
      d. quantifier: not many, so few, too far ·

Jackendoff (1977), who discusses degree words at length, says very little about *not*. He treats *so* and *too* as degree words and generates them as daughters of X'''. However, in his theory, they only occur to the left of the head X. The examples (68) and (69) have these words to the right of the modal, and Jackendoff says nothing about their occurrence in this position. Certainly, the homophony of the emphatics (*so* and *too*) and the negative (*not*) with the degree words in (76) at least suggests that they can also be analyzed as degree words, i.e., characterizers, even in their specialized use as postmodifiers of modals.

The third fact is that *not* can freely occur in C_9''', *so* can occur there only with verbs permitting intensification, and *too*, in that position, has the meaning *also*:

(77) a. You can't not go.
      b. He does so want to go. (ambiguous)
      c. He too wants to go.

The ambiguity of (77b) is important, and RG has a way to account for it: *so* is either an emphatic in C_8''' or an intensifier in C_9'''.

The fourth fact is that degree words and phrases can occur in posthead position in other categories. Consider (78).

(78) a. in verb phrases: He loves her *so.*
      b. in adjective phrases: Bill is as tall *as John.*
      c. in prep. phrases: Mary is as behind the times *as her mother.*
      d. in adverb phrases: He snores as loudly *as my grandfather.*

Summarizing these facts, we can stipulate that the grammar must specify the following:

(79) a. A position for degree words (phrases, etc.) must be base generated to the left and to the right of the head as X''' level residents of V''' and C'''.
      b. When generated as X''' level posthead residents of AUX, *too* and *so* are interpreted as emphatics.

The observation embodied in (79a) is fundamental to any attempt to write a nontransformational grammar of English. Without allowing for the generation of degree words both to the left and to the right of the head, many of the facts mentioned above cannot be accounted for. A theory such as Jackendoff's (1977), which base generates DEG only to the left of the head, therefore fails to reach descriptive adequacy. As we have seen, failure to recognize this left-of-head/right-of-head distribution is a major deficiency in previous accounts of English phrase structure, even when transformations are available.

Of course, these remarks do not mean that any particular word, e.g., *too,* must be able to occur with exactly the same interpretation in every position generated. In fact, quite the opposite often occurs: specific positions, e.g., C_8''' as opposed to C_9''', are often associated with specific uses (cf. the ambiguity in (65) and 77b)). A mechanism must be provided to account for these specific cases without obscuring the generality behind them; that is, for stating facts like (79b) within the framework of a generalized theory concerning the linear and hierarchical positions possible. Such a mechanism has been provided above by RG. In short, a variety of thorny facts associated with the words *not, too, so,* etc., fall into place naturally, given the structures justified in previous discussion. I shall return to a consideration of further examples of what might be called the "generality/specificity dichotomy" in Chapter 6.

4.3 QUANTIFIERS AND NOUN PHRASES IN AUX AND VP

The word *well* is usually classified as an adverb by traditional grammarians. However, one is tempted to consider it a quantifier since, alongside of such sentences as *He pretty much can do as he likes* we have *He pretty well can do as he likes*. Furthermore, *well* is apparently the only word in the entire English language that can conceivably be considered a modal adverb, i.e., one that can be generated in C_{11}''' or C_{12}''' of Figure 1, the way manner adverbs, generated in C_9''' or C_{10}''', are associated with verbs. In a language as fecund in vocabulary as English, this seems perverse.

The most exceptional usage of *well* is as a modifier of modals, particularly *may*. It is necessary therefore to examine carefully the modal *may*.

The first thing to observe is the commonly known fact that *may* denotes either permission or possibility. Thus (80) has the two meanings indicated.

> (80)   John may go.
>   a. John has permission to go.
>   b. There is a possibility that John will go.

Second, when a negative is placed between the modal and the main verb in (80), something unexpected occurs. Consider (81) with the permission sense of *may*, i.e., the meanings indicated.

> (81)   John may not go. (permission sense)
>   a. John doesn't have permission to go.
>   b. John has permission not to go.

This is easily handled within our framework: the negative can be associated either with C_8''' or C_9'''. But notice that if one reads the possibility sense of *may* in a sentence with a negative following *may*, the negative can only be interpreted as occupying C_9''', i.e., as being part of the verb phrase. Thus (82) means only (82a), not (82b).

> (82)   John may not go. (possibility sense)
>   a. There is a possibility that John will not go.
>   b. There isn't a possibility that John will go.

In short, the grammar must state that the possibility sense of *may* cannot occur with a negative in C_8'''.

As confirmation of this, note that the passive cannot be used with the permission sense of *may*:

> (83)   You may be invited.

(83) seems very odd when interpreted as meaning (84).

(84)   ?You are permitted to be invited.

Thus the negative of (83) should have only one meaning, as indicated in (85). It does.

(85)   You may not be invited. (= It is possible that you will not be invited).

Further, there is no sentence (86), since all the meanings are ruled out.

(86)   *You may not # not be invited. (# signifies the division between AUX and VP)

Another telling point is that the perfective cannot be used with the permission sense of *may*. Thus (87a) only has the possibility sense of *may*, and (87b) does not occur.

(87)   a. He may # have gone.
      b. *He may not # not have gone.

Notice also that a question such as (88) cannot have the possibility sense of *may*.

(88)   ?May not he go? (cf. May not I help you?)

This rather peculiar state of affairs offers a possible explanation for the rarity of *mayn't* in American English. The argument might be summarized as follows:

(89)   a. Contraction of a negative is not possible unless the negative is in AUX. (= (71))
      b. The modal *may* occurring with a negative in C_8''' only has permission sense.
      c. Most Americans use *can* for permission.
      d. The sequence *may not* occurring at all in AUX is unlikely.
      e. *Mayn't* would rarely arise.

Notice that the information in (89b) is like (79b) in character. Thus, we have another example of what is needed in a phrase structure grammar of English: a mechanism for expressing the relationship between linear/hierarchical position and semantic interpretation, and, in particular, a mechanism which is based on a more elaborate description of English phrase structure, i.e., one which allows for more instances of particular categories at various levels than has been provided in the past.

Returning to the matter of *well*, note that when it occurs with *may*, *may* cannot have the permission sense:

(90)   a. He well may go.
      b. He may well go.

We now have an explanation for the fact that the sentences in (91) are no good, whereas those in (92) are fine: *may* with a negative in C_8''' must have the permission sense (cf. (89b)); *may* with *well* cannot have the permission sense (cf. (90)).

(91) a. *He well may not # go.
      b. *He well may not # so love his wife that he is blind to her infidelity.
      c. *He may well not # go.
      d. *He may well not # so love his wife that he is blind to her infidelity.

(92) a. He well may # not go.
      b. He well may # not so love his wife that he is blind to her infidelity.
      c. He may well # not go.
      d. He may well # not so love his wife that he is blind to her infidelity.

In brief, any occurrence of *not* with *well* must be interpreted as occupying C_9'''; that is, it must be in the verb phrase. We know from (90) that *well* must be generable both to the left and to the right of the modal. Its position to the right of the modal is now straightforward: it must precede C_8'''. Consider also (93).

(93) a. He may well so # not go. (heavy stress on the emphatic *so*)
      b. *He may so well # not go.

Its position to the left of the modal is as diagrammed in Figure 1, namely, N_7'':

(94) He very well may # not go.

The analyses of the sentences in (95) are therefore as indicated.

(95) a. He [pretty much] can [so] # do as he likes.
               N_7 C_8
      b. He may [very well] [so] # [not] care [that much].
               N_8 C_8 C_9 N_6

If all this is correct, then *well* must be analyzed as a quantifier like *much*, i.e., $[+N, +Q]$. It certainly appears to be used that way in (96), (97), and (98).

(96) a. I wish her well.
      b. I wish her luck.

(97) a. She is well known.
      b. She is much loved.

(98) a. We are well off.
      b. We are well on our way to insanity.

Now recall that *much* is an X''' level resident only. While *these many apples* is ambiguous depending upon whether *many* is on the X''' level or X'' level; *this much butter* is unambiguous. *Much* must be an X''' level resident; it has only a [+Q] reading. Consistency demands that *well* therefore be generated in either N_7''' or N_8'''. The examples above support this.

In short, while the V'' level of verbs dominates manner adverbs in C_9'' and C_{11}'', and the N'' level of nouns dominates descriptive adjectives, as we saw in Chapter 2, the C'' level of the AUX does not dominate any corresponding special group of modal modifiers. The one candidate for such status has just been elimated. This frees positions C_{11}''' and C_{12}''' for the so-called sentence adverbs, to which I turn in the next section.

As additional support for our analysis of *well*, consider the following:

(99)   a. John says he will go, and well he may.
      b. Sue said Sally would go, and well she might have.

In these sentences, the position of *well* is not as peculiar as one might suppose. As a quantifier, it is free to "float" (actually, it is base generated) to other N''' positions than N_7'' and N_8'''. Apparently, as (99) suggests, it can occur in N_3'''.

All the evidence suggests that *well* is a quantifier, [+N, +Q], not an adverb.

4.4 SENTENCE ADVERBS

Into positions C_3''' and C_4''', I propose also that we can generate sentence adverbs. Some of these adverbs, like *happily*, *maybe*, and *surprisingly*, cannot occur between the subject and auxiliary or between the auxiliary and main verb. We have the following examples:

(100)   a. Surprisingly, he can go.
       b. *He surprisingly can go.
       c. *He can surprisingly go.
       d. He can go, surprisingly.

Other sentence adverbs can however occur in intrasentential position, e.g., *probably*, *clearly*, and *ultimately*:[8]

(101)   a. Ultimately peace will prevail.
       b. Peace ultimately will prevail.
       c. Peace will ultimately prevail.
       d. Peace will prevail ultimately.

Following the remarks made in the last section, I propose to base generate these adverbs in positions C_{11}''' and C_{12}''' of Figure 1, when they occur in intrasentential position. As we noted, there do not appear to be any modal or auxiliary adverbs in English other than the so-called sentence adverbs. Thus it seems natural to generate these adverbs in the positions just mentioned. Recall that

TNS is an obligatory element on the X‴ level of sentences. TNS, modal, and *do* are in effect precisely those elements that give V categories their sentential status. Notice that we do not have the following:

(102)   a. *For him to probably go . . .
         b. *The man clearly leaving . . .

Given that the characterizer TNS is the distinguishing feature of sentences, it is not surprising that sentence adverbs like *probably* can occupy X″ level characterizer position when the head is TNS. Thus we have four common positions for the sentence adverbs: C_3''', C_{11}''', C_{12}''', and C_4'''. Some adverbs like *ultimately* can occur in all four positions; others like *surprisingly* can occur only initially or finally. Any changes in meaning can be linked to the command properties of the words in the individual positions exactly in the manner as before (cf. (65) and (77b)).

Combining this analysis with the analysis of quantifiers in Section 4.3, we can account for each of the following:

(103)   a. Ultimately both of the men will want to visit each other.
         b. Ultimately the men both will want to visit each other.
         c. Ultimately the men will both want to visit each other.
         d. Both of the men will want to visit each other, ultimately.
         e. The men both will want to visit each other, ultimately.
         f. The men will both want to visit each other, ultimately.
         g. Both of the men ultimately will want to visit each other.
         h. Both of the men will ultimately want to visit each other.
         i. The men both ultimately will want to visit each other.
         j. The men both will ultimately want to visit each other.
         k. The men ultimately will both want to visit each other.
         l. The men will both ultimately want to visit each other.
         m. The men ultimately both will want to visit each other.
         n. The men will ultimately both want to visit each other.

Recursion of the X″ level of AUX is required in (103m) and (103n) since in these cases the characterizer *ultimately* precedes the noun *both*. I believe this is related to the fact that the best readings of (103m) and (103n) have pauses on each side of *ultimately*, but I shall not pursue the matter here (cf. Note 4.).

It should be noted that although TNS is an obligatory element on the X‴ level of V phrases, when there is an X‴ level, i.e., when there is a V‴, TNS is not a permanent resident of V phrases for several reasons. First, there are V phrases without TNS: namely, all infinitives and participles. Second TNS is an affix in surface structure which cannot be considered an independent element in the way, say, POSS, can. Recall that POSS simply follows a noun phrase and is never directly incorporated into the head (cf. *The man who is standing over there's mother is young* versus **The man's who is standing over there mother is young*). Third, TNS does not have a fixed position in the way that, say, articles do. Recall that in direct questions the characterizer TNS precedes the subject noun phrase. It is never the case however that articles occur in any other position than first prehead position X''' level. We have *all those many intelligent children*, not **those all many intelligent children*. Even when POSS is in posthead position signalling the double possessive construction, there is an article in first prehead position, as in *those books of John's*. To summarize, we can say that while articles are permanent residents, TNS and other auxiliary elements are not. This is a reflection of rule (1) in Chapter 3: the category verb is the one category that does not have to begin with an X''' level. This is one of the principle syntactic motivations for the claim that there are only two major syntactic categories in English: verbs and adjuncts.

Consider now adjuncts which might occur in position N_6''' and C_6''' in Figure 1. In accordance with previous arguments, restrictive modifiers of the main verb should occur on the X'' level of V, i.e., on V'' (= VP in TG). The manner adverbs occur in such positions; so do predicate nominatives and adjectives and many other phrases which refer back to the subject of the sentence. To be consistent, positions N_6''' and C_6''' should contain expressions of quantification, comparison, etc., which modify the main verb. The predictions of RG are borne out. Consider these examples:

(104) a. John wants to go [more] [than you can believe]. (Actually:
                       N_4 C_4

           John wants to go [x-much] [more] [than you can believe (he
                      N_6 N_4 C_4

           wants to go x-much)].

       b. *John more wants to go than you can believe.

       c. John loves his work [very much].
                       N_6

       d. *John very much loves his work.

       e. John becomes [sick] [a lot].
                   N_{10} N_6

       f. *John becomes a lot sick.

       g. That tenor sings [fortissimo] [too much].
                   C_{10} N_6

       h. *That tenor sings too much fortissimo.

As these examples illustrate, expressions of quantification and comparison occupy position N_6''' of V phrase. Most examples with such expressions in prehead verbal position are dubious (104d) or downright ungrammatical (104b). Our theory provides an explanation for this: the prehead nominal position on the X''' level of V is obligatorily filled by the subject of the sentence in English; accordingly, there is no position for prehead expressions of quantification and comparison. It is therefore not an accident, the way it is in TG, that comparison of the verb takes the form (104a), not (104b), unlike comparison in adjuncts which has the quantifier in prehead position (cf. *more beautiful than you can imagine*, not **beautiful more than you can imagine*; *more marbles than John has*, not **marbles more than John has*). This is therefore another syntactic reason for separating verbs and adjuncts into two categories as RG does.

Notice also that we do not have examples like **John more will swim than is necessary*, because modals or TNS, like articles, cannot be compared: no X''' level prehead constituent can, as we saw in Chapter 2 with our discussion of Filter (128).

Summarizing, we have examples like (105) and (106), which were discussed above.

(105)   a. John [pretty much] can do as he likes.
N_7

        b. John may [very well] go.
N_8

(106)   a. The two men [both] could have gone.
N_{11}

        b. The two men could [both] have gone.
$N_{12 \text{ or } 9}$

        c. The two men could have [both] gone.
N_{13}

Conversely, we do not have (107), as discussed:

(107)   a. *The two men could have been both going.
        b. *The two men could have been both seen.

We can also directly base generate manner adverbs like those in (108).[9]

(108)   a. The two men could have both gone [enthusiastically].
C_{10}

        b. For him to [so enthusiastically] eat [as voraciously as he does]
                C_9 C_{10}
        indicates that he has a problem.

Lastly, in recursion we account for (109).

(109) a. The two men could have both carefully done their work.

   b. He has happily been carefully slicing all of the salami evenly.

Putting all of these analyses together we can account for such complex examples as those in (110) through (112).[10]

(110) [Against each other] [these two men] [would too] [both] have

   C_3 N_5 C_5 N_9

   [never] fought _____.

   N_{13}

(111) [Brilliant] [these fifteen men] [may have [probably]] [never] [all]

   C_3 N_5 C_5 C_{12} N_9 N_{13}

   been _____.

(112) [Ultimately] [these ten men] [probably] will [all][not] do what

   C_3 N_5 C_{11} N_{12} $C_{8\ or\ 9}$

   you expect.

Note that (112) is ambiguous depending on whether the *all* falls within the domain of *not*. If *not* is in C_8, we have the reading (113a); if *not* is in C_9, we have the reading (113b).

(113) a. Not all of these ten men will do as you expect.

   b. All of these ten men will not do as you expect.

Despite the complexity and verbosity of these examples, all relevant relationships between the individual constituents can be described within the RG framework; further, no transformational rules are involved, and in fact the analyses proposed attain a higher level of descriptive adequacy than possible in current TG models.

NOTES TO CHAPTER 4

1. Throughout the following discussion, I shall assume a nontransformational statement of the active/passive relation such as that discussed in Bresnan (1978). Her analysis, based on a TG phrase structure, can, I believe, achieve even greater generality within an RG phrase structure. For example, as the diagram in (3) indicates, the passive participle in RG is formed from two separate constituents: C, which is the passive morpheme *-en*, and V. Such an analysis allows for the statement of passive in terms of the passive morpheme, rather than, say, in terms of the verb *be*. This allows passive to be generalized to other verbs, in particular, *get*, as in *It got broken*. Furthermore, it allows passive to be generalized even to cases lacking an auxiliary verb, such as *The plate broken by the child*

was an heirloom. Here *broken* is clearly passive, yet there is no *be* (or *get*) with which to construe it in the surface sentence.

In addition, as we shall see in Chapter 6, RG assigns constituent status to CASE, also allowing for greater generality in the statement of passive in those languages in which grammatical function is signalled by desinences. For further discussion, see Binkert (in preparation).

2. (5d) is ungrammatical if intended to mean (5a); that is, if *both* is to be understood as referring to *the two men*. There is a rather marginal reading in which (5d) *is* grammatical, e.g., *The two men could have been both linguists for Halloween*, which parallels *The three men might have been all the people that survived*. This reading is irrelevant here. Also, in sentences like *The three men could have been all finished*, *all* does not refer to *the three men*; rather, it is a quantifier modifying *finished* (cf. **The two men could have been both finished*.) Sentences like *The two men were both finished* will be discussed presently.

3. For a discussion of *do*-replacement, see Emonds (1976) and Culicover (1976).

4. Notice that to be grammatical this sentence requires parenthetical pauses around *inadvertently*, a fact directly related to the RG account. Thus the order of adjuncts on the same level must be nouns before characterizers, as in (33b), where *both*, a noun, precedes *inadvertently*, a characterizer, on the same V″ level. In order to obtain the order *inadvertently both* in (33c), we need to have a recursion of V″, which, I believe, shows up as the parenthetical pauses because of the unexpected order of adjuncts.

5. The structures in (42) are necessary for strings like the following:

(i)   for the men to have both gone/the men having both gone

(ii)   for the men both to have gone/the men both having gone

(iii)   for the men to both have gone

6. This is different from the formulation in Akmajian et al., 1979, where *not* is reduced to *n't* first, and then *n't* is placed in AUX.

7. Care must be taken not to confuse manner adverbs with subject oriented adverbs. Note the ambiguity in the following: *John cleverly answered the question*. For discussion, see Jackendoff, 1972, 56 ff., and the comment in Note 9 below.

8. Many speakers report subtle and elusive meaning differences in examples like those in (101) and the following:

(i)   Probably John will come.

(ii)   John probably will come.

(iii)   John will probably come.

(iv)   John will come probably.

With the RG framework it is clear that we should connect such meaning differences with the different command properties of the various positions, however it is not at all clear what the nature of these meaning differences is. Furthermore, it does not seem possible to treat all of the so-called sentence adverbs globally simply as adverbs: they comprise a very mixed bag of expressions (Quirk et al., 1972, Chapter 8), some having subject orientation, some speaker orientation, and some functioning like degree words. For example, note the ambiguity of both variants in (v).

(v)   John certainly can sing./John can certainly sing.

Because of the complexity of the issues, I leave the matter to future work.

9. We can render adverbs like *cleverly* in *John cleverly answered the question* unambiguous, as follows: when they are subject oriented, such adverbs occur in C''_{12}; when they function as manner adverbs, they occur in C'''_9.

10. In Table 1 of Chapter 3, adverbs and adjectives are designated as $[-X''' \; LEVEL]$; therefore their occurrence on the X''' level in some of the above examples requires comment. Specifically, consider manner adverbs and descriptive adjectives in examples like the following:

(i)   [[reluctantly] [John PAST [pay his taxes [△]]]]
     V''' C'''   V'''   V''   C'''

(ii)   [[stable] [John may [never be [△]]]]
     V''' C'''   V'''   V''   C'''

In both of these cases (and all other similar ones), the modifiers are V''' level prehead residents bound to an empty node in V'' level posthead position. To account for such cases, suppose we say that the feature $[-X''' \; LEVEL]$ designates categories that normally do not occur on the X''' level and can occur there only if they are bound to an empty node which is *not* an X''' level adjunct. This broader definition of $[-X''' \; LEVEL]$ will account for cases like (i) and (ii) in a very natural way. Observe that strings like (i) and (ii) without the empty node present must be marked ungrammatical.

Unfortunately, for reasons mentioned in Note 8, we cannot extend this analysis globally to the sentence adverbs, since, among other things, we would be forced to say that a word like *maybe*, occurring initially, must be bound to a position it can never occupy (cf. *John maybe can go*). I believe that this indicates that sentence adverbs should not be considered adverbs at all; that is, they are not $[-X''' \; LEVEL]$. At present however, all we can say of these words is that they are, as a group, $[-\text{NOMINAL}, -\text{NEIGHBOR}]$.

CHAPTER FIVE

ON THE RULE MOVE *a*

As the previous chapters indicate, I believe that it is possible to remove all syntactic transformations from the grammar described here. Since movement rules, in particular the rule Move *a*, would appear to offer the most serious challenge to attempts to write nontransformational generative grammars, let us now consider this rule more carefully, beginning with the RG analysis of WH-questions like (1a), which has the structure (1b).

(1) a. What did John put into the closet?

b.

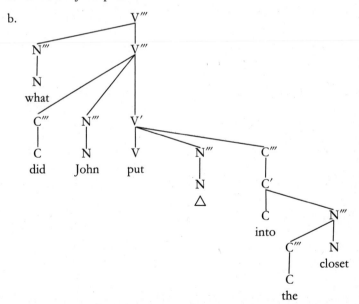

As we have observed, the left to right order of the X''' level prehead adjuncts in (1) is reversed: the normal order is nouns before characterizers. In RG this is treated as a standardized exception to the general order used in English to signal

questions. The rule subject-aux inversion is therefore unnecessary as a transformation. This seems straightforward enough since both nouns and characterizers are members of the category adjunct: that is, (1) can still be generated by
rule (40) of Chapter 1.

Suppose now that we replace movement rules with binding conditions
between a specialized subset of elements, for example, question words, and
empty constituents, such as the dummy symbol in (1b). If no binding relation
can be established for an item like a question word, then the structure is marked
ungrammatical. This would occur if, for example, the direct object slot of *put*
were filled in (1b) with, say, *the coat*. It would also occur if there were no N''' at
all in X' level posthead position after *put*. I believe that this approach to *moved*
constituents solves the problems raised by Bresnan (1978) in arguing for the
existence of transformations like Move *a*.[1]

Extending these ideas, restrictive relative clauses like (2) are given the
structure in (3).

(2)   the men that I saw

(3)

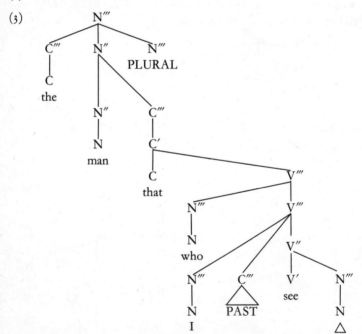

A binding relation exactly parallel to the one described above is possible for
(3); thus the sentence is grammatical. In this manner the last set of rules that
seem to be candidates for transformational status, namely, the rules described as
Move *a*, can be eliminated.

Notice that many of the conditions on rules like WH-movement, *each*-movement, etc., that have appeared in the literature (Chomsky, 1973, 1977; Chomsky and Lasnik, 1977), would require very little "translation" if one wished to incorporate them into the theory proposed here. Thus in an early seminal work on such conditions (Chomsky, 1973, 238), Chomsky proposes (4) to account for the data in (5), (6), and (7).

(4)   No rule can involve X, Y in the structure $\ldots X \ldots [\ldots Y \ldots] \ldots$
$$a$$

where a is a tensed sentence.

(5)   a. The candidates each hated the other(s).
      b. The candidates each expected the other(s) to win.
      c. The candidates each expected that the other(s) would win.

(6)   a. The candidates hated each other.
      b. The candidates expected each other to win.
      c. *The candidates expected that each other would win.

(7)   a. Who did the candidates hate ____?
      b. Who did the candidates expect ____ to win?
      c. *Who did the candidates expect that ____ would win?

Chomsky attributes the ungrammaticality of both (6c) and (7c) to a violation of (4).

In our framework reciprocals require an R-commanding antecedent. This explains (8).

(8)   a. *Each other will win.
      b. *They could each other have seen.

In all of the sentences in (6), *candidates* R-commands *each other*; thus our theory must also find a way to rule out (6c). We might simply appeal to (4) in the form as written, changing "rule" to "binding relation." However I think that this misses a generalization: the ungrammaticality of (6c) is related to the ungrammaticality of (8a). Reciprocals must be R-commanded by an antecedent within their own clause or noun phrase. Suppose we add the following concept to our theory.

(9)   Neighborhood:
      A neighborhood embraces all categories that are R-commanded or L-commanded by one and the same X''' level prehead characterizer.

Now there are two types of X''' level prehead characterizers that we have discussed: TNS (in V''') and articles or POSS (in N'''). C''', as we have seen, has no characterizer permissable in this position. Thus infinitives and participles, having characterizers as their heads, never constitute neighborhoods though they are often embedded within neighborhoods. In fact no characterizer ever constitutes a neighborhood, since characterizers are C′′′ having no X′′′ level first prehead adjuncts (cf. position C_1'' in (52) of Chapter 4, which as we discussed must be empty). There are therefore only two types of neighborhoods: verbal neighborhoods, distinguished by TNS, and nominal neighborhoods, distinguished by POSS or an article.

We may now revise (81) of Chapter 3 to the following:

(10)   The antecedent of a reciprocal must R-command either the reciprocal or an anaphor bound to the reciprocal, *and* both the antecedent and the reciprocal or bound anaphor must be within the same neighborhood.

Note that (10) is not a mere notational variation of the tensed S condition (4), since (4) does not block (8) whereas (10) does. Crucially, (8b) must be blocked since the grammar must account for the following pair:

(11)   a.   They could both have seen each other.
       b.   *They could each other have seen both.

The stipulation "one and the same" in (9) is also crucial; essentially the antecedent and the reciprocal (or bound anaphor) must be within the same simple sentence. This accounts for (12).

(12)   a.   *The men left, after Bill avoided each other.
       b.   The men left to avoid each other.

Thus (10), based on (9), rules out not only (6c) but also (11b), (12a) and both of the examples in (8).

Turning now to examples involving WH-constituents like (7), notice that we could also appeal to (4) without much change in its form if we wished. However the facts here are different. The verb *expect* governs a sentential complement (among others) introduced by a permanent resident. Thus in accordance with (70) of Chapter 3, (7c) is ruled out. And so are these:

(13)   a.   *Who did the candidates sneer that _____ would win. (cf. The candidates sneered that they each would win.)
       b.   *The candidates expected/sneered they each would win.
       c.   *Who did the candidates expect/sneer they each would nominate _____?
       d.   *Who did the candidates expect/sneer that they each would nominate _____?

In short, I think that it is a mistake to try to account for both (6c) and (7c) with the same condition (4). Actually two distinct factors are involved in these data: neighborhood in (6c); permanent residency in (7c) and (13).

Consider now some of the classic cases involving *picture noun phrases*: namely, those in (14) and (15) which have the structures (16) and (17), respectively.

(14) a. all of those twelve pictures *that* the men took of each other
        b. all of those twelve pictures *which* the men took of each other
        c. all of those twelve pictures _____ the men took of each other

(15) a. all of those twelve pictures of each other *that* the men took
        b. all of those twelve pictures of each other *which* the men took
        c. all of those twelve pictures of each other _____ the men took

(16)

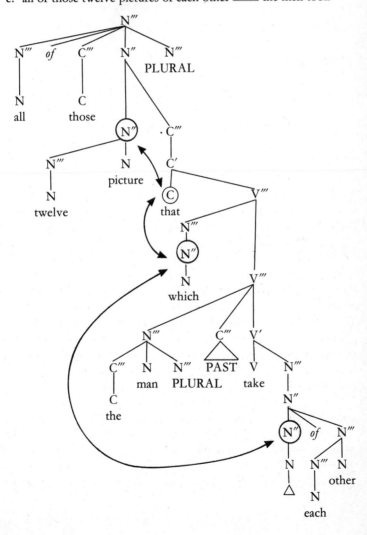

(17)

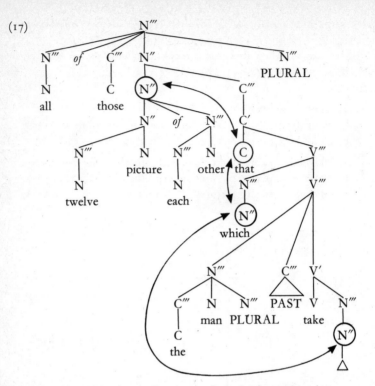

In (16) we see that *the men* R-commands *each other* within the same verbal neighborhood (under the command of PAST). *Which*, also in the same neighborhood,[2] can be bound to the dummy symbol by principles that we have suggested. Suppose now that we say the restrictive relative *that* is bound to the N″ that is the left-sister of the entire restrictive relative clause, as discussed in Chapter 2. In this way, we specify the characterizer as a bound constituent. Further suppose we say that the restrictive relative *that* must also be bound to an immediately following WH-constituent, which would be *which* in (16). We thus have a *chain of binding* indicated by the arrows in (16). *Twelve pictures* can fill the gap indicated by the dummy symbol. That produces the N‴ *twelve pictures of each other* which is grammatical in the context given. Therefore without modification (10) accounts for (14), provided we allow for the optional occurrences of *that* and *which* and the non-occurrence of both together.

Turning to (17), we note that *the men*, as above, R-commands the dummy symbol, so that a reciprocal can be connected with this position. Further, in the manner just discussed, a chain of binding can be established between *twelve pictures of each other* and the dummy symbol, as indicated by the arrows. I believe that this chain of binding is responsible for the grammaticality of (15).

This analysis represents a significant gain in descriptive adequacy over those available with a TG model, since that model requires special conditions to handle data like (14) and (15) (see Chomsky, 1973, for discussion).

The production of the variant cases in both (14) and (15) is apparently a separate issue. Assuming the structures (16) and (17), we may propose that the node dominating *which* is empty to produce the (a) cases, that the node dominating *that* is empty to produce the (b) cases, and that both nodes are empty to produce the (c) cases. Empty nodes in RG of course must be bound to some constituent in order for their occurrence not to be blocked. In the cases above this simply entails allowing the chain of binding represented by $N'' - [\beta] -$

$$\underset{C}{}$$

$[\gamma] - [... [\Delta]...]$ to contain *that* or Δ for β and *which* or Δ for γ, but not both
N''' $V'''N'''$
that and *which*.

To summarize the above analysis, a reciprocal may precede its antecedent provided a chain of binding can link the reciprocal to a position the antecedent R-commands within the same neighborhood.

Consider now Chomsky's "specified subject condition" (Chomsky, 1973, 239) repeated here as (18).

> (18)   No rule can involve X, Y in the structure $...X...[...Z...\text{-}WYV\text{-}...]...$
> a
>
> where Z is a specified subject of WYV in a

This condition is designed to account for examples like (19b) and (20b), which Chomsky derives from (19a) and (20a), respectively.

> (19)   a.   The candidates each expected [PRO to defeat the other].
>   S
>
>   b.   The candidates expected to defeat each other.

> (20)   a.   The men each expected [the soldier to shoot the other].
>   S
>
>   b.   *The men expected the soldier to shoot each other.

Again we could easily incorporate a condition like (18) into the grammar developed here; however there is no need to do so. Condition (18) is necessary because Chomsky's theory contains PRO and derives the infinitive phrases above from underlying clauses. In our theory there is no PRO, and the structures for (19b) and (20b) parallel, respectively, (36a) and (36b) of Chapter 3. A sentence like (20b) is blocked because, while *the soldier* is the subject of *shoot* and R-commands *each other*, it cannot be the antecedent of *each other* because of the conflict in number. In the theory proposed here (18) is thus unnecessary.

The above analysis extends to cases in which a in (18) is a noun phrase. The examples discussed by Chomsky (1973, 239) are the following:

(21)   a.   The men each saw [pictures of the other]
                                NP

            b.   The men saw pictures of each other.

(22)   a.   The men each saw [John's pictures of the other]
                                  NP

            b.   *The men saw John's pictures of each other.

(23)   a.   COMP you saw [pictures of who]
                            NP

            b.   Who did you see pictures of?

(24)   a.   COMP you saw [John's pictures of who]
            b.   *Who did you see John's pictures of?

Ruling out examples like (22b) has already been implicitly accomplished in previous discussion. Recall that the definition of *subject* and *direct object* in (41) and (42), respectively, of Chapter 3 was modified in the course of discussion to include both nouns and verbs. I repeat the emended definitions here for convenience, making use of the feature NEIGHBOR:[3]

(25)   a.   The subject of [+NEIGHBOR]''' is the N''' which most immediately L-commands [+NEIGHBOR]''' or which itself is the antecedent of an anaphor that most immediately L-commands [+NEIGHBOR]'''.

           b.   The object of [+NEIGHBOR]''' is the N''' which most immediately R-commands [+NEIGHBOR]''' or which itself is the antecedent of an anaphor that most immediately R-commands [+NEIGHBOR]'''.

According to (25a), *John* in (22b) is the subject of *pictures*. In our framework *John* is also the noun phrase that most immediately R-commands *each other*; therefore *John* should be its antecedent. As we just saw in (20b) however a conflict in number makes this impossible (cf. *John saw the men's pictures of each other*, which is grammatical). Accordingly (22b) is blocked for the correct reason: namely, the conflict in number. The ungrammaticality of (22b) has nothing to do with the specified subject that intervenes between *the men* and *each other*.

Before discussing (24b), there is an ambiguity of structure associated with phrases like *pictures of someone* that must be discussed. Consider first these examples:

(26)   a.   John delivered the letter to Mary.
           b.   John destroyed the letter to Mary.
           c.   John attributed the letter to Mary.

There is an ambiguity in (26a) associated with the structures (26b) or (26c). In the (26b)-reading, *letter to Mary* is within the same noun phrase; in the (26c)-reading, *letter* and *to Mary* are separate constituents. The relevant structures, respectively, are diagrammed in (27).

(27) a.

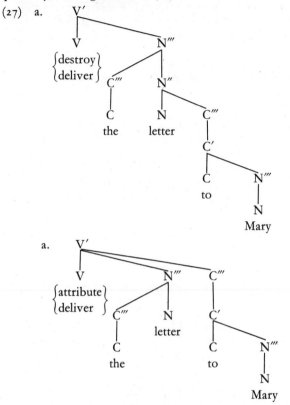

a.

The structure (27a) is associated with sentences like the following:

(28) a. John delivered the letter to Mary (to Sue by mistake).
      b. The letter to Mary is what John delivered.
      c. The letter to Mary was delivered by John.

(27b) underlies examples like these:

(29) a. The letter was delivered to Mary.
      b. The letter is what John delivered to Mary.

The same ambiguity of structure is involved in the following sentences containing *of*:

(30) a. John took pictures of Mary.
      b. John makes friends of his enemies.

In (30a), *took* (= *stole*) has a structure like (27a), whereas *took* (= *photographed*) has a structure like (27b). Similarly, in (30b), *makes* in its sexual sense is associated with a structure like (27a), whereas *makes* in the sense of *fashions* is associated with a structure like (27b). The only difference—an irrelevant one here—is that the *of*-phrase associated with the single constituent structure (27a) is, I believe, a genitive of quality and not a full prepositional phrase.

Now consider the following examples from Bach and Horn (1976, 281):

(31) a. Pictures of Gerald Ford are seen every day.
      b. Pictures are seen of Gerald Ford every day.

In our framework these two examples would be assigned structures parallel to the N‴ and C‴ in (27a) and (27b), respectively.

In addition to (31) there are similar examples which to my knowledge have not been observed, including these:

(32) a. The pictures of Gerald Ford are seen every day.
      b. ?The pictures are seen of Gerald Ford every day.

(33) a. Nixon's pictures of Gerald Ford are seen every day.
      b. *Nixon's pictures are seen of Gerald every day.

I believe that these data are related to Chomsky's observation (Chomsky, 1973, 239, Note 19) that there is a three-way gradation of acceptability associated with examples like (24b), as follows:

(34) a. Who did you see pictures of?
      b. ?Who did you see the pictures of?
      c. *Who did you see John's pictures of?

To account for these judgements, Chomsky proposes that reference to the feature [+Definite] be incorporated into (18). Suppose however that we say that the grammar contains PSFs which allow structures like (35a), (35b), and (35c), but not ones like (35d).

(35) a. V′

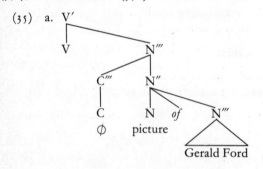

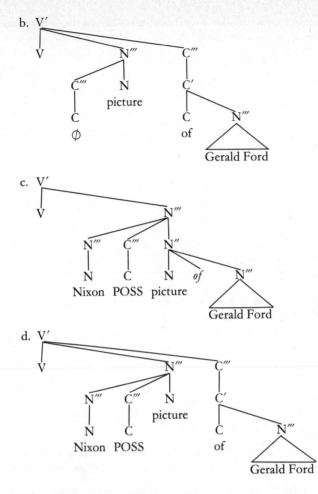

The noun phrase in (35a) is structurally related to (31a); the one in (35b), (31b); and the one in (35c), (33a). The nonexistence of (35d) accounts for (33b). Notice that the noun phrase immediately dominating Gerald Ford in (35c), if empty, cannot be bound to a constituent outside of the N''' whose head is *picture*, because it is R-commanded by POSS (cf. the discussion of (84) in Chapter 3). Furthermore, we note from previous discussion that (35b) is related to (34a).

To rule out structures like (35d), we add the following PSF, specifying the *of-*phrase as a *complementary genitive*:

(36) *Noun phrases containing POSS followed by a complementary genitive.

This PSF invented to rule out (33b) is also needed elsewhere in the grammar. Thus while (30a) is ambiguous, (37) is not.

(37)   John took Bill's picture of Mary.

Furthermore we do not have (38).

(38)   *Bill's picture was taken of Mary.

Despite the fact that (36) or something like it is necessary, I see no reason why the grammar of English should contain it.

Given (36), we may now say that the marginal acceptability of (32b) is due to the insertion of an article other than $\emptyset$ into (35b). This I believe requires a separate PSF, because judgements are very uncertain whereas structures like (35d) always lead to ungrammaticality. Consider these:

(39)   a. ?Those pictures are seen of Gerald Ford every day.
        b. ?A picture is seen of Gerald Ford every day.
        c. ?A certain picture is seen of Gerald Ford every day.

I shall not attempt to formulate the required PSF here.

Summarizing, we may say that (24b) is blocked for the same reason the examples in (84) of Chapter 3 were blocked: elements within the domain of a permanent resident (here, article or POSS) cannot be bound to constituents outside that domain. It should follow from this that questions based on the ambiguous (30a), associated with both (35a) and (35b), are unambiguous. This is the case. *Who did John take pictures of* means only "Who did John photograph?".

In the new analysis of WH-elements we have suggested, all of the above facts can be embodied in (40).

(40)   *A binding relation between a WH-constituent and an element R-commanded by an X''' level prehead characterizer of a noun phrase.

Since such characterizers are permanent residents, and such conditions are also applicable in characterizer phrases and verb phrases, (40) is actually part of the much more general (41).

(41)   *A binding relation between a WH-constiuent and an element within the domain of a permanent resident.

(41) rules out (24b), as well as (7c), (13c), (34c), all of the examples in (84) of Chapter 3, (82h) and (82i) of Chapter 3, and many others.

Let us now turn to some more complicated examples involving "floating" quantifiers and reciprocals. In particular consider (42) which has the structure (43) in RG.

(42)   Which two men does John think [$\triangle$] could have both seen each other?

(43)

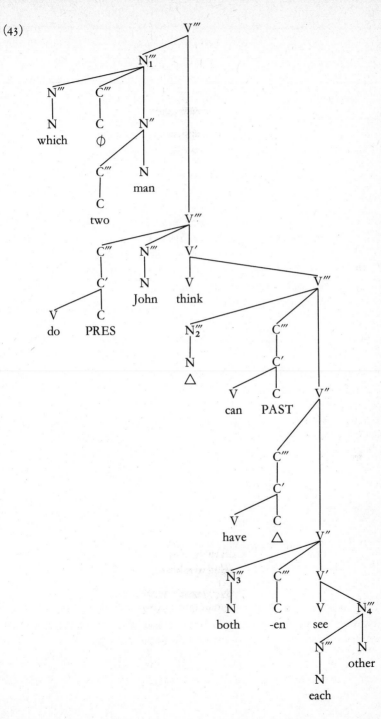

We see in (43) that the WH-constituent, N_1''', can be bound to the empty node, N_2''': there is no permanent resident or free resident present to block such a binding as there would be in the structure underlying (44).

(44)   *Which two men does John think that [△] could have both seen each other?

Since N_2''' L-commands the "floating" quantifier, N_3''', and R-commands the reciprocal, N_4''', the structure is grammatical, and (42) has a proper interpretation. By the same methods we account for these examples:

(45)   a. Which two men does John think [△] could have both wanted to see each other?
        b. Which two men does John think [△] could have both wanted these women all to see each other?
        c. Which two men does John think [△] could have both wanted to see pictures of each other?
        d. *Which two men does John think [△] could have both wanted to see Bill's pictures of each other?
        e. What does John think that these two men could have both wanted to see [△] of each other's?

Notice that (45d) is ungrammatical because of the conflict in number between *Bill* and *each other*. Further, (45e) *is* grammatical because *that* is a free resisdent which accordingly allows a binding relation to exist between a WH-constituent and an item *not* L-commanded by *that* (the gap is to the right of *want*).

Consider now the structure in Figure 2. Notice that a chain of binding can be established between *pictures of each other* and the dummy symbol in the manner described above. Since *men* R-commands the dummy symbol, it is the antecedent of *each other*, since *men* L-commands *all*, it is the antecedent of *all*.

Now suppose that the boxed N''' in Figure 2 is filled by *the women*. In this case we have the phrase (46).

(46)   the pictures of each other that the men all may want the women to continue distributing.

In (46), the referent for *each other* is now *the women*, as in (47).

(47)   The men want the women to continue distributing pictures of each other.

The reason for this change in reference is of course that *the women* now R-commands *each other*, not *the men*. Accordingly the phrase (48) is grammatical even though the subject of *want* is now singular.

(48)   the pictures of each other that John may want the women to continue distributing.

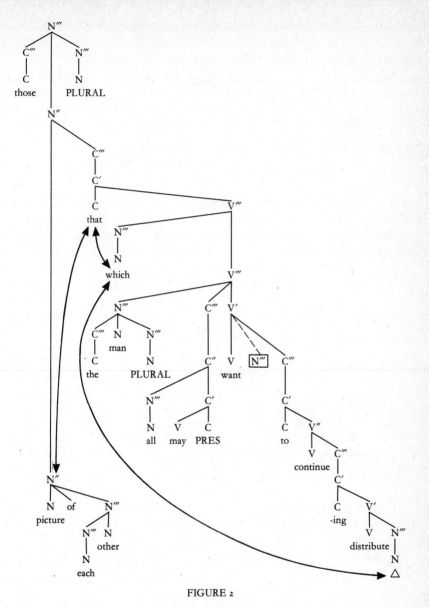

FIGURE 2

Despite examples of extraordinary complexity, there is therefore no reason to appeal to transformations or conditions on transformations, given the RG model of phrase structure and the concepts of command and residency discussed above. I know of no relevant relationship expressed by a transformation, in regard to any of the examples we have considered, that cannot be expressed in RG terms. Indeed RG has often attained a higher level of descriptive adequacy than TG. To take one further example, consider (49).

(49)   a.   Brilliant, that man standing over there certainly is not _____.
       b.   Graciously, John will no doubt accept the award he has been offerred _____.[4]

Notice that *brilliant* and *graciously* are not noun phrases and, further, do not contain a WH-element—conditions which are necessary for a WH-movement analysis. In RG *brilliant*, *graciously*, noun phrases, WH-constituents, etc., are all adjuncts subject to binding conditions of the types we have discussed:

(50)   a.   *What does John wonder whether Sue bought _____?
       b.   *That book, John wonders whether Bill read _____.
       c.   *Brilliant, John wonders whether Bill is _____.
       d.   *Graciously, John wonders whether Bill will accept the award _____.

In short, it is not NP status, WH status, or anything of the like that blocks (50). Simply put, constituents, no matter what their particular structure, cannot be bound to others that are within the domain of a permanent resident or that are L-commanded by a free resident.

NOTES TO CHAPTER 5

1. There are remaining difficulties involving rules like subject-verb agreement (number agreement) in examples like (i), which is from Bresnan (1978, #124):

(i)   Which problems did your professor say she thought were unsolvable?

Note that in (i) *which problems* will be bound in RG to an empty node in subject slot of *be* (*were*). Phonological rules cannot of course handle such matters as agreement between a node bound to some other node. However, suppose we allow number to be freely chosen as a constituent of AUX, specifically, N_8''' of Figure 1 (Chapter 4). This exactly parallels the position for NUMBER in noun phrases, i.e., N_3''' in (3) of Chapter 2. We may now add the following PSF to the grammer:

(ii)   *[[...N''[a]...] [...C''[β]...] V''...]
       V'''N'''   N'''   C'''   N'''

   where $a \neq \beta$

What (ii) says is the the nominal adjunct in X''' level first posthead position of the subject N''' and the AUX (C''') must be the same. Utilizing the concept *chain of binding*, to be discussed presently, we may account for cases like (i), where the subject N''' is not in its normal position. Thus I do not feel that Bresnan's examples offer any challenge to RG. I shall return to this discussion in Chapter 7.

One might argue that the above account shows more promise than the standard TG account of agreement, when performance factors are considered. Clearly, speakers are more likely to make an error in agreement in a sentence like (i) than in one like (iii) where subject and agreeing verb are adjacent.

(iii)   Which problems were unsolvable?

In a TG framework, the assignment of number to *be* in (i) and (iii) is identical; that is, number is assigned to *be* in (i) at a stage of the derivation when *which problems* is adjacent to *be*. Accordingly, the greater chance of an error in agreement in examples like (i), where the subject is separated some distance from its agreeing verb, would be unexplained. In RG, on the other hand, (i) involves the use of more complex mechanisms than (iii); hence the difference between them. I return to such performance considerations in more detail in the next chapter.

2. Recall that the command relations are not sensitive to rewrites of the same X^n level, n being constant. The relevant level here is V'''.

3. The category [+NEIGHBOR], it will be recalled, embraces both nouns and verbs (cf. Table 1, Chapter 3).

4. Notice that, as the above discussion predicts, *graciously* cannot be understood as a modifier of *offer*, which is within a relative clause. I am grateful to Pat Dennen for pointing this out to me.

CHAPTER SIX

6.0 THE DEVELOPMENT OF RG

Residential Grammar did not arise as an attempt to write a generative grammar without transformations; rather, it began as an effort to explore the potential of X′ syntax. In fact the original version of parts of this monograph (Binkert, 1981, MS) was largely a criticism of Jackendoff (1977).

At first I was concerned with how X′ syntax might contribute to the solution of a number of problems in the syntactic analysis of English; in particular, the status of articles and degree words, the representation of complex nominals and inflectional categories, the manner of accounting for the multiple positions which various word classes like sentence adverbs and quantifiers can occupy, and in general the cross-categorial relationships among the syntactic categories of English. At the same time it seemed important to consider various transformational rules in terms of the surface structures they produced; for example, the form of *there*-insertion, passive, and affix hopping in terms of the main verb nature of the passive and progressive *be* and the participial nature of the verb forms associated with these auxiliary elements.

It soon became clear that X′ syntax could not solve these sorts of problems by itself. The categorial problem alone was formidable: attempting to construct a series of context-free phrase structure rules in the form of Jackendoff (1977) proved to be an impossible task when the goal was to account for data such as those mentioned above. As the model of RG began to take shape with the realization that there was a need to think in terms of very general syntactic categories, it became clear that many transformations, as rules of the familiar type, could be eliminated. Among the first to go were rules like relative clause reduction, modifier shift and *there*-insertion. In short, the enrichment of the phrase structure component had the expected effect of reducing the number of transformations needed. Whether or not RG holds up under close critical scrutiny, it seems to me that other linguists will ultimately reach the same conclusion; namely, that a solution to the Categorial Problem and the Level Recursion Problem renders syntactic transformations superfluous.

This prediction requires immediate clarification: what can be eliminated from a generative grammar is the transformational rule in its familiar form; the relationships that such rules have expressed in the past of course remain. This is not to suggest that RG is a mere notational variant of TG. On the contrary, a generative grammar containing transformational rules as formal objects of a particular type makes predictions about the nature of language that are very different from those made by a generative grammar without such formal objects. Most generally, a TG claims that a descriptively adequate grammar of a language must assign to each sentence in that language at least two levels of structure. An RG makes no such claim. The implications of this one difference alone are considerable. Furthermore, the inclusion of transformational rules into a generative grammar, these rules being themselves subject to severe restrictions of form and functioning, places restrictions on all other components of the grammar. Thus in a grammar containing transformations, phrase structure rules must be of a particular type (cf. Bach, 1964): the phrase structure rules must provide unique derivations. Hence no PS Rule can rewrite a symbol beginning or ending with itself. This precludes rules of the type used in RG, in particular, rule (40) of Chapter 1. Again, the ramifications of restrictions of this type are far-reaching.

Two points therefore must be kept distinct. Since those syntactic relationships that transformations have attempted to capture remain to be captured in a nontransformational grammar, it may appear that the two grammars are notational variations of each other: both are attempting to account for the same data, so there will naturally be some descriptive overlap. In this sense one may interpret the binding conditions discussed in the last chapter as notational variations of conditions on WH-movement, such as the tensed-S condition and the specified subject condition. However the RG claim that all items are base generated in their surface positions—that is, that only one level of syntactic representation is required to attain descriptive adequacy—is *not* a notational variation of the TG claim that items are first generated in position β by one set of rules (phrase structure rules) and then subsequently moved from position β to position γ by another set of rules (transformations). The TG claim that two distinct levels of syntactic representation—the deep and the surface structures—are required for descriptive adequacy supports a very specific conception of grammatical characterization, universal grammar, and language acquisition. Consider for example the following excerpt from *Language and Mind* (Chomsky, 1968, 31):

Knowledge of a language involves the ability to assign deep and surface structures to an infinite range of sentences, to relate these structures appropriately, and to assign a semantic interpretation and a phonetic interpretation to the paired deep and surface structures. This outline of the nature of grammar seems to be quite accurate as a first approximation to the characterization of "knowledge of a language."

Since Chomsky made these comments, TG has undergone considerable extension (Newmeyer, 1980). In fact I consider RG the natural outcome of an evolutionary process that began in the early 1970s with Chomsky's work on constraints on transformational rules. An RG constrains the transformational component in the maximal way possible: it eliminates it. Accordingly, the RG conception of grammatical characterization, universal grammar, and language acqusition is very different from the standard version of TG (Chomsky, 1965) which emphasizes a duality of structure in grammatical representation.

In view of these remarks and in order to give the proper focus to the following discussion, further arguments in this chapter will be directed against the claim of the standard version of TG (Chomsky, 1965). The RG position is that description (and explanatory) adequacy can be achieved in generative grammars *without* appeal to a formal level of deep structure related to a distinct formal level of surface structure by a set of formal syntactic transformations.

6.1 THE FUNDAMENTAL EMPIRICAL PROBLEMS

In Chapter 1, following Bresnan (1978), I noted that there are two fundamental empirical problems facing modern linguistic theory: the grammatical characterization problem, which involves accounting for the linguistic competence of the mature native speaker; and the grammatical realization problem, which entails accounting for all those phenomena relating to linguistic performance.

In regard to these problems, Chomsky (1965, 9) makes the following comments:

(1) a. To avoid what has been a continuing misunderstanding, it is perhaps worth while to reiterate that a generative grammar is not a model for a speaker or a hearer. It attempts to characterize in the most neutral possible terms the knowledge that provides the basis for actual use of language by a speaker-hearer.

     b. No doubt, a reasonable model of language use will incorporate, as a basic component, the generative grammar that expresses the speaker-hearer's knowledge of the language . . .

The distinction drawn by Chomsky in 1965 was for one thing cautionary: it did not seem reasonable at that time to propose a theory of how native speakers use language (linguistic performance) because the linguist's understanding of the nature of competence was so limited. Put another way, it made little sense to make proposals about how a person uses what he knows without first having a firm understanding of what it is that he knows.

In the twenty-five year history of TG, very significant gains have been made in our understanding of linguistic competence so that it now seems appropriate to investigate statement (1b)—to ask the question, Can TG form part of a reasonable model of language use? Beyond mere appropriateness the study of linguistic competence may well be advanced significantly by considering the results of investigations of various aspects of performance, in its most general sense, including the study of emerging competence in normal children (Brown, 1973), of the degenerative effects on competence owing to cerebral trauma (Whitaker, 1971), and the like. The dates of the last two references is significant: for quite some time now the study of various aspects of performance has yielded results to which linguistics ought to be responsive in their effort to achieve a better understanding of competence. To be more specific, the many diary studies of child language development have revealed that there is a two-word stage that all children pass through, the description of which has come to be known as *pivot grammar*. (See Brown, 1973, for a comprehensive review and discussion). Although originally received with much enthusiam, pivot grammar eventually met heavy criticism, in particular because the pivot-open dichotomy did not relate to adult classes. Brown (1973, 95) has put the matter as follows:

One thing that has bothered many people about the pivot-open distinction is the fact that it seems to make no particular linguistic sense. If these are the primal classes why are they so? They have nothing obvious to do with the adult standard languages.

This particular criticism derives from a TG bias: transformational grammars do not recognize any syntactic categories that pivot and open classes of words might develop into. The point is that the issue could have been looked at the other way around. Could it not be the case that the syntactic classes of TG are wrong? This question does not seem to have received much attention from workers in the field.

In mentioning this it is not my purpose to marshall support for pivot grammar, a defense of which involves many questions. Nor do I claim that the matter of word classes was the only factor which drove Brown to suggest that the "notion of pivot grammar should simply be jettisoned altogether" (1973, 111). Rather, I wish to raise the question, in the case of pivot grammar, did linguists miss an opportunity to enhance their understanding of syntactic word classes because the particular classes that seemed to be relevant in child language did not mesh with the prevailing model of adult competence? I think one must admit that this is a distinct possibility.

Clearly, the cautionary aspect of (1) was entirely appropriate in 1965 and remains instructive today. However, consider the following more recent remarks of Chomsky (1980b, 226):

Study of performance relies essentially on advances in understanding of competence. But since a competence theory must be incorporated in a performance model, evidence about the actual organization of behavior may prove crucial to advancing the theory of underlying competence. Study of performance and study of competence are mutually supportive. We must simply try to be clear about what we are doing in attempting to investigate something as complex and hidden as the human faculty of language and its exercise.

Therefore, realizing that a TG of, say, English was never intended to be a model of *how* native speakers of English produce and understand sentences, one can still raise questions about the possible relevance of TG to a theory of performance, in an effort to ascertain what contributions to the study of competence might derive from discussing various competence models in terms of performance issues.

Notice that there is nothing particularly unorthodox about taking this approach to the study of language. Consider the following comments from Chomsky (1981, 55):

The question of the nature of empty categories is a particularly interesting one for a number of reasons. In the first place, the study of such elements [PRO and trace], along with the related investigation of anaphors and pronouns, has proven to be an excellent probe for determining properties of syntactic and semantic representations and the rules that form them. But apart from this, there is an intrinsic fascination in the study of properties of empty elements. These properties can hardly be determined inductively from observed overt phenomena, and therefore presumably reflect inner resources of mind. If our goal is to discover the nature of the human language faculty, abstracting from the effects of experience, then these elements offer particularly valuable insights.

The intent of these comments is clear: the innateness hypothesis, as an explanatory theory of human language acquisition, will accrue dramatic support if it can be shown that it is impossible to describe the syntax of the world's languages without appeal to empty categories. The reason is that if descriptive adequacy cannot be achieved without reference to empty categories, then it seems reasonable to say that empty categories are part of *core grammar* (Chomsky and Lasnik, 1977; Chomsky, 1981). If they are part of *core grammar*, then the child approaches the task of language acquisition unconsciously knowing that the language to which he has been fortuitously exposed may contain empty categories. It is therefore reasonable for psycholinguists to entertain questions on the effect that empty categories, i.e., gaps, have on sentence comprehension, a performance task, and this is just what has been done. (See, for example, J. D. Fodor, 1978.)

Along the same lines, we may ask questions like, Is there any "psychological reality" to the kinds of deep structures produced by a TG; or to the kinds of derivations constructed by a TG; or to the very idea that sentences must contain two levels of syntactic representation? These are the sorts of questions we will entertain below in terms of the Grammatical Realization Problem.

Summarizing these remarks, we can describe the major difference between transformational and residential grammars in the following way. A *generative grammar* (GG) is a grammar which attempts to characterize the linguistic competence (knowledge) of the mature adult native speaker. A *transformational generative grammar* (TGG or TG, for short) is a model which claims that this characterization must include transformational rules, while a *residential generative grammar* (RGG or RG, for short) claims that it does not.

6.2 GRAMMATICAL CHARACTERIZATION AND DESCRIPTIVE ADEQUACY

We have seen in many cases above the RG attains a much higher level of descriptive adequacy than TG, because RG is able to generalize facts in a way that is beyond the descriptive power of TG. The purpose of this section is to examine more carefully the descriptive apparatus of the two theories.

6.21 PHRASE STRUCTURE FILTERS

In the preceding chapters, the PSFs of RG have been stated informally to facilitate exposition. Examining such filters in more detail, we find that they serve two purposes: (i) to express restrictions on the sequences of items in phrase structure, and (ii) to express restrictions on semantic interpretation such as the binding conditions that can exist between anaphors and their antecedents. In the former capacity, PSFs operate like context sensitive phrase structure rules; in the latter, like conditions on transformations.

Considering the former type first, we have noted that an adequate grammar of English must contain PSFs like the following:

(2)   Noun phrases must have an article or POSS generated in X''' level first prehead position on the last rewrite of N''' to N''.

(3)   Noun phrases must have the category NUMBER generated in X''' level first posthead position on the last rewrite of N''' to N''.

In RG, we have seen (Chapter 3) that terms like *article* and *POSS* are really abbreviations for a syntactic feature matrix as follows:

(4)   a. Article:
        $[-\text{Nominal}, +\text{Prehead}, +X''' \text{ Level}, + \underline{\hspace{1cm}} N, \ldots]$
   b. POSS:
        $[-\text{Nominal}, \pm\text{Prehead}, +X''' \text{ Level}, + \underline{\hspace{1cm}} N, \ldots]$

The feature $[-\text{Nominal}]$ means that articles and POSS are characterizers; $[+\text{Prehead}]$ signifies items that can occur to the left of the head; $[+X''' \text{ Level}]$ signifies items that can be residents of the X''' level, i.e., items that can be dominated by X'''; and, $[+ \underline{\hspace{1cm}} N]$ indicates items that can occur in noun phrases as modifiers of the noun head. The last feature is used to distinguish articles and POSS from degree words like *too, as, so,* etc., which are $[- \underline{\hspace{1cm}} N]$ (see Chapter 3, Section 3.0).

PSFs like (2) and (3) are actually *node admissibility conditions* in the sense originally suggested by Richard Stanley (see McCawley (1968)). To express such statements formally, we employ labelled brackets, a formalism which has also appeared recently in Gazdar (1981). In this way, (2) and (3) are stated as (5).

(5) $[\quad (N''') - [- \text{COMP}]''' - N'' - [- \text{COMP}]''' - (C''')]$
     N'''

Both $[-\text{COMP}]$ categories in (5) must be $[+/\underline{\quad}/N]$ and $[+X''' \text{LEVEL}]$, because of the occurrence of N'' and the label on the outer brackets, respectively. Thus what (5) constitutes is a specification of the items that can occur in rule (6), which is based on the more general (7), which in turn is based on the still more general (8), the rule that began this inquiry.

(6) $N''' \to (N''')(C''') N'' (N''')(C''')$

(7) $N''' \to /A''' - A'''/ N''$

(8) $X^n \to /A''' - A'''/ X^m, m \leq n$

An RG, of course, need explicitly contain only (5) and (8).[1]

Rule (8), as we have noted, is inadmissable in TG because it allows a category to be written as a string beginning or ending with itself, a condition necessary in a GG which contains transformations. To express the contents of PSF (5), TG has available a phrase structure rule like (9).

(9) $NP \to ART + N + NUMBER$

However (9) is by no means equivalent to (5); furthermore, it is not possible to attain the level of generality implicit in (5) within TG.

(5) is part of a generalized system which reduces all syntactic categories except noun and verb to one, the category characterizer, thereby allowing for the expression of many cross-categorial generalizations, as we have seen. Within the standard theory of TG (Chomsky, 1965) and various EST (extended standard theory) versions, e.g., Jackendoff (1977), the simplicity and generality of expression that constitute (8) and (5) are impossible. Both the standard theory and the EST must ultimately resort to devices like curly brackets, the evils of which have been noted elsewhere (McCawley, 1970, 1972). More specifically, within RG, articles are $[+X''' \text{Level}]$ and adjectives are $[-X''' \text{Level}]$ (when they occur in noun phrases). Both categories are $[-\text{Nominal}, +\underline{\quad}N]$. Furthermore, some adjectives, e.g., *available*, can occur either before or after the head noun: that is, they are $[+/\underline{\quad}/N]$, where the slashes denote possible occurrence on either side of the head, as in rule (8). This system allows therefore for both generality and specificity; TG allows only for specificity. Any phenomenon involving both articles and adjectives, e.g., agreement in Latin, German, etc., cannot be expressed without appeal to curly brackets, which because they are used specifically for the phenomenon at hand are *ad hoc*.

To avoid misunderstanding, recall that the argument here is not that one cannot extend various EST versions of TG in the needed direction. Of course this can be done. However once it is done, transformations are no longer necessary. In short, to incorporate the analyses of this monograph into a TG— any TG—is to render transformations unnecessary, and hence to produce a phrase structure grammar.

Consider now the second type of PSF, like (10).

(10)   *A binding relation between an adjunct and an anaphor, when the anaphor is within the domain of a permanent or free resident.

We define residential domains as follows:

(11)   a. Permanent resident (PR)
           The domain of a permanent resident embraces all items it either
           L-commands or R-commands.
       b. Free resident (FR)
           The domain of a free resident embraces all items it L-commands.

We now make (10) more precise as follows:

(12)   *A binding relation between X and Y in the structure ...X...
        [...Y...]..., where *a* is a residential domain.
        a

(12) looks very much like Chomsky's conditions discussed in the last chapter, but it is far more general. For example, with (12) we can eliminate, as special statements, Ross's constraints (Ross, 1967). Consider, for example, Ross's sentential subject constraint (Ross, 1967; Baker, 1978). This constraint says that no item can be extracted from a sentential subject; thus from (13a) we cannot derive (13b).

(13)   a. That John won WHAT upset Bill? (an echo question)
       b. *What did that John won upset Bill?

The *that* complementizer which introduces the sentential subject in (13a) cannot be deleted. There are no sentences like (14).

(14)   *John won the race upset Bill.

Since this complementizer cannot be deleted (see Chomsky and Lasnik, 1977, for a possible explanation), it is a permanent resident in RG. Hence, the grammar need contain Ross's sentential subject constraint as a special constraint: (12) blocks (13b) already.

Consider now Ross's complex NP constaint (Ross, 1967; Baker, 1978). This constraint prevents the extraction of an item from within a complex NP, blocking (15b) derived from (15a).

(15) a. Bill believes the claim that John won WHAT? (an echo question)
      b. *What does Bill believe the claim that John won?

The direct object NP in (15a) has the structure (16) in RG.

(16)

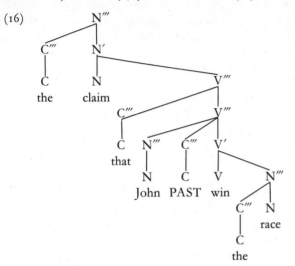

In (16) *the race* is within the domain of the permanent resident *that*. Observe that the complementizer cannot be deleted from these complex noun phrases:

(17) a. *Bill believes the claim John won the race.
      b. *The fact Bill dated Sue upsets John.

Accordingly, (12) also blocks (15b), and the grammar need not contain the complex NP constraint as a special constraint.

We see from the above examples that RG, using the concepts of residency that we have discussed, can achieve a higher level of descriptive adequacy than TG can, using Chomsky's conditions. Thus phrase structure filters, when constrained to a particular format, say, (5) and (12), have the effect of achieving considerable generality within a system that still allows for the statement of specific details.

At the categorial level we see that an RG can also express both the very specific and the highly general. For example, we can make reference to articles ([−NOMINAL, +PREHEAD, −POSTHEAD, +X‴ LEVEL, +____N) or tense ([−NOMINAL, +PREHEAD, −POSTHEAD, +X‴ LEVEL, −____N), using the syntactic features in Table 1 of Chapter 3. But within the same system we can collapse articles and tense to one category, i.e., [−POSTHEAD]. This is necessary to ensure that there will be at most one article modifying the head per noun phrase, and one tense modifying the head per verb phrase. Thus the filter (ii) or (iii) proposed in Note 1 extends easily to tense, by replacing the final N''' with X''', i.e., *[N''' − [−NOMINAL, X'''

−POSTHEAD, +X''' LEVEL] − X'']. This filter blocks any occurrence of articles or tense from occurring before an X''', i.e., either N''' or V''' here. Since articles or tense can now only occur before X'', there will be at most one article or tense per X''' phrase. Notice that it is impossible for either category to be repeated before successive recursions of X'' since they are X''' level categories. Articles and tense can occur only on the last rewrite of X''' to X'', exactly as the filter ensures. This sort of generality, in the midst of a phrase structure system that still admits great specificity, is impossible to attain in all current versions of TG phrase structure. Again, RG attains a higher level of descriptive adequacy than TG. We shall see further examples of this when we return to a more formal discussion of PSFs in the next chapter.

6.22 TRANSFORMATIONAL RULES

In this section let us examine the adequacy of transformational rules as expressions of semantic and syntactic relations. Consider first the rule *there*-insertion. This rule is designed to capture the relationships between pairs of sentences like the following:

(18)   a. A man is on the phone.
       b. There is a man on the phone.

The important fact for a grammar of English to account for is that the subject of (18b) is *a man*, making (18b) virtually synonymous with (18a). That it is the subject is clear from the number on the verbs in the following:

(19)   a. *There are a man on the phone.
       b. *There is two men in the garden.

As we have noted, the structural change of the *there*-insertion transformation is fraught with difficulties. In some versions, e.g., Burt (1971), the moved NP has even ended up dominated by the progressive node. Let us assume however that these difficulties can be worked out. Now consider (20).

(20)   a. A man could have been on the phone.
       b. *There a man could have been on the phone.
       c. *There could a man have been on the phone.
       d. *There could have a man been on the phone.
       e. There could have been a man on the phone.

As these data indicate, the moved NP must end up to the right of the verb *be*.

This is the case whether *be* is the main verb *be*, the progressive *be* or the passive *be*. Consider these:

(21) a. A man could have been lurking in the garden.
       b. *There a man could have been lurking in the garden.
       c. *There could a man have been lurking in the garden.
       d. *There could have a man been lurking in the garden.
       e. There could have been a man lurking in the garden.

(22) a. A man could have been murdered in the garden.
       b. *There a man could have been murdered in the garden.
       c. *There could a man have been murdered in the garden.
       d. *There could have a man been murdered in the garden.
       e. There could have been a man murdered in the garden.

Again, assuming that a TG can generalize (20) to include (21) and (22), a very generous assumption indeed, the thing to note is that the moved NP ends up to the right of the verb *be*. The question is, Why? Within TG, there is no explanation whatsoever. This seems only to be a quirk of the English language.

Now consider the RG analysis discussed above in Chapter 4. In all of the above sentences, the main verb is *be*, and the moved NP occurs to the right in predicate nominative position. Further, the moved NP, being in predicate nominative position, is R-commanded by the permanent resident *there*. Notice we do not have (23), so *there* must be considered a permanent resident.

(23)   *Could have been a man on the phone.

We see now why the moved NP is to the right of the verb *be*. All items in RG that occupy predicate nominative position refer back to the subject and are R-commanded by the subject. This includes all the italicized items in the following:

(24) a. A review appeared *of the book that John wrote.*
       b. A man walked in *wearing a mink coat.*
       c. Three men showed up *that I want to meet.*

Since *there* in (18b) is a morpheme having no sematic content, *a man*, in this case, is the subject of the sentence. In short, RG accounts for the synonymy of (18a) and (18b), and, at the same time, provides an explanation for the most perplexing aspect of these sentences: namely, the position of the moved NP.

Now notice that the number on the verb in (18b) is singular, agreeing with *man*. We can account for this in RG as suggested in Note 1 of Chapter 5; only in the case of sentences containing *there*, matters are not so straightforward. In particular, we must utilize the concept of *chain of binding* to locate the subject in predicate nominative position. This is clearly more complicated than the TG analysis which always simply looks to what is in the deep structure subject slot to determine the number on the verb. However, in this case, the added complication seems warranted. Notice that many speakers of *Standard English* accept (25a), whereas none accept (25b).

(25) a. ?There's three men lurking in the garden.
      b. *Three men is lurking in the garden.

In TG these two sentences have the same degree of deviance since the assignment of number to the verb is the same in each. In RG, on the other hand, the assignment of number in (25a) is more complicated than the assignment of number in (25b), for the reasons just given. Thus in RG, the marginal acceptability of (25a) is related to the relative difficulty of finding the subject. This seems intuitively correct since the subject of (25a) is less clear than the subject of (25b).

Now consider these examples:

(26) a. *It a man could have been on the phone.
      b. *It could a man have been on the phone.
      c. *It could have a man been on the phone.
      d. It could have been a man on the phone.

The analysis of (26) in RG is straightforward: *it* simply has to be identified as another morpheme without semantic content that R-commands a constituent in predicate nominative position. Notice also the following parallels with the above:

(27) a. It could have been a man lurking in the garden.
      b. It could have been a man murdered in the garden.

To account for these data TG presumably would allow either *there* or *it* to be inserted in the structural change of some *there/it*-insertion rule. But this will not work, because the insertion of *there* is under different constraints from the insertion of *it*. Observe the following:

(28) a. There are three men in the garden.
      b. *It are three men in the garden.

Again, the generality/specificity dichotomy mentioned above cannot be captured within TG. Since there is no movement involved at all in RG, the differences between the two constructions can be stated easily in terms of PSFs. We might, for example, include the following:

(29) *[it $-$ C''' $-$ [... be [... [+ PLURAL] ...] ...] ...]
         V'''   V''   N'''

Of course one would hope to find a better reason than (29) for ruling out

(28); perhaps (29) derives from the inherent singularity of *it*. Assuming this to be the case, it is clear that such reasons can be stated in RG terms without any loss in generality in accounting for (20), (21), (22), and (26).

Consider now a rule like relative clause reduction, which has been proposed, e.g., Baker (1978), to account for pairs like the following:

(30) a. the books *that are available*
      b. the books *available*

(31) a. the man *that was murdered*
      b. the man *murdered*

Semantically these pairs pose no problems for RG, since the italicized constituent are all N″ level characterizers. Now consider these:

(32) a. the books available
      b. the available books

(33) a. the man murdered
      b. the murdered man

To account for these, many TG analyses propose a rule of modifier shift, e.g., Baker (1978). But again this kind of analysis is fraught with problems: some relative clauses cannot reduce, e.g., (34); some postnominal modifiers cannot be the result of reductions, e.g., (35); some modifiers do not shift, e.g., (36); and so on.

(34) a. the books that appeared available
      b. *the books appeared available (are over there)

(35) a. *the man who is with ambition/the man who is without ambition
      b. the man with ambition/the man without ambition

(36) a. the debris that is adrift
      b. the debris adrift
      c. *the adrift debris

Incorporating these idiosyncrasies into the transformational rules mentioned is next to impossible. This is another case of the generality/specificity dichotomy. In RG the treatment of the above data is intuitively correct: all N″ adjuncts, whether prehead or posthead, are modifiers of the head. All idiosyncrasies are consigned to the lexicon, e.g., *adrift* is marked [− Prehead]. The crucial point here, I think, is that pairs like those in (30) are semantically related not because one is derived from the other, the TG account, but because each of the italicized sequences is a characterizer residing on the same level in the same position within the N‴ hierarchy, the RG account.

6.3 GRAMMATICAL REALIZATION AND EXPLANATORY ADEQUACY

In this section I shall address the questions, Can RG be incorporated into a realistic model of linguistic performance, and, if so, what advantages does it have over TG in this regard?

6.31 LANGUAGE ACQUISITION

I assume that a child has an innate predisposition to acquire language and that he is born with unconscious knowledge of core grammar, which I take simply to be a reflection of the human language apparatus. The evidence for this appears to be overwhelming, but I choose only one example here to make the point, and that example is a phonological one.

It is a well known fact that there are three ways of forming the past tense of regular English verbs: one suffixes either [t] or [d] or [əd] to the verbal base. The question is, Does the child have to learn in particular which ending goes with every verb separately, or is there some general principle which predicts which ending goes with which verbs? The answer is overwhelmingly that there is a principle. That principle is embodied in the following phonological rules:

(37) a. PAST → [əd] / [t], [d] ——
      b. PAST → [t] / [−voiced] ——
      c. PAST → [d] / [+voiced] ——

It has been known for a long time that children have knowledge of (37), because they will, like adults, choose the correct ending even for nonsense verbs (Berko Gleason, 1958). The question is, Do children have to learn (37); and the answer is, Not entirely. What a child must learn is that English chooses to signal past tense by the suffixation of an *unreleased* alveolar stop to the verbal base. Which particular consonant goes with which verb is not a matter of choice, either on the part of the child or English. Given the nature of the human vocal apparatus, if the past is signalled by an *unreleased* alveolar stop, the only choice of the three endings for a verb like [prad] is [əd]; one cannot articulate either *[pradt] or *[pradd]. Similarly, while forms like [drept] and [sevd] are natural, forms like *[drepd] and *[sevt] are not. The reason: it is very difficult to end a word with two stops that differ in voicing. In short, for a good many verb forms, the past tense is completely predictable given constraints on human articulation. It is for this reason that children often pronounce the past tense of *hurt* as *hurted*; they don't yet know that it is an irregular verb.

The preceding paragraphs offer a real explanation for the rapidity with which children acquire knowledge of the past tense in English. The explanation is given in terms of core grammar, which is simply a reflection of the human language apparatus. Unfortunately such explanatorily adequate descriptions of linguistic competence are very hard to uncover, particularly in the area of syntax where matters are not so obvious.

In light of these remarks, consider again the matter of word classes in the speech of English–speaking children. We have such data as the following (from Brown and Bellugi, 1964; see also McNeill, 1966):

(38) a. My stool.
      b. That knee.
      c. More coffee.
      d. Two shoes.
      e. Poor man.
      f. Two tinker toy.

Both Brown and Bellugi (1964) and McNeill (1966) describe a process whereby, beginning with utterances like (38), children gradually increase their mean length and start to differentiate the members of the modifier (pivot) class, that is, the first word in each of the examples of (38). Initially the modifier class consists of possessives, demonstratives, quantifiers, numerals, and adjectives. Gradually however the children studied began to make distinctions among the members of this all inclusive modifier class, so that Brown and Bellugi (1964, 155) note "in three-word utterances that were made up from the total pool of words and that had a noun in final position, the privileges of *a* and *the* were different from the privileges of all other modifiers. The articles occurred in initial position followed by a member of the class M other than an article."

As I noted in Section 6.1, most psycholinguists have now rejected the analysis of child language in terms of modifier or pivot class because, for one thing, such a class does not correspond to any class of words in adult speech. This is correct if the model of adult speech is a TG; it is not correct if that model is an RG. All of the members of the modifier (pivot) class are adjuncts. In other words, given an RG framework, it is possible to say that one global class, adjuncts, is gradually differentiated by the children over time.

Notice also that RG allows directly for the early formation of complex nominals like the one in (38f). Consider also the following examples, taken from the speech of my own son at 24 months (Binkert, 1974):

(39) a. Dump truck.
      b. Milk truck.
      c. Cement truck.
      d. Tow truck.
      e. Motor cycle.
      f. Motor scooter.
      g. Big dump truck.
      h. Two garbage mans.

And, about two months later, the following:

(40)   a. Kevin take big bubble bath.
        b. Kevin ride that big wheel.
        c. Where's the washcloth?
        d. See that steam shovel down there?
        e. See that sail truck. (A picture that looks like a truck with a sail)

Clearly the data in (40) indicate a creative use of complex nominals. One must assume that by this time in the child's speech ambiguous sequences like *big wheel*, which is either a complex nominal or an adjective + noun construction, were also understood. Given the level hierarchies of RG, data like (40) can also be described in a very straightforward way (see Chapter 2).

Essentially RG provides for a description of English syntax that can capture the generalizations that children appear to be operating with over time. This is not true of TG. What this may mean is that the categorical breakdown in RG reflects more accurately the breakdown in core grammar: beginning with two global categories, verb and adjunct, in both children and adults, these categories are subdivided into smaller ones by increasingly specific syntactic features. The first feature extracted by children is apparently $[+X''' \text{ Level}]$, which identifies the articles. While it is beyond the scope of this monograph to pursue these ideas in detail, nonetheless the above account seems quite promising and natural.

6.32 SENTENCE COMPREHENSION IN ADULTS

In this section, I shall investigate three areas of English syntax from the point of view of a theory of linguistic performance. In each case, I shall entertain a question like, Which of the two GGs discussed, TG or RG, is more in accord with the facts regarding performance?

Consider first the matter of self-embedded constructions, mentioned in Chapter 2, Section 2.6. Chomsky (1965, 12–14) discusses five types of constructions from the point of view of acceptability. Of the five, Chomsky notes that "self-embedding contributes ... radically to unacceptability" (p. 13). In addition to the examples presented in Section 2.6, consider these:

(41)   a. John passed up the opportunity to look up the information.
        b. John passed the opportunity to look the information up up.

(42)   a. John passed by the opportunity to look over the information.
        b. John passed the opportunity to look the information over by.

Both of the (b) sentences above sound equally incomprehensible to me; so it is not the repetition of the same word (*up*) in (41b) that makes it so difficult to understand. Rather it is the fact that both (41b) and (42b) contain instances of self-embedding.

Now notice that in most cases involving self-embedding English provides alternative sentences that are not unacceptable, e.g., (41a) and (42a) above. Other examples are as follows:

(43) a. It is not surprising that it worried Mrs. Jones that her children were constantly ill.
b. That that her children were constantly ill worried Mrs. Jones is not surprising.

(44) a. The cat that was chased by the dog that was bitten by the rat fled into the woods.
b. The cat that the dog that the rat bit chased fled into the woods.

Now consider (45).

(45)   John had as many more opportunities to do that than Bill as Bob.

Interestingly, there does not appear to be any direct way to unravel (45) so that an acceptable sentence results. To render (45) acceptable, we must resort to circumlocution:

(46)   John had more opportunities to do that than Bill, in fact, he had as many more as Bob.

None of the analyses of the comparative that have appeared in the literature of TG (Selkirk, 1970; Bresnan, 1973; Bowers, 1975; Jackendoff, 1977) directly generates sentences like (45); to produce (45), a transformation is necessary— usually one which extraposes the comparative clause.

In a transformational analysis of the sentences (41) through (45), we have an unnatural and perplexing set of circumstances, particularly from the viewpoint of a theory of linguistic performance. First, we have sentences in which a rule, particle movement, has applied to produce an unacceptable self-embedded construction. This is what occurs in the derivation of (41b) and (42b) from (41a) and (42a), respectively. Second, we have cases in which the application of a transformational rule, extraposition in (43) and passive in (44), has the effect of unravelling an unacceptable self-embedded construction to produce acceptable right-branching constructions (Chomsky, 1965). Both of these situations seem perfectly feasible. However the derivation of (45) is another matter altogether.

As noted above, (45) is not a base structure in any TG analysis of the comparative; it can only be arrived at by transformation. Further, there is no other way, except through periphrasis, to say (45). The question is, Why would a language contain only one means of derivation for a construction, when that means always produces unacceptable self-embedding? From the standpoint of the theory of performance, this hardly seems natural or expected. Thus, in this case, the grammar of competence (here the TG analysis of comparatives) will benefit from a consideration of performance issues. If this perception is correct, then all TG analyses of the comparative, which have the effect of producing constructions like (45) through transformation, must be rejected.

Now notice that the same criticism cannot be directed against the RG analysis of comparatives. Sentences like (45) are base generated as self-embedded sentences. It is odd that the grammar of English does not have a direct way out of such sentences, but that appears to be exactly what the situation is.

If transformations were involved in the derivation of comparatives, one would surely think that historical pressures would at least have evolved some transformation that promotes comprehensibility in these cases. Notice, incidentally, that (45) *is* a possible acceptable structure in English; we have sentences paralleling (45) like (47).

(47)   John has had so many more opportunities to do that than Bill that it is downright unfair.

The acceptability of (47) derives from the fact that the higher clause, *so many . . . that it is downright unfair*, is consecutive, not comparative. In other words, (47) is not entirely self-embedding. Thus the RG analysis of comparatives presented in Chapter 2 produces exactly the correct structures both from the standpoint of the theory of competence and the standpoint of the theory of performance.

Consider now the so-called garden path sentences (Marcus, 1980) like (48).

(48)   The horse raced past the barn fell.

Why are most English speakers dumbfounded when they read (48)? I believe that the answer lies in a perceptual strategy discussed in Chomsky and Lasnik (1977) and repeated here as (49).

(49)   In analyzing a construction C, given a structure that can stand as an independent clause, take it to be a main clause of C.

When speakers read (48), they naturally assume that *the horse* is the main subject and *raced* is the main verb, in accordance with (49).

But it is exceedingly difficult to co-ordinate (49) with the TG analysis of (48), which proceeds through steps like the following:

(50)   a. the horse which someone raced past the barn fell
       b. the horse which was raced past the barn by someone fell
       c. the horse which was raced past the barn fell
       d. the horse raced past the barn fell

Whether or not steps (a) → (b), the passive, and (b) → (c), agent deletion, are involved in the derivation of (48) is immaterial here; I am concerned about step

(c) → (d), which involves the rule, relative clause reduction (RCR), mentioned previously.

Clearly, a mature speaker of English has knowledge of the relationship between pairs of sentences like the following:

(51) a. The man who was awarded the prize jumped for joy.
       b. The man awarded the prize jumped for joy.

(52) a. A man who is that intelligent will succeed.
       b. A man that intelligent will succeed.

TG has represented that knowledge in the form of the rule RCR. Let us now ask the question, in regard to (48), Does it seem reasonable to assume that RCR is an accurate representation of the speaker's knowledge? From the point of view of competence, we have already shown that RCR is fraught with difficulties. Putting this aside, it should be the case that knowledge of RCR would aid in the comprehension of (48), but it doesn't. Even after staring at a sentence like (48) for a very long time, most speakers remain nonplussed. Further, in my own experience, even when speakers are told what (48) means, they often deny that it's possible to say the sentence. Thus it seems that the pressures of the perceptual strategy (49) are so great that knowledge of RCR, in this case, is completely suppressed. Alternatively, we may follow the suggestion (J. D. Fodor, 1978, 427) "that the human sentence comprehension routines may be able to interpret at least some transformed sentences directly, without first reconstructing their underlying phrase markers." In other words, RCR is not necessarily used in the perception of every reduced relative clause.

Again, we have an unnatural and perplexing set of circumstances. If knowledge of a relationship expressed in the form of a transformational rule can be so easily suppressed or is not utilized to begin with in the perception of sentence meaning, then what is the function of a transformational rule in performance? It appears that there is none. Thus, since TG fails as an adequate representation of competence and fails to play a discernible role in performance, we should reject transformations as a means of expressing linguistic relationships.

Now notice that RG does not encounter the same difficulties. Sentences like those in (48), (51), and (52) are all base generated. Accordingly, the stunning effect of (48) is due to (49), and perhaps other similar strategies. Despite this, RG can simply express the relationship between pairs of sentences like those in (51) and (52). The answer lies not in deriving one sentence from the other; it lies in the similarity of the structural relationships that sequences like *who was awarded the prize* and *awarded the prize* have in relation to the head: both are X″ level posthead characterizers.

Consider now the matter of empty elements, in particular, trace, which is a conspicuous feature of many recent accounts of TG (Chomsky, 1977, 1980a,

1980b, 1981; Chomsky and Lasnik, 1977) and recall that RG contains no trace. The introduction of an element like trace to a GG is an unnecessary complication if it can be shown, as I think it has, that a GG can obtain at least the same level of descriptive adequacy without it. Beyond the element itself, one must consider all the mechanisms necessary for its correct interpretation. For example, trace theory requires some means of indexing traces with each other when they have the same noun as antecedent. Thus Chomsky (1981, 184) proposes structures like (53a) for (53b).

(53)   a.   who [t seemed [t′ to have been killed t″]
                  S   S

        b.   Who seemed to have been killed?

In a structure like (53a), we see that the traces are indexed to each other; all are represented by "t" without subscript, the higher the prime the closer to its source the trace is, in this case, the direct object slot of *kill*. Beyond this, various devices must be invented to turn the underlying representations that form part of trace theory into their surface realizations. For example, the noun phrase (54a), in Chomsky and Lasnik (1977, 462) is derived from (54b).

(54)   a.   a man to fix the sink
        b.   a man [for]   [who to fix the sink]
               COMP S

Movement of the WH-word into COMP in (54b) produces a structure like (55).

(55)   a man [who$_i$ for] [t$_i$ to fix the sink]
         COMP   S

The abstractness of the underlying representation (54b) is due to the fact that Chomsky and Lasnik derive all infinitives from underlying clauses, a derivation that we have argued is unnecessary. In RG the noun phrase (54a) has the representation (56).

(56)

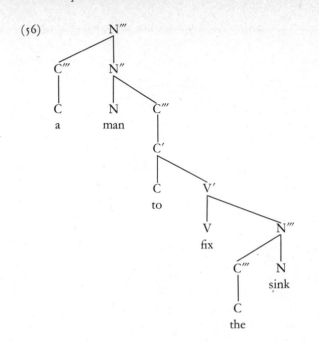

In (56) the infinitive phrase *to fix the sink* is an adjectival phrase modifying *man*, i.e., *man* is the subject, hence its suspension from the N″ level. Therefore in RG, *to fix the sink* in (54a) has a structure identical to *fixing the sink* in *the man fixing the sink*. There is of course a difference in meaning between the infinitive phrase and the participial phrase, and that in RG is attributed to the difference between *to* and *-ing*. The interpretation of infinitival relatives is placed in RG on a par with the interpretation of other N″ level prehead and posthead characterizers as follows:

(57) a. books available = books are available
     b. a man on the run = a man is on the run
     c. a man to fix the sink = a man is to fix the sink
     d. a man fixing the sink = a man is fixing the sink

Comparing the TG and RG analyses of infinitival relatives as we have, it is easy to see that the TG analysis is considerably more involved. In terms of the theory of performance, it is incumbent on proponents of the TG analysis to show that in some way this additional complexity is warranted. In terms of competence, I believe that we have shown that the overall RG approach achieves a higher level of descriptive adequacy than the TG model. Thus structures like (54b) have no claim, unless in fact it can be shown that their abstractness is justified in terms of performance. For example, can it be shown that either of the following pairs of sentences is more difficult to interpret in any way than the other:

(58) a. The man fixing the sink is John's brother.
      b. The man to fix the sink is John's brother.

(59) a. John's brother is the man in the kitchen.
      b. John's brother is the man to fix the sink.

In general, efforts to demonstrate the psychological reality of derivations via transformations have not met with any success. Fodor et al. (1974) say of these efforts that "... experiments which undertake to demonstrate the psychological reality of the structural descriptions characteristically have better luck than those which undertake to demonstrate the psychological reality of the operations involved in grammatical derivations" (p. 241). Bresnan (1978) is more emphatically negative: "the derivational theory of complexity—the theory that the number of transformations operating in the grammatical derivation of a sentence provides a measure of the psychological complexity in comprehending or producing the sentence—cannot be sustained" (p. 2). In short, the prevailing critical opinion is that, in terms of a theory of linguistic performance, transformations have little justification.

As I noted at the beginning of this chapter, I believe that such findings are relevant to the study of competence; the more ways that a grammar is tested, RG included, the more adequate will the theory ultimately become as a description of the human faculty for language.

6.4 LINGUISTIC UNIVERSALS AND CORE GRAMMAR

In this section I shall consider some aspects of RG that can contribute to our understanding of core grammar, which I assume is nothing more than a reflection of the capacities and limitations of the human language apparatus. I have chosen as my point of comparison with English the case system of Classical Latin. I will show that the structures already motivated can produce descriptions which attain a high degree of descriptive adequacy and which are very suggestive in terms of specifying the nature of core grammar.

There is a large number of Latin verbs which govern objects marked for cases other than the accusative, the usual marker for direct objects. Such verbs are *studere* (desire) and *nocere* (harm), both of which take the dative case instead of the accusative. We have examples like the following:

(60) a. Homo gloriae (DAT) studet. (The man desires glory.)
      b. Homo feminae (DAT) nocet. (The man harms the woman.)

Superficially, this use of the dative does not seem to be attributable to the meaning of the verb, i.e., not all verbs in Latin meaning "desire" or "harm" take the dative. For example, *cupere* and *laedere*, whose basic meanings are "desire" and "harm," respectively, are construed with the accusative. Compare the following with those above:

(61) a. Homo gloriam (ACC) cupit. (The man desires glory.)
     b. Homo feminam (ACC) laedit. (The man harms the woman.)

Similar pairs of words, some taking the dative, others taking the accusative, are easy to find (see Binkert, 1970). In addition, there are some verbs which can take either the dative or the accusative without any obvious change in meaning. For example, both of the following mean "The man flatters the woman":

(62) a. Homo feminae (DAT) adulatur.
     b. Homo feminam (ACC) adulatur.

Sometimes the alternation in construction is between a simple noun phrase in the dative and a prepositional phrase. For example, *appropinquare* (approach) is construed with either the dative or a prepositional phrase introduced by *ad* (to):

(63) a. Homo oppido (DAT) appropinquat. (The man approaches the town.)
     b. Homo ad oppidum appropinquat. (The man approaches the town.)

How are the above facts to be captured in a GG?

It would clearly be myopic to assume that the grammar of Latin contains a special transformation which adds a feature, say, [+DATIVE], to the complements of the verbs above. Nor is it possible to say that particular prepositional phrases, say, those introduced by *ad*, are transformed into the dative, since not all phrases introduced by *ad* can be.

One of the major differences between RG and TG is that, in RG, inflections of various kinds can serve as the head of their own construction. To my knowledge, this feature has never been part of TG (but, see Fillmore, 1968, 1969). Making use of this feature of RG, suppose now that we say sentences like (60a) and (60b) have a verb-complement structure like (64).

(64)

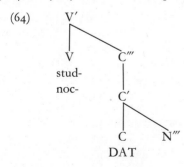

Similarly, verbs taking alternative constructions, like *appropinquare* (cf. (63)), have the structure (65).[2]

(65)

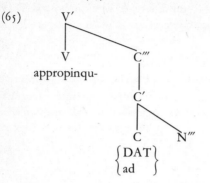

In short, special case uses like the above are characterizers with a structure paralleling that for prepositional phrases. The evidence in Latin suggests that this analysis is correct. Thus verbs taking special cases parallel prepositional phrases in one very important respect: their passives must be impersonal. The passive of (66a) is (66b).

(66) a. Homo ad oppidum it. (The man goes to the town.)
      b. Ab homine ad oppidum itur. (Literally: "There is a going to the town by the man.")

Similarly, the passive of (58) is (67).

(67) Ab homine feminae (DAT) studetur. (Literally: "There is a desire for the woman by the man.")

We find data similar to the above in other ancient Indo-European languages like Greek and in some modern ones as well. For example, in German, the verb *schreiben* can be construed either with the dative or a prepositional phrase introduced by *an*:

(68) a. Ich schreibe ihm (DAT). (I write to him.)
      b. Ich schreibe an ihn. (I write to him.)

The passive, as expected, is impersonal:

(69) a. Ihm (DAT) wird von mir geschrieben.
      b. An ihn wird von mir geschrieben.[3]

One of the major advantages of assuming structures like (64) and (65) is that the grammar of Latin, German, etc., does not change radically from dialect to dialect or from one period in time to another or for poetic usages. This is a significant gain in descriptive adequacy: one does not have to claim that underlying representations differ dramatically in language variation and change. Furthermore, any meaning differences which exist in these alternative constructions can be stated in terms of the difference between, say, DATIVE and a particular preposition.

If the above analysis can be substantiated across a wide variety of languages, it may be possible to formulate the following linguistic universal:

(70) The relationship that a particular noun phrase has to the head (verb, noun, etc.), when not syntactic, is expressed by a characterizer in the form either of an independent word (preposition or postposition) or a case.[4]

Thus the subject and direct object, as we have seen, are signalled structurally in English by the L-command and R-command relations. In Latin, and other languages, the signalling system for such relations often involves either a preposition or a special case. Thus cross-linguistic data, such as the following, can be generalized:

(71) a. The man sprinkled the flowers with the water.
b. The man sprinkled the water on the flowers.

(72) a. Homo flores (ACC) aqua (ABL) aspergit.
the man—the flowers—with the water—sprinkled
b. Homo floribus (DAT) aquam (ACC) aspergit.
the man—on the flowers—the water—sprinkled

The advantage of RG, over TG, in accounting for data like the above, lies in its solution of the Categorial Problem. Here again, as in the case of language acquisition mentioned above, this solution has far-reaching implications. In particular, it is possible to state explicitly what has always seemed rather obvious: prepositions, postpositions, and case endings serve similar functions in different languages. In RG, as we see, for quite independent reasons, all these categories are characterizers which can serve as the head of their own constructions.

6.5 EXTENSIONS

It seems appropriate to conclude this chapter with a discussion of those constructions which played a great part in launching X′ syntax (Chomsky, 1970; Jackendoff, 1977), in particular, nominalizations of various types. I am concerned with data like the following:

(73) Derived nominals, -*ion* type:
a. Bill's nomination of John

   b. the nomination of John
   c. *ϕ nomination of John

(74) Derived nominals, *-ing* type:
   a. Bill's nominating of John
   b. the nominating of John
   c. *ϕ nominating of John

(75) Gerundial nominals:
   a. Bill's nominating John
   b. *the nominating John
   c. ϕ nominating John

Of these three nominals, the first two are clearly noun-like constructions and
the third is clearly a verb-like construction: witness the varying grammaticality
of the (c)-examples. Further, X″ level modifiers of the derived nominals are
adjectives, whereas X″ modifiers of gerundial nominals are adverbs:

(76) a. Bill's sudden nomination of John
   b. *Bill's suddenly nomination of John

(77) a. Bill's sudden nominating of John
   b. *Bill's suddenly nominating of John

(78) a. *Bill's sudden nominating John
   b. Bill's suddenly nominating John

Also, (73b) and (74b) are ambiguous: the *of John* can be interpreted as either a
subjective or objective genitive. Examples like (75b), on the other hand, are not
only unambiguous, they are ungrammatical, except in isolated instances like *this
telling tales of yours has got to stop* (see Schachter, 1976).

   Despite the verb-like character of the gerundial nominal, it can fill all of the
positions noun phrases fill:

(79) a. Bill's nominating John came as a surprise.
   b. I heard about Bill's nominating John.
   c. Bill's nominating John was received with derision.
   d. Bill's nominating John was tough to take.

Herein lies the problem: If the gerundial nominal is essentially verb-like, how
can it fill positions normally associated with noun phrases? It is this question
that I shall attempt to answer. First, I shall discuss some characteristics of the
gerundial nominal. Second, I shall present structures for all three constructions.
Third, I shall show how these structures capture the known facts.

   To begin with, the possessive subject of a gerundial nominal is under severe
restrictions, a fact which seems not to have been noticed before. In particular,
the possessive subject cannot have any of the usual postnominal modifiers.

Consider the following:[5]

(80)   No Restrictive Relatives off N″:
   a. The man that Bill is supporting's *nomination of John* came as a surprise.
   b. The man that Bill is supporting's *nominating of John* came as a surprise.
   c. *The man that Bill is supporting's *nominating John* came as a surprise.

(81)   No Prepositional Phrases off N″:
   a. The man with the beard's *nomination of John* was a typically hippie move.
   b. The man with the beard's *nominating of John* was a typically hippie move.
   c. *The man with the beard's *nominating John* was a typically hippie move.

(82)   No Participles off N″:
   a. The man standing next to the podium's *nomination of John* shocked everyone.
   b. The man standing next to the podium's *nominating of John* shocked everyone.
   c. *The man standing next to the podium's *nominating John* shocked everyone.

Furthermore, the possessive subject cannot have the usual quantifiers in prenominal position:[6]

(83)   a. Each of the senators' *nomination of a relative* was labelled nepotistic.
   b. Each of the senators' *nominating of a relative* was labelled nepotistic.
   c. *Each of the senators' *nominating a relative* was labelled nepotistic.

The following are acceptable:

(84)   Proper noun:
   a. Bill's *nomination of John* came as a shock.
   b. Bill's *nominating of John* came as a shock.
   c. Bill's *nominating John* came as a shock.

(85)   Noun preceded by an adjective:
   a. The antediluvian senator's *nomination of his mistress* surprised no one.
   b. The antediluvian senator's *nominating of his mistress* surprised no one.
   c. The antediluvian senator's *nominating his mistress* surprised no one.

(86) Pronoun:
  a. His *nomination of Mary* came as a surprise.
  b. His *nominating of Mary* came as a surprise.
  c. His *nominating Mary* came as a surprise.

Notice that all of the above data can be accommodated within the analyses we
have suggested. There is one other construction in the language which shares
the same restrictions with the possessive subject of gerundial nominals, and that
construction is the double possessive discussed in Chapter 2. The conclusion
seems ineluctable: in the present case, as in that one, the POSS ending is part of
the N‴ phrase itself. In other words, we propose structures like (87) for the
possessive subject, not (88), which is the expected one.

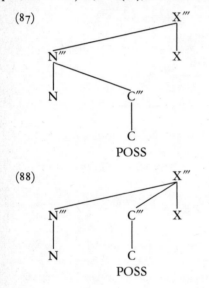

Given (87), all of the ungrammatical examples above are ruled out for the same
reasons discussed in connection with the double possessive construction.
  The next question is, What does X stand for in (87)?
  To answer this, consider the following:

(89) a. *Who do they favor John's nomination of [_____]?
      b. *Who do they favor John's nominating of [_____]?
      c. Who do they favor John's nominating [_____]?

These examples are very significant. Recall that in the last chapter we
proposed a PSF to rule out noun phrases containing a possessive that are
followed by a complementary genitive (cf. example (36)). Thus the genitive in
(89a) and (89b) is part of the X‴ whose head is *nomination/nominating*. In short,

consistent with all the other data above, the *-ing* type nominal must be considered just that, a nominal. But the gerundial nominal does not appear to be a nominal at all; that is, under the usual analysis of the possessive subject. However, given (87), we may say that the three nominals have the following structures:

(90)   Derived Nominal, *-ion* type:

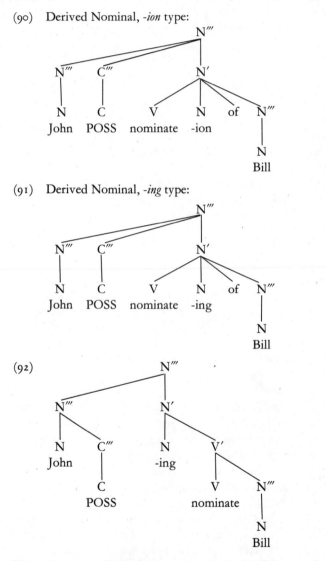

(91)   Derived Nominal, *-ing* type:

(92)

From the point of RG, the structure (92) is the only one of the above three requiring comment, because it is exceptional. It is a noun phrase which has no

X''' level characterizer in first prehead position, the normal position for POSS and articles. However, in this case, the exception seems justifiable for two reasons. First, for reasons just discussed, there is already a POSS in the X''' level prehead noun phrase. Admission of an article or POSS in the normal position would always lead to ungrammaticality. Second, we have already seen that gerundial nominals are modified by adverbs, not adjectives (cf. (78)); it seems only natural that they not be allowed to contain an X''' level prehead characterizer either.

To account for these facts, I propose that the grammar contain the following PSF:

(93)   *[([N — POSS]) C''' — ing — V']
        N''' N'''

Note the generality of (93). Because of the RG framework, in *one* filter, we account for the fact that neither articles, nor POSS, nor adjectives can occur in gerundial nominals. All are characterizers, i.e., they would fill C''' in (93). This sort of generality is beyond the descriptive power of all versions of TG that I have seen. Further, notice that if filter (93) is violated, we can generate those rare and marginal gerundial nominals mentioned by Schachter (1976) like (94).

(94)   This telling tales of yours has got to stop.

Observe the double possessive construction in (94), which, of course, is also generable in our theory.

We now have an explanation for the grammaticality of (89c). Filter (12) does not apply because there is no permanent resident in structures like (92). All relevant data have therefore been accounted for. Of particular significance is the fact that the peculiarities of the gerundial nominal do not have to be described by adding category switching rules to the grammar, in the manner of Jackendoff (1977). This in itself is a very important step in tightening the constraints in a grammar of natural language. The inclusion of category switching rules vastly increases the class of grammars that might be considered grammars of natural language. We have avoided that dreaded step.

A decisive argument supporting the preceding analysis is that all *ing*-forms in English are now assigned parallel and related descriptions both in terms of syntactic features and syntactic structures. All *ing*-forms are adjuncts, that is, [+ADJUNCT]. Two of them, in addition, are characterizers, i.e., [+ADJUNCT, −NOMINAL]: those which are adjectives like *interesting* in *a very interesting book* and those which are participles like *appearing* in *anyone appearing tired* or *being* in *They are being noisy*. The other two *ing*-forms are nouns, i.e., [+ADJUNCT, +NOMINAL]: derived nominals like *nominating* in (91) and gerundial nominals like *nominating* in (92). Frequently a given *ing*-form can be ambiguous in all four ways, e.g., *charming, imposing, searching, demanding*, etc.

The four structures are as follows:

(95)   a. Adjective, as in *a very charming lady*:

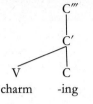

b. Participle, as in *the lady (who is) charming her escort*:

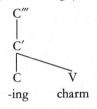

c. Derived nominal, as in *such charming of snakes*:

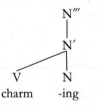

d. Gerundial nominal, as in *Charming candy from a baby is easy*:

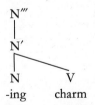

These structures are parallel to the adjectives and past participles discussed in Chapter 4, repeated here as (96).

(96)   a. Adjective, as in *a charmed life*:

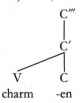

b. Participle, as in *the snake (which was) charmed by an expert*:

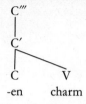

-en   charm

Each of the six structures above has been given independent and individual justification in the course of the preceding discussion, thereby making our proposals especially cogent. Further, the internal consistency of the final analyses is highly supportive of the RG framework. Lastly, it is important to observe that all relevant relationships among the six forms above and between each individual form and its putative transformational source have been accounted for without recourse to syntactic transformations.

NOTES TO CHAPTER 6

1. (5) is actually part of a much more comprehensive filter needed to incorporate the facts mentioned in (130) of Chapter 2: namely, the filter (i).

(i)   [(N''') − [−COMP] − N'' − [−COMP] − [−COMP]]
    N'''

Again, because of the form of (i), all [−COMP] categories are [+/___/N] and [+X''' LEVEL]. Also, the first [−COMP] must be [+PREHEAD], which means, according to Table 1 of Chapter 3, that it can contain only either an article or CASE, i.e., POSS. Further, the second and third occurrence of [−COMP] in (i) must be, respectively, [+Nominal], [−Nominal], since, as we have seen, that is always the order of adjuncts on the same level. In short, the second [−COMP] must be NUMBER, and the third [−COMP] must be CASE, again referring to Table 1 of Chapter 3. Thus, given (i), we rule out the possibility of generating partitives, appositive relatives, and comparatives on the rewrite of N''' to N'' (cf. (130a) in Chapter 2); and, we also stipulate that the last [−COMP] in (i) must be a CASE, thereby satisfying (130b) in Chapter 2.

What we need now, in addition to (i), is a filter allowing successive N''' levels to contain POSS, but not articles, in prehead position allowing structures like (118a) of Chapter 2. That filter is as follows:

(ii)   *[N''' − [−NOMINAL, −POSTHEAD] − N''' ...]
     N'''

or, stating the matter positively,

(iii)   [N''' − [−NOMINAL, +POSTHEAD] − N''' ...]
      N'''

Adopting this formalism, we can replace (128a) of Chapter 2 with (iii) and (128b) with (iv).

(iii) *[[... N''' − C'''] ... N'' ...]
        N''' N'''

(iv) *[[...CASE − N'' ...] ... N'' ...]
        N''' N'''

Further generalization is possible, but the issues involve more discussion of CASE, which is beyond the scope of this monograph (see Binkert, in preparation).

2. Further examples in Latin include the following:

(i)   (a) Imagines in corpora obrepunt.
      (b) Imagines corporibus (DAT) obrepunt.
           (Images into the body creep, i.e., Images creep into the body.)

(ii) (a) Homo feminam de foedere admonet.
      (b) Homo feminam foederis (GEN) admonet.
           (The man the woman about (of) the agreement warns, i.e., the man warns the woman about (of) the agreement.)

3. Further examples in German include the following:

(i)   (a) Ich erinnere mich an ihn. (I remember him.)
      (b) Ich erinnere mich seiner (GEN). (Archaic)
      (c) An ihn wird sich erinnert. (Impersonal passive)
      (d) Seiner (GEN) wird erinnert. (Impersonal passive; used only in very formal speech)

(ii) (a) Ich übergebe das Buch an ihn. (I hand over the book to him.)
      (b) Ich übergebe ihm (DAT) das Buch.
      (c) Das Buch wird an ihn übergeben. (Personal passive of the direct object *Buch*)
      (d) Das Buch wird ihm (DAT) übergeben. (Personal passive of the direct object *Buch*)

(iii) (a) Ich denke an ihn. (I think of him.)
      (b) Ich denke seiner (GEN). (Archaic)
      (c) An ihn wird gedacht. (Impersonal passive)
      (d) Seiner wird gedacht. (Impersonal passive; formal and archaic)

I am indebted to Renate Gerulaitis for help with the German examples.

4. In Binkert (1970), I discuss the difference between syntactic and semantic uses of cases. When the use of a case is occasioned by a particular structural configuration, i.e., a particular set of dominance and/or precedence relations, that use is syntactic. For example, in many Indo-European languages, the noun phrase immediately dominated by S is put into the nominative cases signaling that it is the subject of S. In contrast, when the use of a case is not structural, but the result of a meaning relationship that the noun phrase has to some other word, then the use is semantic. From this use, come expressions like *dative of agent*, *ablative* of *comparison*, etc.

Indo-European is not the only language family to have semantic uses of cases. In virtually every language having case, some uses are purely semantic, meaning that expressions having similar meanings are put in the same case. For example, in Indo-European languages having a genitive case, partitive expressions and expressions like *about God* in *I want to speak to you about God* are often put into the genitive case. Likewise, in his grammar of Innuit, an Eskimo language spoken on the western coast of Alaska, Barnum (1901, 14) observes a use of the modalis case:

(i)   chūyămŭk (Modalis) pēyŭqtoa. (I want some tobacco.)
(ii) Agīyutmŭk (Modalis) kăthlăuchŭwămkĭn. (I want to talk to you about God.)

Clearly, in both Innuit and Indo-European a phrase like *about God* is understood as being semantically related to a partitive expression, hence the same case is used for both types of noun phrases. A glance at a grammar of any language having case confirms that case often has purely semantic functions like this which take the place of prepositions and postpositions in other languages. In RG, all of these categories are manifestations of the category characterizer, and all are heads of their phrases. For further discussion, see Binkert (in preparation).

5. I have italicized the nominals in the following examples to call the reader's attention to the presence of the word *of*, which is crucial for distinguishing the *-ing* type derived nominals from the gerundial nominals. Further, while I have included examples with *-ing* type derived nominals, most of them seem rather marginal, probably because of the rarity of the construction.

6. Note that the word *senators* is plural in these examples. Also, I have not included here examples with the pseudopartitive construction, since most of them sound rather dreadful, e.g., *A bunch of the senators' nominations of relatives*. . . In such examples, there are just too many plurals. Also, in examples like *A bunch of the senators' mail was lost*, where *mail*, not *bunch*, is the head, trying to keep the heads straight becomes very difficult.

CHAPTER SEVEN

In this chapter, I shall investigate in more detail than previously the nature of PSFs and of syntactic features. My purpose will be to provide an illustrative fragment of an RG of English so that comparisons of RG and TG can be meaningful.

7.1 SYNTACTIC FILTERS AND SYNTACTIC FEATURES

In this section, I shall summarize and extend previous discussion of PSFs. We shall examine in turn a variety of formal statements necessary to capture the facts of English phrase structure. Ultimately we shall provide a specific set of PSFs to characterize the syntactic structures we have examined (cf. (31) below).

The major syntactic categories of RG, namely, verb (V), noun (N), and characterizer (C), have the feature specifications given in Table 2, which expands the matrix given in Table 1 of Chapter 3 taking intervening discussion into consideration. At this point, I view Table 2 as a working hypothesis of the syntactic distinctive features for English. It allows for reference to each of the important groupings of categories that we have found to be necessary: nouns and characterizers, [+ADJUNCT]; verbs and nouns, [+NEIGHBOR]; and, verbs and characterizers, [−NOMINAL]. As before, we shall continue to abbreviate [+ADJUNCT] as A.

Given the feature matrix in Table 2, previous discussion indicates that the maximally generalizable phrase structure schema for English is (1).[1]

(1) $[/[+\text{NOMINAL}]^i - [-\text{NOMINAL}]^i / X^m]$
     X^n
     where $m \leq n$ and $i = \{0, 1, 2, 3\}$.

(1) embraces both (2), the phrase structure schema of Chapter 1, and (3), the schema we have proposed for all sentence embedding in RG.[2]

(2) $[/[+\text{ADJUNCT}]''' - [+\text{ADJUNCT}]'''/X^m]$, where $m \leq n$
     X^n

	VERB	CHARACTERIZER										
		NOUN	NUM	TNS	CASE	DEG	ART	ADV	ADJ	PREP	CPL	CONJ
ADJUNCT	−	+	+	+	+	+	+	+	+	+	+	+
NOMINAL	−	+	+	−	−	−	−	−	−	−	−	−
NEIGHBOR	+	+	−	−	−	−	−	−	−	−	−	−
PREHEAD	+	+	−	+	+	+	+	+	+	−	+	−
POSTHEAD	+	+	+	−	+	+	−	+	+	+	+	+
/___N	+	+	+	−	+	−	+	−	+	+	+	+
/___V	+	+	−	+	−	+	−	+	+	+	+	+
/___C	+	+	+	−	−	+	−	+	−	+	+	+
X''' LEVEL	−	+	+	+	+	+	+	−	−	+	+	+
X'' LEVEL	−	+	−	−	−	−	−	+	+	+	+	+
X' LEVEL	+	+	−	−	−	−	−	−	+	+	−	−
COMP	+	+	−	+	+	−	−	−	+	+	+	+

[+NEIGHBOR] = can have a characterizer in X‴ level prehead position
[+PREHEAD] = can occur in prehead position
[+POSTHEAD] = can occur in posthead position
[+/___/N] = can occur in N‴ immediately dominated by some N level
[+/___/V] = can occur in V‴ immediately dominated by some V level
[+/___/C] = can occur in C‴ immediately dominated by some C level
[+X‴ LEVEL] = can occur in the X‴ LEVEL, i.e., as a daughter of X‴[3]
[+X″ LEVEL] = can occur in the X″ LEVEL, i.e., as a daughter of X‴
[+X′ LEVEL] = can occur on the X′ LEVEL, i.e., as a daughter of X″
[+COMP] = can govern an adjunct on the X′ level

TABLE 2

(3) $[/[+\text{ADJUNCT}]''' - [-\text{ADJUNCT}]^i/\text{X}]$, where i = {0, 1, 2, 3}.
$\quad$ X′

Notice that (2) and (3) ensure that all the adjuncts are dominated by an A‴
level, a provision not made in (1). As we have noted (Section 4.4), Verb is the
only category that need not be dominated by an X‴ level. Notice further that
(2) and (3), together with (1), directly relate structures like the following:

(4) a. [V — N‴ — C‴]
$\quad\quad$ V′

$\quad\quad$ make$\quad$ him$\quad\quad$ ill
$\quad\quad$ put$\quad\quad$ him$\quad\quad$ in the first row
$\quad\quad$ keep$\quad\quad$ him$\quad\quad$ away
$\quad\quad$ leave$\quad\quad$ him$\quad\quad$ alone

$\quad$ b. [V — N‴ — V]
$\quad\quad$ V′

$\quad\quad$ let$\quad\quad$ him$\quad\quad$ go
$\quad\quad$ make$\quad\quad$ him$\quad\quad$ stay

Observe that the head of (4b) is unambiguously the leftmost verb, i.e., *let/make*.
If *go/stay* were in head position, the order of prehead constituents would have to
be [−NOMINAL] − [+NOMINAL], an order which violates (1).

As this discussion indicates, the syntactic component of an RG contains rules
of the form (1)–(3) in place of context-free rewrite rules associated with the
syntactic component of a TG. Within the RG system, a familiar PS rule like (5)
becomes (6).

(5) S → NP + AUX + VP
(6) [N‴ − C‴ − V″]
$\quad$ V‴

The advantage of the RG system is that it allows for greater generality. Schema
like (1), (2) and (3) cannot be formulated within the theoretical framework of
currently available versions of TG.

Now notice that PS rule (5) claims that a sentence *must* consist of an NP
(the subject), an AUX, and a VP. In a grammar without transformations this
rule becomes impossible, since there are some sentences which lack subjects:
namely, imperatives. Conversely, in a grammar with transformations, there is
no way to generalize (5) so that it includes NP structures like those in (7).

(7) a. all — the — books
$\quad$ b. John — ’s — books
$\quad$ c. $\quad\quad$ a — book

This dilemma is solved in RG with (8).

(8) $[([+\text{NOMINAL}]''') - [-/\underline{\quad}/C]''' - [+\text{NEIGHBOR}]'' - ...]$
$[+\text{NEIGHBOR}]'''$

(8) stipulates that in the rewrite of X''' to X'' in [+NEIGHBOR] categories, i.e., in V and N, there *must* be a $[-/\underline{\quad}/C]$ category in first prehead position and there *may* be a [+NOMINAL] category in second prehead position. The form of (8) specifies that this $[-/\underline{\quad}/C]$ category must be $[+X''' \text{ LEVEL}]$— note that the outer brackets are labelled with an X'''—and must be either $[+/\underline{\quad}/N]$ or $[+/\underline{\quad}/V]$—note that the head is a [+NEIGHBOR] category. According to Table 2 therefore, if the [+NEIGHBOR] category in (8) is a noun, then in X''' level first prehead position there must be either an article or CASE, i.e., POSS. If the [+NEIGHBOR] category is a verb, then in X''' level first prehead position there must be a tense.[4] Notice that the only [+X''' LEVEL] categories that are also $[-/\underline{\quad}/C]$ are ART and CASE and TNS. Of these only ART and CASE are $[+/\underline{\quad}/N]$, and only TNS is $[+/\underline{\quad}/V]$, according to Table 2. Therefore (8) states that all noun phrases must have an article or POSS, as we have argued they must, that all sentences must have a tense/mood marker, and that these required categories must occur in first prehead position only, and on the rewrite of X''' to X''. Further, all [+NEIGHBOR] categories *may* have an N''' in second prehead position.[5]

Since the discussion in previous chapters has provided ample motivation for (1), (2), (3), and (8), let us assume that they are part of the syntactic component of an RG of English.[6] Essentially, as (2), (3), and (8) indicate, all PSFs in an RG of English can be viewed as ever more specific variations of (1). Thus (1) embraces both (2) and (3), and (2) in turn embraces (8) and many other PSFs. Further, PSFs in an RG may be stated positively or negatively, as we have seen (Chapter 6, Note 1). Determining whether the form should be positive or negative is viewed here as an entirely empirical matter. Compare (9) and (10).

(9) $[\qquad\qquad ([+\text{NOMINAL}]''') - [-\text{NEIGHBOR}]'' - ...]$
$[-\text{NEIGHBOR}]'''$

(10) $*[\qquad\qquad [-\text{NOMINAL}]''' - [-\text{NEIGHBOR}]'' - ...]$
$[-\text{NEIGHBOR}]'''$

(9) stipulates that, on the rewrite of [−NEIGHBOR] categories from X''' to X'', if there is anything in prehead position, it must be a noun. (10), on the other hand, rejects all structures where the rewrite of [−NEIGHBOR]''' to [−NEIGHBOR]'' contains a non-noun in prehead position. Both of these PSFs attempt to cover the same fact: characterizer phrases may not have a characterizer on their own X''' level in prehead position. But they are not equivalent; (9) is more general, since it allows for a [+NOMINAL] category in

prehead position, as is needed in such characterizer phrases as *far down the road*, *more clearly*, etc.

Two points need to be emphasized here. The first is that a TG does not have the option of choosing from alternatives like (9) and (10). This is a significant advantage of RG since RG does not have to generate a structure by one system of rules only to have that structure blocked by another system of rules, the route a TG must take. For example, within the PS rules of a TG there is no way to prevent the generation of structures that have AUX realized as the imperative marker and, at the same time, have the NP subject realized as something other than *you*. Thus a sentence like (11) must be blocked by some system other than the categorial rules.

(11)   [[John] [ϕ]   [go]]
       S NP   AUX   VP

Ruling out such structures in an RG is straightforward. Assuming that λ is the imperative marker and that λ only occurs in (12), then (12) stipulates that all sentences containing λ must, if they have a subject, have *you* as their subject.

(12)   [([*you*]) − [λ] − V″ − ...]
      V‴ N‴   C‴

Notice that (12) is merely a very highly specific instance of (1).

The second point to be emphasized about PSFs like (9) and (10) is that, in an RG, all PSFs are in force simultaneously, which is precisely why the grammar can contain statements like (9) and (10). In other words, every phrase must *both* contain structures of the type and arrangement specified in positive PSFs like (9) *and* not contain structures of the type and arrangement specified in negative PSFs like (10). A structure like (13) does not occur because it violates (2); one like (14) does not occur because it violates (10).

(13)   [[+NOMINAL] − [+NOMINAL]‴ − V‴]
      V″

(14)   [[−NOMINAL]‴ − C″]
      C‴

Observe that (13) violates (2) in two ways: it contains two nominal categories in succession on the same level; and it allows a V″ to dominate a V‴, i.e., allows *m* to be greater than *n*. On the other hand, (14) violates (10) as well as (9) in only one way: it allows a category to the left of C″ on C‴ to be [−NOMINAL].[7]

PSFs (8) and (9) exhaust the rules needed for the rewrite of X‴ to X″ in prehead position; however there is a slight problem with (9). Since [−NEIGHBOR] includes the category NUM, (9) will allow a noun in X‴ level prehead position of a NUM phrase, which is not possible. To prevent this and other impossible structures as well, we add (15) to the grammar.[8]

(15)   [NUM^i]
       NUM^i

(15) permits NUM phrases to contain only a head; any NUM phrase having adjuncts on any of its internal levels will therefore not occur.

Continuing to explore the syntactic component of an RG, consider now PSF (16), which we discussed above (Chapter 6, Note 1) and which we must now change for a number of reasons.

(16)   [(N''') − [−COMP]''' − N'' − [−COMP]''' − [−COMP]''']
       N'''

First, notice that the adjuncts referred to in (16) are specified as [−COMP], a specification made possible by Table 1 of Chapter 3 which labelled CASE as [−COMP]. Discussion in Chapter 6 however indicated that CASE should be labelled [+COMP] to allow for structures like those in examples (64) and (65) of that chapter. Thus in Table 2 above, CASE is so labelled.

Second, given (8), (16) redundantly specifies what can occur in prehead position on the rewrite of N''' to N''. We can solve these two problems by replacing (16) with (17).

(17)   [...N'' − [−COMP]''' − [−X'' LEVEL]''']
       N'''

(17) specifies that there *must* be two X''' categories in posthead position on the rewrite of N''' to N''. Because of the form of (17), these X''' categories must be [+X''' LEVEL], [+POSTHEAD], and [+/___/N]. Further, the first must be [+NOMINAL] and the second must be [−NOMINAL] in accordance with (1) which specifies the order of adjuncts on every level in both prehead and posthead position. The specification [−COMP] in (17) indicates that the first X''' category must be NUM; the specification [−X'' LEVEL] indicates that the second must be CASE.[9]

As (17) now stands, it unfortunately is too strong. As we have noted in previous chapters, some heads of noun phrases have inherent number, e.g., pronouns, mass nouns, proper nouns, and so on. The choice of number in such noun phrases is therefore not free, and, as we have suggested, there is no NUM in posthead position on N'''. In short, while all noun phrases have a CASE, not all noun phrases have a NUM category, their number being inherent. This necessitates dealing with the two X''' categories of (17) separately. Taking NUM first, we replace (17) with (18).

(18)   [...   N''   − [−COMP]''' ...]
       N'''   [±PLURAL]

(18) says that an N''' containing a head with a free choice of number, which we indicate with "±Plural," must have a NUM category in posthead position on

its X''' level. That NUM category, indicated above with "[−COMP]," will itself contain a free choice of number, either [+PLURAL] or [−PLURAL]. Thus the PSFs allow for structures like the following:

(19)

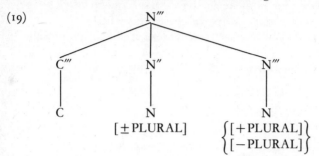

However structures like (20) will not occur since (18) specifically states that NUM can occur only when the head is marked [±PLURAL].

(20)

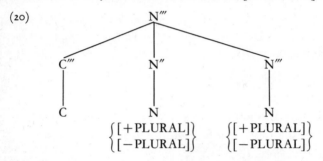

The above analysis means that words whose number does not change— that is, words inherently marked [+PLURAL] OR [−PLURAL]—do not undergo the phonological rules for plural formation. However words marked [±PLURAL] occurring in N''' containing a NUM which is [+PLURAL] do. For the purposes of this monograph we can assume therefore a rule like (21).

(21) $\emptyset \rightarrow z$ / [+voiced] _____ ... [+PLURAL]

Turning to CASE, we add (22) to the grammar.

(22)   [... N'' − ([+NOMINAL]''') − [−X'' LEVEL]''']
       N'''

(22) stipulates that, although NUM, which is indicated by "[+NOMINAL],"
is optional in N''' except as specified by (18), CASE, which is indicated by "[−X'' LEVEL]," is obligatory. (22) ensures that every N''' will have a CASE on its own X''' level in posthead position.

The specification of CASE is a highly complex matter which I deal with elsewhere (Binkert, in preparation). Here I shall only note that syntactic uses of cases can be specified with PSFs. For example, (23) specifies that the subject of a sentence must be in the nominative case, (24) that the direct object of a verb is in the accusative.

(23) $\quad$ [$\quad$ [$\quad$ ...N″ (N‴) [+NOM]‴] − C‴ − V″ − ...]
$\quad\quad$ V‴ N‴

(24) $\quad$ [...V − [$\quad$ ...N″ (N‴) [+ACC]‴] ...]
$\quad\quad$ V′ $\quad\quad$ N‴

Assuming that individual cases are a free choice within the category CASE, then all occurrences of cases other than [+NOM] and [+ACC] in frames like (23) and (24), respectively, do not occur. (23) specifies that the subject N‴ must contain [+NOM] on its own X‴ level in posthead position on the rewrite of N‴ to N″; (24) specifies that the direct object N‴ must contain [+ACC] there. Since no other cases are specified in these frames, no others occur.

For structures like (25) (cf. (64) in Chapter 6), we may add the PSF (26).

(25)

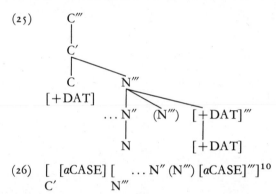

(26) $\quad$ [$\quad$ [aCASE] [$\quad$ ...N″ (N‴) [aCASE]‴]¹⁰
$\quad\quad$ C′ $\quad\quad\quad$ N‴

(26) stipulates that the direct object of some [+CASE] that is in head position functioning like a preposition must be in the same [+CASE]. Non-identical combinations will, accordingly, not occur. Thus the category [+DAT] will govern objects in the dative, the category [+GEN] will govern objects in the genitive, and so on. To ensure that only dative objects go with verbs that take the dative, genitive objects with verbs that take the genitive, etc., we may add (27).

(27) $\quad$ [$\quad$ [[aCASE]] [... [aCASE] ...]]
$\quad\quad$ V′ V $\quad\quad\quad$ C‴

(27) stipulates that a verb whose lexical entry contains the feature [aCASE] will occur only in frames followed by a characterizer with that same CASE in head position. Clearly, we can combine (26) and (27) to (28), a maximally general account of the facts in a language like Latin.

(28)   [[[*a*CASE]] [... [*a*CASE] [... N″ (N‴) [*a*CASE]]]]
    V′ V   C‴   N‴

The level of descriptive adequacy reached by (28) is far greater than that attainable within a TG framework; therefore further comment regarding (28) is in order. Notice that a comparable transformational account is possible only at great cost to the theory of TG, unless the theory is radically altered in the direction of RG. In RG a feature like [+DAT] is simply another syntactic feature along with [−ADJUNCT], [−NOMINAL], etc.; that is, [+DAT] is part of a more elaborate feature matrix than the one suggested in Table 2. Just as (1) is the maximally generalizable PSF in RG and PSFs can become as specific as (12), so syntactic features can be as general as [+ADJUNCT], i.e., all categories of words except Verb, and as specific as [+DAT]. In short, there is no appreciable cost in mentioning a feature like [+DAT] in a syntactic rule, any more than there is a cost to mentioning a feature like [+NOMINAL] in, say, (22). It is just that some syntactic features are more general than others. Recall that a sequence like (29) is merely an abbreviation for a more precise formulation like (30).

(29)   V‴   (30)   [−ADJUNCT, −NOMINAL, ... +DAT, ...]‴
     | |
     V″   [−ADJUNCT, −NOMINAL, ... +DAT, ...]″
     | |
     V′   [−ADJUNCT, −NOMINAL, ... +DAT, ...]′
     | |
     V   [−ADJUNCT, −NOMINAL, ... +DAT, ...]

In TG, on the other hand, the situation is quite different. Transformational rules operate on categories, not features, and any rule that transferred a syntactic feature from a verb to an object would greatly expand the power of the transformational component. Chomsky (1965, Chapter 4) discusses extending the theory of transformations to allow for rules that refer to features. Subsequent to *Aspects*, features figured prominently in transformational accounts of English. (See, especially, Baker, 1968, Chapter 10, which offers a discussion of number and case). Within the extended standard theory, however, a major thrust of research has been to constrain the form and functioning of transformations. (See, for example, Chomsky 1973, 1976, 1977, etc.) Accordingly, one might argue plausibly that transformations referring to syntactic features are permissable only at a cost to the overall system. The addition of X′ syntax complicates the matter, raising anew the whole question of the relation between syntactic categories and syntactic features in TG. In any case, there seems to be no expression of comparable generality to filter (28) in any version of TG that distinguishes syntactic categories from syntactic features.

Naturally, one goal of every GG must be to search for the most highly constrained theory. This is precisely the intent behind many of the conditions on transformations that have been proposed. In RG, this effort translates into a search for conditions on the forms of PSFs and on the nature of syntactic distinctive features. Clearly, one would hope, for example, to be able to propose a set of universal syntactic features ultimately. However, even at this point, one must be clear about the status of syntactic categories in RG: a syntactic category is a bundle of syntactic features, just as a phonological segment is a bundle of phonological features. Therefore, it is completely appropriate and not at all costly, in terms of RG, for filter (28) to refer to features like $[+\mathrm{DAT}]$. Hopefully, such case features will turn out to be universal.

Similar concerns about conditions on grammars apply to all parts of RG discussed in the preceding chapters. For example, it is certainly appropriate to explore whether the command relations investigated at various points in the preceding discussion extend to other languages. Clearly, languages with different word orders will require different definitions of subject and object; however an appropriate question is, Can subject and object be universally defined in terms of dominance and precedence relations? That they can be in English is clear from previous discussion. Whether they can universally is a question that is completely open. In an SOV language, perhaps subjects must be distinguished from objects by reference to specific X levels since both subject and object are to the left of the verb. Whatever the answer to this particular matter is, the goal of an RG, like that of a TG, is to search for the most general and most highly constrained description.

Summarizing, we may state that our grammar now contains the following PSFs, which I shall name for ease of reference and identification:

(31)   a. General PSF schema ($= $(1)):

$$[/[+\mathrm{NOMINAL}]^i - [-\mathrm{NOMINAL}]^i/ X^m]$$
$$X^n$$

where $m \leq n$ and $i = \{0, 1, 2, 3\}$

     b. Non-embedding PSF ($= $(2)):

$$[/[+\mathrm{ADJUNCT}]''' - [+\mathrm{ADJUNCT}]'''/ X^m]$$
$$X^n$$

where $m \leq n$

     c. S-embedding PSF ($= $(3)):

$$[/[+\mathrm{ADJUNCT}]''' - [-\mathrm{ADJUNCT}]^i/ X]$$
$$X'$$

where $i = \{0, 1, 2, 3\}$

     d. TNS/ART PSF ($= $(8)):

$$[(N''') - [-/\underline{\quad}/C]''' - [+\mathrm{NEIGHBOR}]'' - \ldots]$$
$$[+\mathrm{NEIGHBOR}]'''$$

e. C in C''' PSF (= (9)):
$$[(N''') - [-NEIGHBOR]'' - ...]$$
$$[-NEIGHBOR]'''$$

f. Imperative PSF (= (12)):
$$[\quad ([you]) - [\lambda] - V'' - ...]$$
$$V'''N''' \qquad C'''$$

g. NUM PSF (= (15)):
$$[NUM^i]$$
$$NUM^i$$

h. PLURAL PSF (= (18)):
$$[\quad ... \qquad N'' \qquad - [-COMP]''' ...]$$
$$N''' \quad [\pm PLURAL]$$

i. CASE PSF (= (22)):
$$[...N'' - (N''') - [-X'' \text{ LEVEL}]''']$$
$$N'''$$

j. NOM PSF (= (23)):
$$[\quad [...N'' (N''') [+NOM]''] - C''' - V'' - ...]$$
$$V'''N'''$$

k. ACC PSF (= (24)):
$$[...V - [...N'' (N''') [+ACC]''] ...]$$
$$V' \qquad N'''$$

To determine the relevance of these filters to particular structures, it will be necessary to establish some criteria for applicability. For example, we do not want to interpret the Imperative PSF as meaning that there must be an imperative marker in every TNS. Similarly, the ACC PSF should apply only when a sentence has an object; it should not be interpreted to mean that every sentence must have an object. If it meant the latter, it would of course rule out all intransitive verbs. I assume that such matters can be specified in terms of some universal set of criteria based on the nature of natural language. In other words, it seems ill-advised at this point to introduce some *ad hoc* method of stipulating the relevance of a filter, say, by italicizing the focal point of each filter, e.g., the imperative marker in (31f) and the object category in (31k). Such italics might be interpreted to mean that a structure containing an italicized category is grammatical only if it contains all other categories mentioned in the filter as specified. Thus, the Imperative PSF would be interpreted to mean that a structure containing the imperative marker in the TNS characterizer must have *you* in second prehead position if there is anything in second prehead position. Similarly, italicizing the N'''/N'' expansion in (31k) would mean that a noun in the specified position must be marked [+ACC]. While such facts are clearly correct, it seems to me that the relevance of a filter, as opposed to the contents of a filter, would follow from principles that are part of core grammar in the sense discussed above (cf. Chapter 6, Section 6.31). Thus it seems entirely reasonable to assume that all human languages offer speakers a variety of tense/mood options, however such options are realized, e.g., by verb conjugation, by a system of auxiliary verbs, by adverbs, etc. It follows therefore that interpreting the imperative PSF to mean that every TNS category in English must contain an imperative marker is rather absurd; in effect, it would mean that English only contains commands. Similarly, it seems entirely reasonable to assume that all human languages contain the equivalent of what in English are called transitive and intransitive verbs; that is, they have some expressions whose meaning at least implicitly requires an object and others whose meaning does not, however such expressions in fact are realized. We therefore do not understand (31k) to mean that every verb in English must be followed by a noun phrase object; rather, it means that a noun phrase in direct object position must be marked $[+ACC]$. The former interpretation is tantamount to ruling out all intransitive expressions in English, which is as bizarre as saying that English has no sentences which are not commands.

Viewing the matter somewhat differently, notice that a more detailed categorial breakdown than that specified in Table 2 would indicate several possible realizations of TNS, only one of which would be the imperative marker. Also, some verbs will be lexically specified as transitive, i.e., $(+/\underline{\hspace{1em}}N''')$, others as intransitive, i.e., $[-/\underline{\hspace{1em}}N''']$. Given these stipulations, the imperative PSF and the ACC PSF become contradictory when interpreted to mean that every TNS must be realized as the imperative marker and every verb must be followed by a direct object. For this reason, it seems correct at this point to adopt the position that the relevance of a particular filter to determining the grammaticality of a particular structure will be predictable from principles of core grammar, and accordingly such relevance should not be directly encoded into the filter itself.

The content of each filter, on the other hand, is not predictable on the basis of core grammar for the most part; it is precisely for this reason that there is such a thing as the particular grammar of English. For example, there appears to be no particular reason why the subject of imperatives in English must be second person: other languages, including earlier stages of English, conjugate the imperative for other persons; sentences like *Don't he touch that*, paralleling *Don't you touch that* syntactically, are certainly imaginable. Nevertheless, modern English contains a second person restriction for imperatives, a restriction which we have recorded in filter (31f).

In view of these remarks, we interpret a filter like (31f) as follows: given a λ in a V''' level prehead characterizer, then any N''' in second prehead position must contain *you*; that is, it must contain the second person personal pronoun. Similarly, we interpret (31k) as follows: given a noun phrase in direct object position, i.e., one that immediately R-commands a V, then that noun phrase must have the case marking [+ ACC] on its own X''' level in posthead position. The given part of both of these interpretations—what I have been calling the "relevance" of a filter—is predictable from principles of core grammar, we assume.

Turning now to other concerns, recall that PSFs such as those in (31) can be stated negatively as well as positively (cf. (9) and (10)); however, in some cases, doing so results in very cumbersome and unrevealing rules. For example, the imperative PSF (31f) stipulates that a sentence containing the imperative marker must have *you* in subject position if there is anything in subject position. This is straightforward. The reverse, stating that all N''' except those with *you* as subjects of imperatives are blocked, is not straightforward. Similarly, the Latin case PSF (28) is preferable to the many PSFs that would be required to block all of the possible ungrammatical combinations of case features, if the facts were stated as a negative PSF. (28) even seems preferable to (32).

(32) $*[\ [\ [\alpha CASE]] \ [\dots [\beta CASE] \ [\dots N'' \ (N''') \ [\gamma CASE]]]]$
       $\quad$ V'V $\qquad\qquad$ C''' $\qquad\qquad$ N'''

where $\alpha CASE \neq \beta CASE \neq \gamma CASE$

In view of this, let us adopt the following hypothesis as a step toward constraining the form of PSFs:

(33) All PSFs dealing with the heirarchical arrangement of syntactic feature matrices must be stated positively.

Consider now the second type of PSF mentioned in Chapter 6: namely, those like (34) (= example (12), Chapter 6):

(34) *A binding relation between X and Y in the structure ...X... [...Y...]..., where a is a residential domain.
       a

Before examining alternative ways of stating (34), it is necessary to define what is meant by a "binding relation." Let us say that X and Y form a binding relation under the following conditions.

(35) X and Y form a binding relation if X and Y have equivalent syntactic feature matrices, if X dominates a fully specified lexical item, if Y dominates e, the identity element,[11] and if X can occur in the same context as Y.

Given a structure like (36), we may say, according to (35), that *bagels* and [e] form a binding relation.

(36)

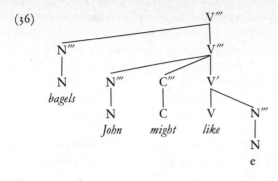

Given (35), attempting to state (34) as a positive PSF similar to those in (31) produces (37).

(37)   ... [x] [...[e]...] ...,
       A''' a   A'''

where x is a lexical item, e is the identity element, x and e form a binding relation, and *a* is not a residential domain.

To interpret (37), definitions are needed of *lexical item*, *binding relation*, and *residential domain*. No similarly abstract definitions figure into the positive PSFs in (31). Since (34) is simpler than (37), let us adopt, as a corollary to (33), the following hypothesis:

(38)   All PSFs dealing with the interpretation of syntactic feature matrices must be stated negatively.

Notice that it is not at all surprising that (33) and (38) are formulated dichotomously. (33) involves PSFs that deal with the *arrangement* of syntactic feature matrices, which is basically a syntactic issue, replacing among other things the PS rules of a TG. (38) involves PSFs that deal with the *interpretation* of syntactic feature matrices, which is basically a semantic issue, replacing many conditions on transformations or interpretive filters in TG. However, for reasons emphasized in Chapter 6, one should not mistake an RG for a notational variation of a TG. In particular, nowhere in any of the above discussion is any reference made to more than one level of syntactic representation or to "stages" in the derivation of a sentence. To simplify matters, let us hereafter refer to rules like (31) as syntactic filters and those like (34) as semantic filters.

We may further strengthen (38) as follows:

(38)   All PSFs dealing with the interpretation of syntactic feature matrices must be stated negatively. Only negative filters may make reference to abstract concepts like "binding relation," "lexical item," etc.

This dichotomy between syntactic and semantic filters is based on a long tradition in GG. In general, syntactic information has been formalized positively, most commonly in the form of permissable rewrite rules. Such rules have traditionally specified what structural configurations may occur in a language. Conversely, filters like the specified subject condition and the tensed S condition, discussed in Chapter 5, have traditionally been viewed as interpretive, that is, as based on already generated syntactic structures. In an RG, such filters also have an interpretive function. A filter like (34), for example, does not block a particular syntactic structure for syntactic reasons; rather, it blocks the structure because an inappropriate semantic interpretation is being imposed on it. Thus a sentence like *The boys said that the girl saw themselves* is deviant, while *The boy said that the girls saw themselves* is not; however their syntactic structure is virtually identical. Similarly, the question, *Who did the boys say [e] saw themselves?* is acceptable only if *who* is plural and only with *themselves* not referring to *boys*. In an RG, just as in a TG, these are interpretive matters handled by semantic filters which necessarily refer to abstract concepts like *subject*, *R-command*, and so on.

Consider now the filter regarding number agreement between verbs and subjects discussed in Chapter 5, Note 1, which I repeat here as (39).

(39) $*[\quad [\ldots N'' - [a]\ldots] - [\ldots C'' - [\beta]\ldots] - V'' - \ldots]$
       $\quad\; V''' N''' \qquad N''' \qquad C''' \qquad N'''$
       where $a \neq \beta$

As it stands, filter (39) is inadequate to account for those cases where number is marked on the head, i.e., in nouns and pronouns with inherent number. To account for these cases too, we modify (39) to (40), adding also the specification "PL" for PLURAL.

(40) $*[\quad [\quad \ldots N'' - ([aPL])\ldots] - [\ldots C'' - [\beta PL]\ldots] - V'' - \ldots]$
       $\quad\; V''' N''' [aPL] \qquad N''' \qquad\quad C''' \qquad N'''$
       where $a \neq \beta$

(40) stipulates that the number on the subject noun phrase, marked either inherently on the head or freely in X''' level posthead position, must be the same as the number marked on TNS.

As we noted in our previous discussion of this filter, a fully adequate account of verb-subject agreement in RG must deal with those cases where the subject is represented by an empty node bound to some adjunct not in subject position. To handle these cases, we sharpen the concept of *chain of binding* as follows:

(41)   X, Y, and Z form a chain of binding if X and Y form a binding relation and if, when X is substituted for Y, Y and Z form a binding relation.

Stated as (41), a chain of binding is seen as a propagating link between a fully specified adjunct and an empty adjunct.

Given (41), we can directly account for those cases of agreement in which the subject is represented by [e] with filter (40) just as it is stated. To see this, consider (42) (= Bresnan, 1978, #(124a)), which has the structure (43) in our framework.

(42) Which problems did your professor say she thought were unsolvable?

(43)

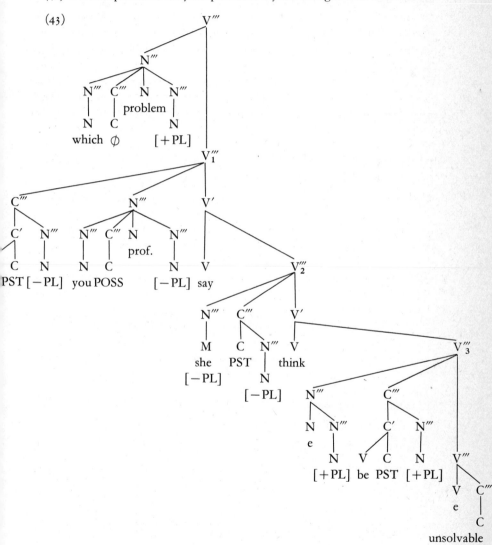

Notice that the agreement between verb, i.e., the TNS phrase, and subject in both V_3''' and V_2''' satisfies (40). Further, the N''' *which problems* and [e] form a binding relation in accordance with (35). Therefore, the "displaced" subject *which problems* in (42) does not present any difficulties to our theory of agreement.

There is of course a problem with (43), and that concerns the reversal of subject and AUX, i.e., C''', in V_1'''. Let us therefore consider now the matter of adjunct order in questions.

The order characterizer before nouns in questions is clearly exceptional. So far as I am aware, this is the only clear cut case where the order of adjuncts is not nouns before characterizers in both prehead and posthead positions. Other reversals that we have seen, e.g., in connection with examples (103m) and (103n) of Chapter 4, have been associated with a pause break. No such pause occurs in questions. In fact there is frequent palatalization between the AUX and subject is examples like (44a), flapping of alveolars in examples like (44b), and so on.

> (44)   a.   Did you eat? [jiyt]
>   b.   Did he eat? [diDiy#iyt]

In view of (44), it does not seem reasonable to assume that there is a recursion of V''' involved, that is, that AUX occurs on the highest V''' in questions and is bound to an empty AUX on the next lower V'''. It would be difficult to justify the phonological effects in (44) if the AUX and subject were not on the same level.

It seems therefore that the grammar must somehow allow for the unexpected order of adjuncts in questions. Revising the general PSF (31a) does not seem advisable. This could easily be done, so that the new order could be accommodated; however that solution obfuscates the exceptional nature of the problem. I assume therefore that the reversal occurs only at the cost of ignoring (31a).[12] In other words, we say that structures like (43) are marked exceptions; they can be obtained only when schema (31a) is not in force.

Returning to the matter of agreement, some way must now be found to allow filter (40) to apply in questions. To accomplish this, let us add the symbol "∞" to our grammar with the definition (45).[13]

> (45)   A ∞ B: {A − B, B − A}

We now revise (40) to (46).

> (46)   *[[...N'' − ([aPL])...] ∞ [...C'' − [βPL]...] − V'' − ...]
> V''' N''' [aPL] N''' C''' N'''
>   where $a \neq \beta$

This new abbreviatory device will be utilized in a number of similar situations beyond the case just mentioned. For example, we now revise the NOM PSF

(31j) as follows:

(47) $\quad [\quad [\ldots N''\ (N''')\ [+NOM]''']\ \infty\ C''' - V'' - \ldots]$
$\quad\quad\ V'''\,N'''$

Stating verb-subject agreement as filter (46) results in classifying it as a semantic filter. This seems counterintuitive. Moreover, now that we have seen that abstract concepts like *binding relation* are not directly part of the filter, it is appropriate to reformulate (46) positively; that is, as a syntactic filter. The result is (48).

(48) $\quad [\quad [\quad \ldots N'' - ([aPL])\ldots]\ \infty\ [\ldots C'' - [\beta PL]\ldots] - V'' - \ldots]$
$\quad\quad\ V'''\,N'''\,[aPL]\quad\quad N'''\quad\quad\quad C'''\quad\quad N'''$

$\quad\quad$ where $a = \beta$

(48) stipulates that the number on the subject noun phrase, either inherent or free, must be the same as the number on the TNS phrase. Since the filter is now positive, we can simplify it further by removing the differing Greek letters, giving (49).

(49) $\quad [\quad [\quad \ldots N'' - ([aPL])\ldots]\ \infty\ [\ldots C'' - [aPL]\ldots] - V'' - \ldots]$
$\quad\quad\ V'''\,N'''\,[aPL]\quad\quad N'''\quad\quad\quad C'''\quad\quad N'''$

The decision to reformulate (46) positively now seems entirely appropriate: notice the similarity between the revision (49) and the Latin case filter (28) rewritten here as (50).

(50) $\quad [\quad\quad V\quad\quad \infty\ [\quad \ldots C''\quad \infty\ [\ldots N''\ (N''')\ [aCASE]]]]$
$\quad\quad\ V'\,[aCASE]\quad C'''\,[aCASE]\quad N'''\quad\quad\quad N'''$

The above discussion supports the hypotheses (33) and (38), so that it seems that the step taken in these restrictions toward constraining the form of filters in RG is warranted. Now notice that (50) is not written exactly as (28), although it says the same thing, and further that (50) could be equivalently written as (51) and (49) could be equivalently written as (52).

(51) $\quad [\quad [aCASE]\ \infty\ [[aCASE]\ \infty\ [\ldots N\ (N''')\ [aCASE]'']]]$
$\quad\quad\ V'\quad\quad\quad\quad\quad C'''\quad\quad\quad\quad N'''$

(52) $\quad [\quad [\ldots [aPL]\ ([aPL]''')\ldots]\ \infty\ [\ldots C - [aPL]'''\ldots] - V'' - \ldots]$
$\quad\quad\ V'''\,N'''\quad\quad\quad\quad\quad\quad\quad\quad C'''$

Since (51) and (52) are clearly simpler than their previous statements, we shall adopt by convention rules of the form (51) and (52). Notice that the first [aCASE] in (51) must refer to a verb that has the feature [aCASE] since V' must dominate a V node. Similarly, the second [aCASE] in (51) must refer to a characterizer with the feature [aCASE]. The third [aCASE] must refer to a noun with the feature [*a*CASE] since only a noun can occur in that position.

In (52), the first [*a*PL] refers to a noun that is marked either [+PL], [−PL], or [±PL]. The second and third [*a*PL] must refer to a NUM with the feature either [+PL] or [−PL]. Recall that the feature specification [±PL] indicates a free choice of number. We therefore say that a noun with this feature is analyzable as either [+PL] or [−PL], so that if such a noun is in subject position of (52), the filter is satisfied when the second and the third [*a*PL] are either both [+PL] or both [−PL].

What makes rules of the form (51) and (52) simpler than those previously given for number and case agreement is the fewer number of syntactic features specifically referred to. Thus (51) and (52) are the preferred statements by virtue of a rather natural convention that rules be written in as maximally general a way a possible; that is, with the simplest feature specification necessary.

7.2 SYNTACTIC FILTERS VERSUS PS RULES

Let us turn now to the matter of how syntactic filters like those in (31) are put into effect. Given a full set of such filters, we have a number of options. Assume first a completely unrestricted rewriting system consisting of the rule (53), where X is any matrix of syntactic features, where the asterisk indicates that X can be iterated indefinitely, and where i = any number.

(53) $X^i \to /X^i/* - X^i$

Assume also a Lexicon consisting of an unordered list of Lexical items (LI) and the rule (54).

(54) $X \to LI$

Clearly, (53) and (54) will generate an indefinite number of structures which never occur in any of the world's languages. All such structures would be blocked because they do not conform to the requirements of any syntactic filter. However, in addition to these ungrammatical structures, (53) and (54) will also generate structures like (43), which does not violate any filters. Let us refer to this system, (53) and (54), as the generative grammar (GG) approach.

Now notice that this GG approach is not the only manner in which filters (31) can be put into effect. Many other approaches are possible. For example, one might propose an augmented transition network grammar of the type discussed in Wanner and Maratos (1978). Such a grammar, call it the ATN approach, requires access to precisely the sort of syntactic information represented in filters like those in (31). Thus, in an ATN, a processor compares an input string like *the old train* with patterns from a noun phrase network describing possible noun phrase structures to see if the input string can be analyzed as a noun phrase. Syntactic filters of the type proposed here could constitute such a network. For our present purposes, the main point is that the *use* of filters like (31) involves entirely different concerns from matters connected with the *content* of such filters.

Since the advent of TG, there has been considerable confusion over the nature of the grammar itself, in particular, whether it is a model of competence or performance, and, if performance, whether a model of the speaker or the hearer. Chomsky (*passim*) has repeatedly insisted that TG is a model of competence, not performance. Still, observe that a PS rule like (55) actually does two things.

(55) $S \rightarrow NP + AUX + VP$

On the one hand, (55) provides structural information about English since it stipulates that a sentence must consist of an NP, and AUX, and a VP. However (55) also *generates* the string $NP - AUX - VP$ from S. Thus PS rules both describe and create structure, which is the probable source of much of the abovementioned confusion.

In contrast to PS rules, filters like those in (31) technically do not create anything. They simply describe structure.[14] We therefore have a very important distinction between TG and RG which we have so far ignored: TG is truly generative, in the sense that the PS rules build structure; however RG has no structure building rules. Thus, in RG, the process of describing structure is completely separate from the process of creating or parsing structure. In other words, the RG system we have proposed can be investigated in terms of a variety of performance theories, whereas TG, because of the very nature of its syntactic component, is locked into a generative approach to performance based on rewriting systems. For this reason, a question like, How can a model of linguistic competence be implemented in a model of linguistic performance, does not have equal openendedness when asked in reference to TG and RG. The phrase "most neutral possible terms" quoted above in (1a) of Chapter 6, when used to describe the PS rules of TG, seems misapplied. There is no other way to interpret a rule like (55) than to say that it creates or builds the string $NP - AUX - VP$ from the string S, since there is no other way to get the string $NP - AUX - VP$ than by applying (55). Since a TG mixes description with creation, it is not the same as the RG system proposed above. (31) merely describes possible structures that exist in English; it says nothing about how such structures are derived in the first place. To make RG (residential grammar) RGG (residential generative grammar), one must add rules like (53) to the filters we have so far proposed. Notice that this move is not ineluctable; RG does not have to become RGG, in particular. What RG becomes depends on how it is intended to be used.

One cannot make a distinction between description and creation of structure in TG by reinterpreting the meaning of the arrow in a PS rule. The GG approach to phrase structure actually makes impossible the statement of many of the filters we have considered. For example, consider the imperative PSF (31f) designed to ensure that the imperative marker occurs with *you* subjects. In TG, the statement of what a subject noun phrase can be and what an auxiliary can be are made in two separate rules, the former in the rule for rewriting NP, the latter in the rule for rewriting AUX. Basically this is a problem of context, and since the mid-1960s at least, TGs have only contained context free PS rules. Thus, within its categorial component of rules, TG cannot relate the imperative marker and the *you* subject. Such problems do not arise in the syntactic filters we have proposed. Since it is not possible to separate the creative and descriptive parts of rules like (55) from each other, PS rules in general do not mesh with many models of performance, e.g., the ATN approach referred to above. Thus one way of describing RG would be to say that it is even more neutral than phrase structure grammar in terms of performance issues.

The preceding discussion involves an issue that has figured in some very significant changes in the theory of TG from its first formulations (Chomsky, 1955, 1957) to the development of the standard theory (Chomsky, 1965) and finally to the emergence of the extended standard theory (Chomsky, 1970; Chomsky, 1977, especially the discussion and references cited on pages 71–78). This issue concerns the differing natures of phrase structure rules, which have been considered "structure building," and transformational rules, which have been considered "structure changing." In other words, the phrase structure rules create constituent structure, whereas the transformational rules alter already generated structure. In the history of TG, this distinction has surfaced frequently as the pivotal point in an argument, perhaps no more clearly than in discussions of the active/passive relation. The particular problem with passives is that they contain a prepositional *by*-phrase, e.g., *by Russia* as in *Germany was defeated by Russia*, which does not occur in actives, e.g., *Russia defeated Germany*. If passives are transforms of actives, then the question is, Where does the PP come from? Akmajian and Heny (1975, 148–149) state the problem very clearly:

In general, transformations have been limited to modifying existing structures (which are originally built by the PS rules), and if, for example, we permitted Passive to create a PP ex nihilo, we would fail to account for the fact that the PP introduced by the transformation is exactly the same in form as any basic PP created by the PS rule *PP → Prep NP*.

This problem prompted changes in the transformational account of the active/passive relation (cf. Chomsky, 1965, 103–106; Emonds, 1976, Chapter III). Basically, analyses of the passive in both the standard theory and the extended standard theory have provided deep structures which already contain the prepositional *by*-phrase, thereby reserving structure building to the phrase structure rules.

Throughout the history of TG therefore a rule like (55) has been viewed as both creative and descriptive. Transformational rules, on the other hand, have been limited to modifying existing structure. Since RG does not contain transformations which modify existing syntactic structures, one should not assume that filters like (31) take over some of the creative and manipulative functions of rules in TG. This is not the case. Filters like (31) only describe structure. As a result, discussing TG in terms of performance issues as well as competence issues involves completely different considerations from discussing RG in the same contexts. Further, RG becomes generative grammar only when rules like (53) and (54) are added.

7.3 LEXICAL INSERTION AND LEXICAL FILTERS

Consider now the syntactic filters of RG in reference to the matter of lexical insertion. Properly, the rules for the actual insertion of lexical items into particular structures are not part of RG itself. However this is achieved, RG will simply deal with the possibilities and results of lexical insertion, that is, with structures which already contain lexical items. Assuming a GG approach allowing completely unrestricted lexical insertion, say, via a rule like (54), RG must deal with structures like the following:

(56) $[\quad [\Phi] - [believe] - [+PL] - [+NOM]]$
$\quad N''' C \quad N$

(57) $[\quad [\Phi] - [belief] - [+PL] - [+NOM]]$
$\quad N''' C \quad N$

The symbols *believe* and *belief* in these structures are abbreviations for full lexical specifications which consist of the following triplet: a phonological specification in the form of a matrix of phonological distinctive features like $[+\text{TENSE}]$, $[+\text{VOICED}]$, etc., which we will refer to as "ϕ"; a syntactic specification in the form of a matrix of syntactic distinctive features like $[+\text{NOMINAL}]$, $[+X'' \text{ LEVEL}]$, etc., which we will refer to as "σ"; and, a semantic specification in the form of a matrix of semantic features like $[+\text{ABSTRACT}]$, $[+\text{CAUSATIVE}]$, etc., which we will refer to as "μ".

Minimally, the grammar must contain the following filter:

(58) $[[\phi,\sigma,\mu]]$, where $X \in \sigma$
$\quad X$

Given (58), (56) is syntactically ill-formed since *believe*, a verb, is $[-\text{NOMINAL}]$ and N is $[+\text{NOMINAL}]$. (57), on the other hand, is well-formed. Notice that (58) says that the feature matrix which constitutes X must be a member of σ, not the other way around, since X need not fully specifiy σ.

Given the above mechanisms, we can now formalize filters discussed in previous chapters. For example, consider the filters for the English auxiliary system which we discussed in Chapter 4 and which we repeat here:

(59)   a.   (= 43a, Chapter 4)
            If *be* occurs in X′ level prehead position before TNS, it must be bound to an empty main verb node.

       b.   (= 43b, Chapter 4)
            If *do* occurs to the left of TNS, there can be no *have* or *be* in the same V‴, except that *do* can occur with the main verb *have*.

Assuming that all auxiliary verbs carry the syntactic feature [+AUX], which means that they *can* occur in the X‴ prehead characterizer of verb phrases, i.e., in the TNS phrase, we replace (59a, b) with (60a,b).[15]

(60)   a. $[\ldots be\ [+\text{TNS}]\ \ldots\ [\text{e}]\ \ldots]$
            V‴

       b. $[\ldots do\ [+\text{TNS}]\ \ldots\ [-\text{AUX}]\ \ldots]$
            V‴

We would like to be able to leave (60a) and (60b) in the very general form in which they are given; however they can range over more than one V‴. To prevent this, we add the following constraint to syntactic filters:

(61)   In filters of the form $[\text{W}a\text{Y}\beta\text{Z}]$, where a and β are syntactic feature
       X^n
       matrices and where W, Y, and Z are left unspecified, a and β must be in the same neighborhood.

Recall (cf. Chapter 5, (9)) that items in the same neighborhood must be either R-commanded or L-commanded by one and the same X‴ prehead characterizer, i.e., by one and the same TNS or ART (or POSS). All of the items in (60) are verbs, excluding [+TNS]. The verbs *be* and *do*, according to (61), must therefore be R-commanded by the same TNS that L-commands the [e] and [−AUX] for them to be in the same neighborhood. As an example, consider (62).

(62)   a. $[do\ \text{TNS N‴}\ have\ \text{N″}]$ (as in *Did the guests have a good time?*)
            V‴

       b. $[do\ \text{TNS}\ [the\ guests\ who\ [[\text{e}]\ \text{TNS}\ leave\ early]]\ have\ \text{N‴}]$ (as in *Did*
            V‴   N‴   V‴

            the guests who left early have a good time?)

In (62a), the TNS R-commands *do* and L-commands *have*; therefore *do* and *have* are in the same neighborhood. In (62b), the first TNS also R-commands *do* and L-commands *have*; but in addition it also L-commands *leave*. However *leave* is further L-commanded by a TNS in its own clause (the one to its immediate left), and that TNS does not command either *do* or *have*. Thus *leave* is not in the same neighborhood as *do* or *have*, and (62b) conforms to filter (60b).

(60a) covers those cases in which any occurrence of *be*[16] is within AUX, i.e., to the left of TNS. This occurs when there is no other auxiliary verb in the same simple sentence, as in *She is sad*. To cover those cases in which there is another auxiliary verb, either a modal, perfective *have* or progressive *be* or a combination of these, we add the following filter:

(63)   [... [+AUX] ... *be* ...]
       V'''

(63) allows *be* to occur in those positions previously discussed (cf. diagrams (36)–(38) in Chapter 4) where there is more than one auxiliary verb in one V'''.

We now feature specifications like the following for auxiliary and non-auxiliary verbs:

(64)   a. perfective *have*   [+AUX]
       b. main verb *have*   [−AUX]
       c. progressive *be*   [+AUX]
       d. passive *be*   [+AUX]
       e. main verb *be*   [+AUX]
       f. modals   [+AUX]
       g. auxiliary *do*   [+AUX]
       h. main verb *do*   [−AUX]
       i. main verbs, e.g., *go*   [−AUX]

As we have noted, [+AUX] means [+/____/TNS], that is, *can* occur in a tense characterizer, whereas [−AUX] means [−/____/TNS], that is, *cannot* occur in a tense characterizer.

If we wish formally to adopt feature specifications like [+AUX] and [−AUX] given in (64), we must investigate more closely the nature of σ in such filters as (58). As we noted above, X in (58) need not duplicate σ. The specific reason is that we would expect individual lexical items to have very detailed environmental restrictions, most of which we do not want to assume as part of the inventory of universal syntactic features. For example, while it seems quite clear that we want to distinguish transitive and intransitive verbs on the basis of some general, perhaps universal, feature as we have, namely, [+COMP] versus [−COMP], it seems unlikely that we would want to propose "universal" features for each of the various types of complements that must occur, e.g., the fact that *rely* takes PP whose head is *on*, whereas *confide* takes PP whose head is *in*. Let us therefore allow X in (58), as well as (53) and (54) if our grammar is to be generative, to be a matrix consisting of any of the features in Table 2 and at least one of them. Let us also continue to assume that Table 2 is a working hypothesis based on an as yet unknown system of universal syntactic features. Further, let us assume that σ in (58) can contain features other than those specified in Table 2, and that such features are language specific. Included among such features would be the pair $[+\mathrm{AUX}]/[-\mathrm{AUX}]$ under discussion. Also included might be features like $[+/\underline{\hspace{1cm}} \textit{-ing}]$, which would specify the progressive *be*, and $[+/\underline{\hspace{1cm}} \textit{-en}]$, which would specify the passive *be*, thereby distinguishing the three verbs *be*. Similarly, we might distinguish the modals and auxiliary *do* from the other auxiliary verbs by marking the former "$[-/\mathrm{PREP}\underline{\hspace{1cm}}]$" thereby indicating that they do not occur as complements of infinitives, which are introduced by the PREP *to*, and participles, which are introduced by the PREP *-ing*. Likewise, we could assume that the nonoccurrence of TNS in infinitives and participles is accounted for by the stipulation that the prepositions introducing these complements are subcategorized as $[-/\underline{\hspace{1cm}} \mathrm{V}''']$, i.e., $[-/\underline{\hspace{1cm}} [-\mathrm{ADJUNCT}]''']$ (Recall that TNS is a feature of V''' only).

The difficulty with the above approach is that we now require a third class of filters in RG: lexical filters, which directly compare the feature specifications of lexical items with the environments in which they occur. The reason is that this group of filters must be either positively or negatively stated depending upon whether the environments involved are positive or negative. As a result, they have one of the characteristics of syntactic filters (positive statement) and one of the characteristics of semantic filters (negative statement). This is perhaps to be expected in filters that deal with the specific structural contexts in which specific lexical items occur. In any case, lexical filters cannot all have the form of (58).

There is no difficulty in stating that items marked positively for occurring in some environment must occur in that environment. Such circumstances produce filters like (65), which has the form of a syntactic filter.[17]

(65) $[\ldots [+/\underline{\hspace{1cm}} [a\sigma]^v] \ldots [a\sigma]^v \ldots],$
        $\mathrm{X^n}$

        where *a* is either $+$ or $-$, σ is a syntactic feature, and v and $n =$
        $\{3, 2, 1, 0\}.$

The problem is handling the negatively specified environments. If we attempt to cast lexical filters as syntactic filters—that is, if we attempt to maintain (33) in the statement of lexical filters—we are prohibited from adopting a filter like (66), a rather simple statement paralleling (65).

(66) $*[\ldots [-/\underline{\hspace{1cm}} [a\sigma]^v] \ldots [a\sigma]^v \ldots],$
        $\mathrm{X^n}$

        where *a* is either $+$ or $-$, σ is a syntactic feature, and v and $n =$
        $\{3, 2, 1, 0\}.$

Attempts to reproduce the intent of (66) positively, i.e., without the asterisk, result in filters like (67).

(67) $[\ldots[-/\underline{\hspace{1cm}}[a\sigma]^{\nu}]\ldots[\beta\tau]^{\mu}\ldots],$
    X^n

  where a and β are either $+$ or $-$,
  where σ and τ are any syntactic features,
  where n, ν, and $\mu = \{3, 2, 1, 0\}$, *and*
  where either $a \neq \beta$ or $\sigma \neq \tau$ or $\nu \neq \mu$.

Clearly, (67) is rather cumbersome, to say the least; moreover, a filter of such latitude would allow an enormous number of ungrammatical structures which would then have to be ruled out by other filters.

The most glaring problem with filters like (67) is that they do not allow us to state the intuitively correct information: that certain lexical items cannot occur in certain environments, even though many, if not most, other items within the same category can, or that certain ones can occur in certain environments where most others cannot. For example, most verbs can occur in either positive or negative sentences; the verb *budge* however requires negative environments:

(68) a. Don't budge.
      I could hardly budge the refrigerator.
    b. *On the count of three, everyone budge!
      *I think I'll budge the refrigerator to get some exercise.

Conversely, while most verbs cannot occur in AUX as main verbs, the verb *be* can:

(69) a. Was John a student?
    b. *Became John a student?
      *Saw John a student?

In view of the above, let us add (70) to our grammar.

(70) Lexical filters, which compare the feature specification of lexical items with the environment of those items, are stated either positively or negatively.

Given (70), we add the following lexical filters to our grammar (in each case, $a = +$ or $-$, σ is a syntactic feature, and ν and $n = \{3, 2, 1, 0\}$):[18]

(71) a. $*[\ldots[-/\underline{\hspace{1cm}}[a\sigma]^{\nu}]\ldots[a\sigma]^{\nu}\ldots]$
        X^n
    b. $*[\ldots[a\sigma]^{\nu}\ldots[-/[a\sigma]^{\nu}\underline{\hspace{1cm}}]\ldots]$
        X^n

(72)   a. $[\ldots[+/\underline{\hspace{1cm}}[a\sigma]^v]\ldots[a\sigma]^v\ldots]$
            X^n

       b. $[\ldots[a\sigma]^v\ldots[+/[a\sigma]^v\underline{\hspace{1cm}}]\ldots]$
            X^n

Both (71) and (72) deal with precedence relations: (71a) and (72a) compare the feature specification of a lexical item with that of an item following in the same neighborhood; (71b) and (72b), with that of an item preceding. Thus (71a) rules out a structure like (73a); (72b) allows a structure like (73b) for perfective *have*.

(73)   a. $[\ldots to - [-\text{ADJUNCT}]'''\ldots]$
            C'

            (*to* is $[-/\underline{\hspace{1cm}}[-\text{ADJUNCT}]''']$, i.e., $[-/\underline{\hspace{1cm}}V''']$)

       b. $[\ldots\text{TNS} - have\ldots]$
            C'

            (perfective *have* is $[+/\underline{\hspace{1cm}}/\text{TNS}]$, i.e., $[+\text{AUX}]$)

If it were possible to remove negative environment features like $[-/\underline{\hspace{1cm}}V''']$ and $[-/\underline{\hspace{1cm}}/\text{TNS}]$ from the grammar, we could eliminate filters like (71), and then all lexical filters would have the same form as syntactic filters. However, elimination of negative environment features or any negative features results in an increase in the total number of features used. For example, if perfective *have* is $[+/\underline{\hspace{1cm}}/\text{TNS}]$ and we cannot used $[-/\underline{\hspace{1cm}}/\text{TNS}]$ to distinguish it from main verb *have*, then some other feature must be used to specify exactly where main verb *have* can occur. The availability of $[-/\underline{\hspace{1cm}}/\text{TNS}]$ means that, instead, we can stipulate where main verb *have* cannot occur. Also, it is sometimes more natural to state some negative feature of an item than to list all possible positive ones. For example, prepositions in English never have sentential complements:

(74)   a.   *We agreed to that John should go.
       b.   *Bill was insulted by that John left so early.

In view of (74), we would say that one of the characteristics of English prepositions is that they are $[-/\underline{\hspace{1cm}}V''']$. This does not mean that in all cases a V'', V', or V can follow any preposition. For example, the V level following the infinitive marker *to* depends on the governing verb. Some verbs permit V'', V', and V:

(75)   a.   They would have allowed him to [have gone].
                                              V''

       b.   They will allow him to [be interviewed].
                                     V'

       c.   They won't allow him to [speak].
                                     V

In view of (75), it seems appropriate to mark *allow* as $[+/\underline{\quad}N''' - to - V^n]$, leaving the V level unspecified since *to* is $[-/\underline{\quad}V''']$. The verb *continue*, in contrast, permits only V′ and V complements:

(76) a. *They would have continued to have done that.
     b. He continued to be interviewed all week.
     c. He continued to speak.

Since there are verbs like *continue* that cannot have a V″ in their infinitive complements, we cannot say that *to*, in particular, is $[+/\underline{\quad}V'']$, $[+/\underline{\quad}V']$, and $[-/\underline{\quad}V]$. It is more natural, as we have argued above, to consider *to* a preposition and mark it $[-/\underline{\quad}V''']$ like all other prepositions. This rules out (74). To account for (75), we mark *allow* as we have suggested, namely, $[+/\underline{\quad}N''' - to - V^n]$; to account for (76), we mark *continue* $[+/\underline{\quad}to - V(')]$. In conclusion, we shall retain negative environment features and add lexical filters of the form (70) to our grammar.

We can now further specify the verbs in (64) as follows:[19]

(77) a. perfective *have* $[+AUX]$ $[+/\underline{\quad}\ldots\text{-}en]$ $[+/PREP\underline{\quad}]$
     b. main verb *have* $[-AUX]$
     c. progressive *be* $[+AUX]$ $[+/\underline{\quad}\text{-}ing]$ $[+/PREP\underline{\quad}]$
     d. passive *be* $[+AUX]$ $[+/\underline{\quad}\text{-}en]$ $[+/PREP\underline{\quad}]$
     e. main verb *be* $[+AUX]$
     f. modals $[+AUX]$ $[-/PREP\underline{\quad}]$
     g. auxiliary *do* $[+AUX]$ $[-/\underline{\quad}\ldots[+AUX]]$ $[-/PREP\underline{\quad}]$
     h. main verb *do* $[-AUX]$
     i. other verbs $[-AUX]$

Adopting the neighborhood constraint (61) for features like the above, a specification like $[-/\underline{\quad}\ldots[+AUX]]$ means that auxiliary *do* cannot precede any other auxiliary verb in the same neighborhood. This is the RG equivalent of TGs *do*-replacement transformation. Thus in RG the very peculiar idiosyncratic fact that *do* cannot occur with other auxiliaries is relegated to a specification within the syntactic feature matrix of *do* itself. This accounts for the following:

(78) a. He could (should, would, etc.) have gone.
     b. He could (should, would, etc.) be studying.
     c. He could (should, would, etc.) be interviewed.

(79) a. *He did have gone.
     b. *He did be studying.
     c. *He did be interviewed.

Despite these contrasts, in other respects *do* behaves like a modal since it does

not occur in infinitives and participles and since it cannot occur with another
modal (*do can, *will can, *can will, etc.). Observe also the following:

(80)   a. He could and, in fact, should do that.
       b. He could and, in fact, did do that.

Such co-ordination would be unlikely if *do* were not a modal. Thus it is very odd
that standard American English does not tolerate (79), a highly idiosyncratic
fact which we can record in the lexical entry of *do* in an RG. In the process,
we eliminate (60b), which was not very satisfactory to begin with (cf. Note 15).

Observe now that in (77) the modals, including auxiliary *do*, are marked
[−/PREP____], whereas perfective *have*, and progressive and passive *be* are
marked [+/PREP____]. Since the complementizers *to* and *-ing* are prepositions
(cf. Chapter 3, Section 3.2), since all prepositions are [−/____ V‴] as we have
just noted, and since only V‴ contains TNS, then all modals, which are
[+AUX], i.e., [+/____/TNS], occur only in tensed clauses and are excluded
from infinitives and participles. This exclusion is recorded in the specification
[−/PREP____], which would not be possible if we had not adopted the
position that *to* and *-ing* are prepositions. Thus several seemingly unrelated facts
are directly interrelated in the RG system we have proposed.

We can capitalize on the dichotomy between [+/PREP____] and
[−/PREP____] and simplify preceding structural analyses, if we assume
the following redundancies:

(81)   a. [+/PREP____] → [+/TNS____]
       b. [−/PREP____] → [+/____TNS]

According to (81a), perfective *have* and progressive and passive *be* occur after
TNS when they are in the tense characterizer; (81b), on the other hand, stipulates that modals, including auxiliary *do*, must occur before TNS. This modification of analyses given in Chapter 4, Section 4.0 yields structures like (82):

(82)

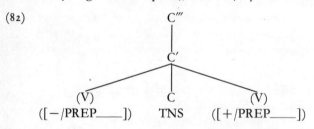

We now modify examples (36)–(38) of Chapter 4 as (83)–(85), respectively.

(83)   *have* in the verb phrase

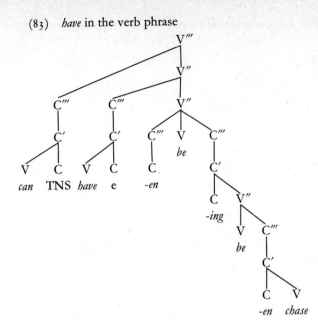

(84)   *have* in the auxiliary

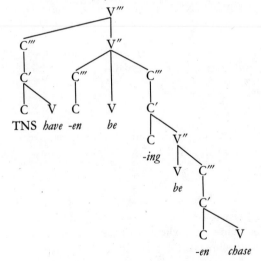

(85) *have* in the auxiliary

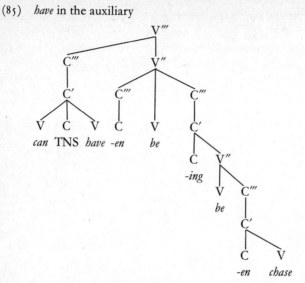

Thus the RG equivalent of TG's (86) is the syntactic filter (87).

(86) AUX → TNS (MODAL) (have -en) (be -ing) (be -en)

(87) [...([−/PREP____]) TNS ... (have ([e]) ... -en) (be -ing) (be -en)...]
      V‴

With (87) we no longer need (63); however we must retain (60a), which we
repeat here with the modifications just discussed:

(88) [... [TNS *be*] ... [e] ...]
      V‴ C′   V

(88) allows *be* to be in AUX only when there is no other auxiliary to its left;
observe that it does not say "[... TNS *be*]" which would allow a modal to
                                C′
the left of TNS.

   Unfortunately there are redundancies between (87) and (77); in particular,
the grammar is saying twice that progressive *be* occurs before *-ing*, that passive
be occurs before *-en*, etc. However, whereas the same redundancies cannot be
eliminated in TG, we can eliminate them by replacing (87) with (89).

(89) [...([−/PREP____]) TNS ... (-en) ... (-ing) ... (-en) ...]
      V‴

Observe that in TG there is no other way to get the auxiliary verbs themselves
into a phrase marker than by assuming a rule like (86). However in RG, since

the creation and description of syntax are separate, filters like (89) are possible, provided that we make some formal distinction between each of the endings associated with AUX. This can be done utilizing the features of Table 2. A full specification of the endings associated with the auxiliary is given in (90).

(90)	TNS	PERF -en	PASS -en	PROG -ing
ADJUNCT	+	+	+	+
NOMINAL	−	−	−	−
NEIGHBOR	−	−	−	−
PREHEAD	+	+	+	+
POSTHEAD	−	+	+	+
/____/N	−	−	+	+
/____/V	+	+	+	+
/____/C	−	−	−	−
X''' LEVEL	+	−	−	−
X'' LEVEL	−	−	+	+
X' LEVEL	−	−	−	−
COMP	+	+	+	+

Observe that the passive and progressive endings share the same features, some of which are different from those assigned to the perfective ending. This is because the passive and progressive endings form participles that have virtually identical environmental distributions, e.g., in noun phrases, on the X″ level like other adjectives, etc. In English there is no perfect active participle of a form like *seen*, e.g., *the man seen the woman left. We have only forms like *having seen* and *having been seen*.

Let us distinguish the passive and progressive by marking the former [+/____ ...by], meaning that it can be directly associated with an agentive phrase, and the latter [−/____ ...by], meaning that it cannot. The symbols in filter (89) we now understand to be abbreviations for the feature matrices just discussed.

There is a remaining problem with a filter like (89) which the neighborhood constraint (61) cannot handle. In RG, infinitives and participles are characterizer phrases, as we have seen; accordingly, they never constitute neighborhoods since they have no characterizer in X‴ level prehead position. This means that a sentence like (91a), which has the structure (91b), would be marked ungrammatical if matters were left as they now stand.

(91)   a. John is known to have done that.
       b. [John TNS be [e] -en know to have -en do that]
           V‴

Notice that all these items are in the same neighborhood: all are commanded by the same TNS and no other TNS. However, in (91), a passive *-en* precedes a perfective *-en*. Although the neighborhood constraint will allow (91), filter (89) will not. According to filter (89), the perfective must precede the passive. This problem has arisen before, but not quite so markedly. To correct matters, we revise (61) as follows:

(92)   In filters of the form [WaYβZ], were a and β are syntactic feature
                X^n
       matrices and where W, Y, and Z are left unspecified, a and β must
       be in the same neighborhood and Y cannot contain [$-$AUX], i.e.,
       a main verb.

In terms of (89), this revised neighborhood constraint stipulates that there cannot be any main verb between TNS and *-en*, *-en* and *-ing*, and *-ing* and *-en*.

It remains to provide explicitly for structures like (83), which contain an *-en* bound to an empty characterizer carrying all of the syntactic features of *-en*. Symbolizing this empty node as [¢ϕ], let us add the feature [$+$/[____[¢ϕ]]] to the specification of perfective *have* in (77) and revise (89) to (93).

(93)   [...([$-$/PREP____]) TNS...((([¢ϕ])...*-en*)...(*-ing*)...(*-en*)...]
       V$'''$

Perfective *have* now carries the specification [$+$AUX] and [$+$/[____[¢ϕ]]], meaning it can occur in the tense characterizer or directly to the left of the empty characterizer [¢ϕ].[20] If it occurs in the TNS characterizer it occurs to the right of TNS, because it is [$+$/PREP____] (cf. (81a)).

According to (93) all V$'''$ in English must dominate a TNS. Furthermore, to the left of this TNS there can be a [$-$/PREP____] verb, i.e., a modal or auxiliary *do*. If it is *do*, then there cannot be any other auxiliary verb in the same neighborhood because *do* is marked [$-$/____...[$+$AUX]]. If it is one of the other modals, there can follow, to the right of tense, perfective *-en*, progressive *-ing*, and passive *-en*, in that order. The same three auxiliary elements can also occur if there is no modal to the left of TNS. Within the framework of (93), the perfective verb *have*, which is marked [$+$/____...*-en*], can occur either within the tense characterizer, because it is [$+$AUX], or to the immediate left of [¢ϕ]. The verb *be*, on the other hand, occurs either in the tense characterizer to the right of TNS (it is [$+$AUX] and [$+$/PREP____]), in which case it must be bound to an empty main verb node (cf. (88)), or it occurs in some other verbal slot before either *-ing* or *-en*.

The preceding analyses raise interesting questions about the nature of linguistic generalizations. Chomsky's affix hopping analysis of the English auxiliary system, which we have represented as (86), was far and away much more general than any analysis achieved by American structuralists. In fact, the elegance of Chomsky's treatment did much to strengthen the TG position.

However, as we have noted, PS rules combine the creation of syntactic structure with the description of syntactic structure. In (86), the nodes specifying the
auxiliary verbs must be there since there is no other way to obtain them. We
cannot even replace (86) with (94) in the standard theory of TG.

(94) AUX → TNS (V) (V − en) (V − ing) (V − en)

(94) becomes inadequate within the total framework of a TG of English. Many
transformations specifically mention modal, *have*, and *be* in their structural
index, a widely accepted indication that some generalization is being missed.[21]
However, it is necessary to mention these verbs specifically, so that they can be
distinguished from non-auxiliary verbs in transformational rules. Accordingly,
(94) is an inadequate representation; one must at least have (95).

(95) AUX → TNS (V   ) (V   − en) (V   − ing) (V   − en)
                  [+AUX]   [+AUX]   [+AUX]   [+AUX]

While (95) is acceptable within X′ syntax, it raises the problem discussed earlier
in this chapter regarding possible restrictions against transformations referring
to features. Thus the essential insight of Chomsky's analysis is buried in matters
that are not directly related to the auxiliary. In an RG, we could of course
replace (93) with (96).

(96) [...([−/PREP____])TNS...(V...([¢ɸ])...-en) (V − ing) (V − en) ...]
      V‴

But (96) is hardly more general than (87). The real generality is (93) which
specifies that the order of auxiliary elements must be perfective, progressive,
and passive, and nothing more. (93) does not tell us what verbs must be to the
left of these affixes, facts accounted for by (77). Further, (93) does not even
stipulate that there *must be* a verb to the left of these affixes, a fact which also is
not properly part of the filter and which should be dealt with elsewhere (cf.
Note 20). Within our framework, these facts can be separated; in TG, they
cannot.[22]

7.4 CONCLUDING REMARKS

Summarizing the preceding discussion, we observe that RG contains syntactic
filters of the form (97), semantic filters of the form (98), and lexical filters of the
form (99).

(97) $+[\ /\Sigma_1 - \Sigma_2/\Sigma_x^\mu]$
      Σ_x^ν

where Σ_1, Σ_2, and Σ_x are syntactic feature matrices and where $\mu \leq \nu$.

(98) $-[\ \ /\Sigma_1 - \Sigma_2/\Sigma_x^\mu]$
     Σ_x^ν

where Σ_1, Σ_2, and Σ_x are syntactic feature matrices and where $\mu \leq \nu$.

(99) a. $+[[\Phi, \Sigma_2, M]]$,
         Σ_1

     where Σ_1 and Σ_2 are syntactic feature matrices, $\Sigma_1 \in \Sigma_2$, Φ is a phonological feature matrix, and M is a semantic feature matrix.

     b. $a[\dots[a/\underline{\hspace{1em}} \infty \Sigma_n] \infty \dots \Sigma_{n'} \dots]$,
         Σ_x

     where Σ_n and Σ_x are syntactic feature matrices and where a is either $+$ or $-$.

To establish some uniformity, these schemata are stated in a somewhat more general form than those given previously. Filter (99a) is based on (58); (99b) is based on (iv) of Note 18. In all of the above cases, syntactic feature matrices (Σ), which must contain at least one syntactic feature, are of the form (100a), where $a, \beta,$ and γ are each either $+$ or $-$, where $\sigma_1, \sigma_2,$ and σ_n are syntactic features, and where $\nu = \{3,2,1,0\}$. An example is (100b), that is, (100c) simply.

(100) a. $\begin{bmatrix} a\sigma_1 \\ \beta\sigma_2 \\ \gamma\sigma_n \end{bmatrix}^\nu$ b. $\begin{bmatrix} +\text{ADJUNCT} \\ +\text{NOMINAL} \\ -\text{NEIGHBOR} \end{bmatrix}'''$ c. NUM$'''$

Within the schema (97), the maximally generalizable syntactic filter for English is (101), a slightly modified version of (1).

(101) $+[\ \ /[+\text{NOMINAL}]^i - [-\text{NOMINAL}]^i/\Sigma^\mu]$,
      Σ^ν

     where $\mu \leq \nu$ and $i = \{3, 2, 1, 0\}$.

If Σ in (101) is $[-\text{ADJUNCT}]$ and $\nu = i = 3$, then (101) describes a structure like (102a,b).

(102) a.

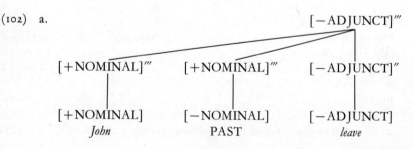

b.

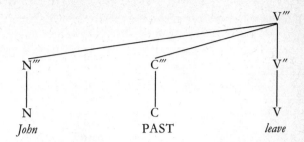

| John | PAST | leave |

Only filters of the form (98) may make reference to abstract concepts like binding relation, R-command, and the like. Furthermore, all syntactic and lexical filters are subject to the neighborhood constraint (92), which is an exceedingly restrictive constraint. In effect, syntactic and lexical filters cannot even mention subjacent clauses, i.e., tensed V'''. There will be, accordingly, no syntactic filter of a form like (103).

(103) $+[\ldots \text{TNS} \ldots [\ldots \text{TNS} \ldots] \ldots]$ (as in [*John said* [*Bill left*]])
$\quad\quad\ \ V''' \quad\quad\quad V'''$

One reason it is possible to invoke the neighborhood constraint in all syntactic and lexical filters is that RG contains no equivalent of rules like raising and equi-NP deletion since surface infinitives and participles do not derive from underlying clauses.

The neighborhood constraint is however much too restrictive for semantic filters, which must be able to embrace unbounded dependencies such as the one in (104).

(104) [what [did John say [Sue believes... [Bill saw [e]]...]]]
$\quad\quad\ \ V''' \quad V''' \quad\quad\quad\quad V''' \quad\quad\quad\quad V'''$

In short, the implicit claim of RG is that above the level of the clause all significant linguistic generalizations, like (34), are essentially interpretive; that is, in our terms, semantic. To see this, consider again the structure (43). Within V_3''' the agreement between subject and verb satisfies filter (52). Recall that the empty subject slot [e] is a fully specified syntactic feature matrix. In this matrix
$\quad\quad\quad\quad\quad\quad$ N'''
there must be some number designation, either $[+\text{PL}]$, $[-\text{PL}]$, or $[\pm\text{PL}]$. In our discussion of (52), we noted that if the NUM slot of the subject N''' and the AUX are both specified as either $[+\text{PL}]$ or $[-\text{PL}]$, then the subject noun itself cannot have inherent number; it must be marked $[\pm\text{PL}]$. Thus V_3''' satisfies (52) if the feature matrix dominating [e] is marked $[\pm\text{PL}]$. In short, (52) does not need to know specifically what the subject noun is, i.e., what the word itself is. Given that agreement is satisfied in this manner on each V''', (43) is syntactically well-formed in terms of (52). The semantic filter (34) examines (43) to check for

the presence of an appropriate referent for [e]. Such a referent is present in the noun phrase *which problems*. The head of this noun phrase is *problem*, which is marked [±PL] since it does not have inherent number. The phrases *which problems* and [e] satisfy the conditions for a binding relation (35). Hence (43) is semantically well-formed. In summary, we may say that despite the "displaced" position of *which problems*, number agreement in RG is still carried out at the local level. So are other referential matters. Consider, for example, the interpretation of the reflexive in (105), which has a structure very similar to (43).

(105)   Which male student did your professor say she thought [e] killed himself?

Here again, the syntax of reflexivization is carried out at the local level, between [e] and *himself*. Finding the antecedent of [e] is then an additional matter—one handled by filter (34) again. Notice that both of the following are ungrammatical:

(106)   a. *Which problems did your professor say she thought that [e] were unsolvable?
        b. *Which male student did your professor say she thought that [e] killed himself?

In RG the ungrammaticality of both of these examples is attributable to the failure of (34) to apply: [e] is within the residential domain of the free resident *that*; therefore [e] cannot be bound to some item outside of that domain. Since [e] has no antecedent, the structures are blocked.

NOTES TO CHAPTER 7

1. The rules in this chapter are given in the form discussed above (cf. Section 6.21). Thus Rule (1) embraces the same structures as (i).

(i) $X^n \rightarrow /[+\text{NOMINAL}]^i - [-\text{NOMINAL}]^i/ X^m$
      where $m \leq n$ and $i = \{0, 1, 2, 3\}$.

Observe that [+NOMINAL] refers only to nouns and that [−NOMINAL] refers to both verbs and characterizers. Rule (1) therefore stipulates that on each X level, nouns must precede all other categories.

In rules like the above, let us adopt the following equations:

(ii) $X^0 = X, X^1 = X', X^2 = X'', X^3 = X'''$

2. Rule (2) is equivalent to Rule (40) of Chapter 1. Rule (3) is based on Rule (1) of Chapter 3, which I repeat here for convenience as (i):

(i) $X' \rightarrow / V^n / X$

Observe that (i) does not allow for the embedding of an adjunct to the left of the verb on the X′ level. However, as other discussion has indicated, this is necessary to generate verb phrases like *make* (*let, see,* etc.) *him go* (cf. example (68) in Chapter 3). The new Rule (3) presented here corrects this deficiency. For the purposes of clarification, let me point out that the following embrace equivalent structures:

(ii) $\quad X' \rightarrow /A''' - V^i/ \ X$

(iii) $\quad [/A''' - V^i/ \ X]$
$\qquad X'$

(iv) $\quad [/[+\text{ADJUNCT}]''' - [-\text{ADJUNCT}]^i/X]$
$\qquad X'$

3. Recall that items marked $[-X''' \ \text{LEVEL}]$ can occur on the X''' level only when they are bound to an empty node which is *not* on the X''' level; see Chapter 4, Note 10 for discussion.

4. Recall that TNS includes here the mood markers for the subjunctive and imperative which are frequently phonologically empty.

5. Further restrictions, some of which will be discussed below, are necessary. For example, if there is a POSS in first prehead position, then there *must* be an N''' in second prehead position; if the mood marker is imperative, then the subject must be *you,* if one occurs; and so on.

6. I shall refer to statements like (1), (2), (3), and (8) variously as schemata, rules or PSFs.

7. These examples indicate that we might formulate a theory of the degree of deviance in terms of the number and types of PSFs violated. Since (1) is more general than, say, (12), we might say that a sentence which violates (1) is more deviant than one which violates (12). In this sense, *John go* is less deviant than *go John,* since the former violates (12), but the latter violates (1).

Observe, incidentally, that the first $[+\text{Nominal}]$ category in (13) is specified without a prime. This is a possible reference. One might also have referred to the same category as $[+\text{NOMINAL}]'''$, $[+\text{NOMINAL}]''$, $[+\text{NOMINAL}]'$, though the latter two references are somewhat unusual. In this regard therefore RG follows TG conventions.

8. The variable i in (15) need not be specified, such specification already being a part of (1). Also, NUM is simply an abbreviatory convenience: the actual rule would contain the syntactic feature matrix which distinguishes NUM from all other categories, i.e., $[+\text{NOMINAL}, -\text{NEIGHBOR}]$.

9. Since the first X''' category must be $[+\text{NOMINAL}]$, we could uniquely specify NUM from all other categories with any of the following instead of $[-\text{COMP}]$: $[-\text{NEIGHBOR}]$, $[-\text{PREHEAD}]$, $[-/\underline{\quad}/V]$, $[-X'' \ \text{LEVEL}]$, or $[-X' \ \text{LEVEL}]$. For the second X''' category in (17), I have specified $[-X'' \ \text{LEVEL}]$ to rule out PREP, COMP, and CONJ.

10. $[a\text{CASE}]$ here abbreviates $[+\text{DAT}]$, $[+\text{ACC}]$, $[+\text{POSS}]$, $[+\text{NOM}]$, etc.

11. Hereafter we shall formally represent empty categories with the identity element e.

12. Observe that the reversal of the expected order does not violate the non-embedding PSF (31b).

13. Observe that ∞ has independent motivation since it is directly related to the slash notation we have adopted and justified in a variety of cases above. In fact, in all instances, the two symbols overlap each other. Note that (i) and (ii) both abbreviate (iii).

(i) $\quad /A/ \ B$

(ii) $\quad A \infty B$

(iii) $\quad$ a. $\ A - B$
$\qquad$ b. $\ B - A$

However there are cases in which expressions require both symbols to avoid ambiguity. Consider (iv), which abbreviates (v).

(iv) $\quad /A \infty B/ \ C$

(v)   a. A — B — C
       b. B — A — C
       c. C — A — B
       d. C — B — A

14. It is for this reason that I have used phrases like "embrace equivalent structures" when comparing RG and TG (cf. Notes 1 and 2 above). While a labelled bracket in TG is associated with both a phrase marker and a rewrite rule, a labelled bracket in RG is associated only with a phrase marker, i.e., the familiar tree diagrams.

For the sake of clarification, recall that McCawley (1976, 39) specifies that "the notion of 'derivation' is dispensed with entirely" in node admissibility conditions. The difference between rule (i) of Note 1 above and rule (1) in this chapter is that the former is descriptive and generative, while the latter is merely descriptive. For a discussion of the nature of PS rules in the standard theory of TG, see Chomsky (1965, 66–68).

15. Notice that in RG, $[+\text{AUX}]$ is a completely syntactic specification. Actually it means $[+\_\_\_/ [+\text{TNS}]]$, i.e., a verb which can occur either before or after a tense characterizer. (60b) does not precisely cover (59b) since it does not rule out sequences of *do* and other auxiliaries. We shall correct this presently.

16. In accordance with the preceding note, the main verb *be* in RG is not specified as $[-\text{AUX}]$, i.e., $[-/\_\_\_/\text{TNS}]$, although most non-auxiliary verbs are. Thus perfective *have* is $[+/\_\_\_/\text{TNS}]$, meaning that it can occur in the tense characterizer, though it need not (cf. examples (36)–(38) in Chapter 4), whereas the main verb *have* is $[-/\_\_\_/\text{TNS}]$, meaning that it cannot occur in the tense characterizer, thereby ruling out **Had the guests a good time?* in American English. In contrast, the main verb *be*, as well as the progressive and passive *be*, is marked $[+\text{AUX}]$. See (64) below.

17. Hereafter in all filters Greek letters refer to constants.

18. We can combine (71a) and (71b) into one rule using the new abbreviatory symbol ∞, if we are willing to stipulate that successive occurrences of ∞ in the same rule be read in the same direction, i.e., by adopting a condition like (i).

(i) $[a_1 \infty \beta_1, a_2 \infty \beta_2, ... a_n \infty \beta_n] =$
       $[a_1 - \beta_1, a_2 - \beta_2, ... a_n - \beta_n]$ or
       $[\beta_1 - a_1, \beta_2 - a_2, ... \beta_n - a_n]$

Given (i), we could replace (71a) and (71b) with (ii).

(ii)   *$[...[-/\_\_\_\_ \infty [a\sigma]^v] \infty ...[a\sigma]^v...]$
       X^n

Similarly, (72a) and (72b) can be combined to form (iii).

(iii) $[...[+/\_\_\_\_ \infty [a\sigma]^v] \infty ...[a\sigma]^v...]$
       X^n

(ii) and (iii) can now easily be reduced to one filter if we interpret the asterisk as a minus and assume β in both places of (iv) is either plus or minus.

(iv) $\beta[...[\beta/\_\_\_\_ \infty [a\sigma]^v] \infty ...[a\sigma]^v...]$
       X^n

19. The individual features in (77) will be discussed in turn below.

20. Nothing in these proposals will prevent perfective *have* from occurring in both places in a structure; however it seems reasonable to assume that the redundancy condition we have discussed before will rule this out. Further, nothing in these proposals, specifically in (93), stipulates that a

verb must occur to the left of perfective and passive *-en* and progressive *-ing*. However these three elements, like TNS, are bound affixes, i.e., they must be attached to something in surface structure. It seems to me therefore that we can assume some general condition on bound affixes stipulating that they must be either preceded or followed by an item to which they can be affixed. In the case of these auxiliary affixes, the verbs with which they are associated are specified in (77).

21. For discussion with examples, see Baker (1968, Chapter 3).

22. There has been a number of attempts to specify the order of auxiliary elements in terms of independent criteria, but none of these is without significant problems. For discussion and references, see Akmajian, et al. (1979, Section 3.).

BIBLIOGRAPHY

Akmajian, A. (1975). "More Evidence for an NP Cycle," in *Linguistic Inquiry* 6.1, pp. 115–129.

Akmajian, A. (1977). "The Complement Structure of Perception Verbs in an Autonomous Syntax Framework," in Culicover et al., eds. pp. 427–460.

Akmajian, A. and F. Heny (1975). *An Introduction to the Principles of Transformational Syntax* (MIT Press, Cambridge, Mass.).

Akmajian, A., S. Steele and T. Wasow (1979). "The Category AUX in Universal Grammar," in *Linguistic Inquiry* 10.1, pp. 1–64.

Amritavalli, R. (1980). "Expressing Cross-Categorial Selectional Correspondences: An Alternative to the $\bar{X}$ Syntax Approach," in *Linguistic Analysis* 6.3, pp. 305–343.

Anderson J. (1971). *The Grammar of Case: Towards a Localist Theory* (Cambridge University Press, London).

Anderson, J. (1977). *On Case Grammar* (Croom Helm, London).

Anderson, S. R. and P. Kiparsky, eds. (1973). *A Festschrift for Morris Halle* (Holt, Rinehart, and Winston, New York).

Andrews, A. (1971). "Case Agreement of Predicate Modifiers in Ancient Greek," in *Linguistic Inquiry* 2.2, pp. 127–152.

Aronoff, M. (1976). *Word Formation in Generative Grammar* (MIT Press, Cambridge, Mass.).

Bach, E. (1962). "The Order of Elements in a Transformational Grammar of German," in *Language* 38, pp. 263–269.

Bach E. (1964). *An Introduction to Transformational Grammars* (Holt, Rinehart, and Winston, New York).

Bach, E. and R. Harms, eds. (1968). *Universals in Linguistic Theory* (Holt, Rinehart, and Winston, New York).

Bach, E. and G. Horn (1976). "Remarks on 'Conditions on Transformations,'" in *Linguistic Inquiry* 7.2, pp. 265–299.

Baker, C. L. (1978). *Introduction to Generative-Transformational Syntax* (Prentice-Hall, Englewood Cliffs, New Jersey).

Barnum, F. (1901). *Grammatical Fundamentals of the Innuit Language* (Ginn, New York).

Berko Gleason, J. (1958). "The Child's Learning of English Morphology," in *Word* 14, pp. 150–177.

Bever, T., J. Katz and D. T. Langendoen, eds. (1976). *An Integrated Theory of Linguistic Ability* (Crowell, New York).

Binkert, P. (1970). "Case and Prepositional Constructions in a Transformational Grammar of Classical Latin," Unpublished doctoral dissertation (University of Michigan, Ann Arbor).

Binkert, P. (1974). "Kevin's Journal," Unpublished MS.

Binkert, P. (1981). "$\bar{X}$ Syntax and Movement Rules," Unpublished MS.

Binkert, P. (in preparation). "Residential Grammar."

Bolinger, D. (1972). *Degree Words* (Mouton, The Hague).

Bowers, J. S. (1975). "Adjectives and Adverbs in English," in *Foundations of Language* 13, pp. 529–562.

Brame, M. K. (1976). *Conjectures and Refutations in Syntax and Semantics* (North-Holland, New York).

Brame, M. K. (1978). *Base Generated Syntax* (Noit Amrofer, Seattle).

Brame, M. K. (1979). *Essays Toward Realistic Syntax* (Noit Amrofer, Seattle).

Brame, M. K. (1981). "Trace Theory and Filters vs. Lexically Based Syntax Without," in *Linguistic Inquiry* 12.2, pp. 275–293.

Bresnan, J. (1973). "The Syntax of the Comparative Clause Construction in English," in *Linguistic Inquiry* 4.3, pp. 275–344.

Bresnan, J. (1975). "Comparative Deletion and Constraints on Transformations," in *Linguistic Analysis* 1, pp. 25–74.

Bresnan, J. (1976a). "On the Form and Functioning of Transformations," in *Linguistic Inquiry* 7.1 pp. 3–40.

Bresnan, J. (1976b). "Evidence for a Theory of Unbounded Transformations," in *Linguistic Analysis* 2 pp. 353–394.

Bresnan, J. (1977). "Variables in the Theory of Transformations," in Culicover et al., eds., pp. 157–196.

Brensnan, J. (1978). "A Realistic Transformational Grammar," in Halle et al., eds., pp. 1–59.

Bresnan, J. and J. Grimshaw (1978). "The Syntax of Free Relatives in English," in *Linguistic Inquiry* 9.3, pp. 331–391.

Brown, R. (1973). *A First Language/The Early Stages* (Harvard, Cambridge, Mass.).

Brown, R. and U. Bellugi (1964). "Three Processes in the Child's Acquisition of Syntax," in Lenneberg, ed., pp. 131–162.

Burt, M. K. (1971). *From Deep to Surface Structure* (Harper and Row, New York).

Chomsky, N. (1955). *The Logical Structure of Linguistic Theory* (Plenum Press, New York, 1975).

Chomsky, N. (1957). *Syntactic Structures* (Mouton, The Hague).

Chomsky, N. (1965). *Aspects of the Theory of Syntax* (MIT Press, Cambridge, Mass.).

Chomsky, N. (1968). *Language and Mind* (Enlarged Edition) (Harcourt, Brace, and Jovanovich, New York.).

Chomsky, N. (1970). "Remarks on Nominalization," in Jacobs and Rosenbaum, eds., pp. 184–221.

Chomsky, N. (1973). "Conditions on Transformations," in Anderson and Kiparsky, eds., pp. 232–286.

Chomsky, N. (1976). "Conditions on Rules of Grammar," in *Linguistic Analysis* 2, pp. 303–351.

Chomsky, N. (1977). "On WH-Movement," in Culicover et al., eds. pp. 71–132.

Chomsky, N. (1980a). "On Binding," in *Linguistic Inquiry* 11.1 pp. 1–46.

Chomsky, N. (1980b). *Rules and Representations* (Columbia University Press, New York).

Chomsky, N. (1981). *Lectures on Binding and Government* (Foris, Dordrecht).

Chomsky, N. and H. Lasnik (1977). "Filters and Control," in *Linguistic Inquiry* 8.3, pp. 425–504.

Cole, P. and J. Sadock, eds. (1977). *Syntax and Semantics*, Vol. 8. (Academic Press, New York).

Culicover, P. (1976). *Syntax* (Academic Press, New York).

Culicover, P., T. Wasow, and A. Akmajian, eds. (1977). *Formal Syntax* (Academic Press, New York).

Curme, G. O. (1964). *A Grammar of the German Language* (Frederick Ungar, New York).

Dingwall, W. (1971). *A Survey of Linguistic Science* (University of Maryland, College Park).

Emonds, J. E. (1970). *Root and Structure Preserving Transformations* (Doctoral dissertation, MIT, Cambridge, Mass.) (Indiana University Linguistics Club, Bloomington).

Emonds, J. E. (1976). *A Transformational Approach to English Syntax* (Academic Press, New York).

Fiengo, R. (1977). "On Trace Theory," in *Linguistic Inquiry* 8.1, pp. 35–61.

Fillmore, C. (1968). "The Case for Case," in Bach and Harms, eds., pp. 1–88.

Fillmore, C. (1969). "Toward a Modern Theory of Case," in Reibel and Schane, eds., pp. 361–375.

Fodor, J. A., T. G. Bever, and M. F. Garrett (1974). *The Psychology of Language* (McGraw-Hill, New York).

Fodor, J. A. and J. Katz, eds. (1964). *The Structure of Language: Readings in the Philosophy of Language* (Prentice-Hall, Englewood Cliffs, New Jersey).

Fodor, J. D. (1978). "Parsing Strategies and Constraints on Transformations," in *Linguistic Inquiry* 9.3, pp. 427–473.

Frank, M. (1972). *Modern English: Practical Reference Guide* (Prentice-Hall, Englewood Cliffs, New Jersey).

Gazdar, G. (1981). "Unbounded Dependencies and Coordinate Structure," in *Linguistic Inquiry* 12.2, pp. 155–184.

Greenberg, J., ed. (1963). *Universals of Language* (MIT Press, Cambridge, Mass.).

Halle, M., J. Bresnan, and G. Miller, eds. (1978). *Linguistic Theory and Psychological Reality* (MIT Press, Cambridge, Mass.).

Hornstein, N. (1977). "S and the X′ Convention," in *Linguistic Analysis* 3, pp. 137–176.

Hudson, R. (1976). *Arguments for a Non-Transformational Grammar* (University of Chicago Press, Chicago).

Jackendoff, R. (1972). *Semantic Interpretation in Generative Grammar* (MIT Press, Cambridge, Mass.).

Jackendoff, R. (1973). "The Base Rules for Prepositional Phrases," in Anderson and Kiparsky, eds., pp. 345–356.

Jackendoff, R. (1977). *X̄ Syntax: A Study of Phrase Structure* (MIT Press, Cambridge, Mass.).

Jacobs, R. and P. Rosenbaum, eds. (1970). *Readings in English Transformational Grammar* (Ginn, Waltham, Mass.).

Jespersen, O. (1961). *A Modern English Grammar on Historical Principles* (George Allen & Unwin, London).

Johnson, D. (1979). *Toward a Theory of Relationally Based Grammar* (Garland, New York).

Kaplan, R. M. and J. Bresnan (1981). *Lexical-Functional Grammar: A Formal System for Grammatical Representation*, Occasional Paper #13, Center for Cognitive Science (MIT, Cambridge, Mass.).

Kayne, R. (1975). *French Syntax* (MIT Press, Cambridge, Mass.).

Keyser, S. J., ed. (1978). *Recent Transformational Studies in European Languages* (MIT Press, Cambridge, Mass.).

Klima, E. (1964). "Negation in English," in Fodor and Katz, eds., pp. 246–323.

Koster, J. (1978). "Why Subject Sentences Don't Exist," in Keyser, ed., pp. 53–64.

Kühner, R. and C. Stegmann (1955). *Ausführliche Grammatik der lateinischen Sprache* (2 Vols.) (Gottahalk, Leverkusen).

Kurylowicz, J. (1964). *The Inflectional Categories of Indo-European* (Carl Winter, Heidelberg).

Langacker, R. (1969). "On Pronominalization and the Chain of Command," in Reibel and Schane, eds., pp. 160–186.

Langacker, R. (1978). "The Form and Meaning of the English Auxiliary," in *Language* 54, pp. 853–882.

Lederer, H. (1969). *Reference Grammar of the German Language* (Scribner, New York).

Lenneberg, E., ed. (1964). *New Directions in the Study of Language* (MIT Press, Cambridge, Mass.).

Levi, J. (1978). *The Syntax and Semantics of Complex Nominals* (Academic Press, New York).

Lightfoot, D. (1975). *Natural Logic and the Greek Moods* (Mouton, The Hague).

Lightfoot, D. (1976). "Trace Theory and Twice-Moved NPs," in *Linguistic Inquiry* 7, pp. 559–582.

Lightfoot, D. (1979). *Principles of Diachronic Syntax* (Cambridge University Press, London).

Luce, P., R. Bush, and E. Galanter, eds. (1963). *Handbook of Mathematical Psychology*, Vol II. (Wiley, New York).

Marcus, M. (1980). *A Theory of Syntactic Recognition for Natural Language* (MIT Press, Cambridge, Mass.).

McCawley, J. (1968). "Concerning the Base Component of a Transformational Grammar," in *Foundations of Language* 4, pp. 243–269. Reprinted in McCawley (1976) pp. 35–58.

McCawley, J. (1970). "English as a VSO Language," in *Language* 46, pp. 286–299. Reprinted in McCawley (1976) pp. 211–228.

McCawley, J. (1972). "A Program for Logic," in McCawley (1976), pp. 285–319.

McCawley, J. (1976). *Grammar and Meaning* (Academic Press, New York).

McNeill, D. (1966). "Developmental Psycholinguistics," in Smith and Miller, eds., pp. 15–84.

Meillet, A. and J. Vendryes (1960). *Traité de grammaire comparée des langues classiques* (Champion, Paris).

Newmeyer, F. (1980). *Linguistic Theory in America* (Academic Press, New York).

Perlmutter, D. (1971). *Deep and Surface Structure Constraints in Syntax* (Holt, Rinehart, and Winston, New York).

Peters, S. and R. Ritchie (1971). "On Restricting the Base Component of Transformational Grammars," in *Information and Control* 18, pp. 483–501.

Peters, S. and R. Ritchie (1973). "On the Generative Power of Transformational Grammars," in *Information Sciences* 6, pp. 49–83.

Postal, P. and G. Pullum (1978). "Traces and the Description of English Complementizer Contraction," in *Linguistic Inquiry* 9.1, pp. 1–30.

Pullum, G. (1977). "Word Order Universals and Grammatical Relations," in Cole and Sadock, eds., pp. 249–277.

Pullum, G. and P. Postal (1979). "On an Inadequate Defence of 'Trace Theory,'" in *Linguistic Inquiry* 10, pp. 689–706.

Quirk, R., S. Greenbaum, G. Leech, and J. Svartvik (1972). *A Grammar of Contemporary English* (Seminar Press, New York).

Reibel, D. and S. Schane (1969). *Modern Studies in English* (Prentice-Hall, Englewood Cliffs, New Jersey).

Reinhart, T. (1976) *The Syntactic Domain of Anaphora*, (Unpublished doctoral dissertation, MIT, Cambridge, Mass.).

Roby, H. J. (1872). *A Grammar of the Latin Language* (Macmillan, London).

Ross, J. R. (1967). *Constraints on Variables in Syntax*, (Doctoral dissertation, MIT, Cambridge, Mass.) (Indiana University Linguistics Club, Bloomington).

Ross, J. R. (1969). "On the Cyclic Nature of English Pronominalization," in Reibel and Schane, eds., pp. 187–200.

Schachter, P. (1976). "A Nontransformational Account of Gerundive Nominals in English," in *Linguistic Inquiry* 7.2, pp. 205–241.

Selkirk, E. (1970). "On the Determiner Systems of Noun Phrase and Adjective Phrase," MS. (MIT, Cambridge, Mass.).

Selkirk, E. (1977). "Some Remarks on Noun Phrase Structure," in Culicover et al., eds., pp. 285–316.

Stockwell, R., P. Schachter, and B. Partee (1973). *The Major Syntactic Structures of English* (Holt, Rinehart, and Winston, New York).

Smith, F. and G. Miller, eds. (1966). *The Genesis of Language: A Psycholinguistic Approach* (MIT Press, Cambridge, Mass.).

Smyth, H. W. (1956). *Greek Grammar* (Harvard, Cambridge, Mass.).

Van Reimsdijk, H. (1978). *A Case Study in Syntactic Markedness* (Peter de Ridder, Lisse).

Visser, F. Th. (1963). *An Historical Syntax of the English Language* (2 Vols.) (E. J. Brill, Leiden).

Wanner, E. and M. Maratsos (1978). "An ATN Approach to Comprehension," in Halle et al., eds., pp. 119–161.

Wexler, K. and P. Culicover (1980). *Formal Principles of Language Acquisition* (MIT Press, Cambridge, Mass.).

Whitaker, H. (1971). "Neurolinguistics," in Dingwall, ed., pp. 136–251.

Woodcock, E. C. (1959). *A New Latin Syntax* (Harvard, Cambridge, Mass.).